RETHINKING THE SKYSCRAPER

THE COMPLETE ARCHITECTURE OF KEN YEANG

ROBERT POWELL

RETHINKING THE SKYSCRAPER

THE COMPLETE ARCHITECTURE OF KEN YEANG

WHITNEY LIBRARY OF DESIGN
AN IMPRINT OF WATSON-GUPTILL PUBLICATIONS/NEW YORK

Frontispiece

The award-winning Menara Mesiniaga high-rise tower, situated in Subang Jaya, near Kuala Lumpur. (Ng)

Above

The Menara UMNO tower on the island of Penang. The reception pavilion on the 21st floor looks out to sea and inland to Bukit Pinang. (Ng)

Photography by K. L. Ng, courtesy of T. R. Hamzah and Yeang. Additional photography by Robert Powell and Albert Lim K.S.

First published in the United Kingdom by Thames & Hudson Ltd, London

© 1999 Robert Powell

First published in the United States by Whitney Library of Design, an imprint of Watson-Guptill Publications, a division of BPI Communications, Inc., 1515 Broadway, New York, NY 10036

Library of Congress Catalog Card Number 99-62059

ISBN 0-8230-4553-6

Manufactured in Singapore

First printing 1999

1 2 3 4 5 6 7 8 / 03 02 01 00 99

Contents

A European Upbringing

A HYBRID WORLD: PENANG TO CHELTENHAM

The cataclysmic economic upheavals of the late 1990s have demolished conventional trust in financially driven globalization, making many developed nations aware that they must now rely on their own resources. Yet the rapid expansion of media influence that has run parallel with this disillusionment has created a curious paradox. The local specializations prompted by enforced self-sufficiency are now evaluated by a much bigger, global audience. Ken Yeang's background has singularly prepared him to respond to this paradox.

Yeang was born on Penang, a small island off the north coast of Peninsular Malaysia, in 1948. He spent his early childhood in a spacious colonial mansion, a building type perfectly suited to the tropical climate. In 1954, Yeang's parents commissioned a new house in Penang from Berthold M. Iverson, one of the foremost modernists in Southeast Asia at that time, who ran the Ipoh office of Iverson and van Sitteren. He had formed the practice with a fellow-expatriate shortly after the Second World War, when they were among the many who came to Malaya to participate in the reconstruction and development of the region's economy. They set up offices in both Singapore and Ipoh, a thriving commercial town at the heart of the tin-mining industry, where, it so happened, Yeang's maternal grandfather was a *Kapitan China*, or head of the Chinese community .

Significantly, Yeang's earliest childhood memories are of visiting the building site during the construction of the family's new home. Unusually at the time, the house had sliding partitions that permitted all the children's bedrooms on the second storey to be amalgamated into one larger room; Yeang's own bedroom adjoined his parents' room. The switch from a colonial mansion to an early modernist-style villa left a deep impression on Yeang. He recalls vividly the modernist spaces in the house and the lifestyle of a family with an international outlook, and one might speculate that in some subliminal way, these influenced his later choice of career and his lack of nostalgia for the past.

As was the custom with upper-income families in Malaya, in 1961 Yeang's parents sent the thirteen-year-old Ken to boarding school in England, some 12,000 miles away. He left behind a country that was undergoing rapid changes. In 1957 Malaya had become independent from Britain, and in 1963 it formed the Federation of Malaysia along with Singapore, Sabah and Sarawak. (Two years later Singapore would leave the Federation.)

In England, Yeang studied at Cheltenham College, a typical English public school situated in the Cotswolds. It had a strong military ethos and many pupils went on to Sandhurst Military

Opposite

Yeang's Archigram-inspired MBf Tower in Penang. The reinforced concrete frame of the thirty-one-storey building is in the form of two separate rectangular towers with curved ends linked by a service core. (Ng)

Academy. Yeang remembers it as a disciplined life, but mostly enjoyable, and he did reasonably well academically. In 1966, he took the first steps towards a career in architecture, gaining a place at the Architectural Association School of Architecture (AA) in London.

THE ARCHITECTURAL ASSOCIATION: MENTORS AND CONTEMPORARIES

The choice of the AA was influenced in part by Dennis Chung, Yeang's uncle and himself a graduate of the school. The chairman of the Association at the time was Dr Otto Koenigsberger, who had established the AA Tropical School. Soon after Yeang's arrival, Michael Lloyd took over as chairman, and he was followed by Alvin Boyarsky. 'Alvin didn't teach in a conventional way, but informed through conversations. For many, he became much more than a teacher', remembers Yeang. 'For me, he was a paternal figure giving encouragement, as well as criticism. For a summer, I worked for him as a graphic designer at his International Institute of Design, which he ran at the Institute of Contemporary Arts [ICA].'[1]

Yeang's first-year tutor was Elia Zenghelis. Later, in the 1970s, Zenghelis would establish the Office for Metropolitan Architecture (OMA) group with Rem Koolhaas and Zaha Hadid, although at that time the design philosophies of the OMA were not apparent in his teaching. He generated in Yeang an enthusiasm for the modern movement. 'Zenghelis was a very good teacher,' says Yeang, 'he nurtured my interest in architecture and was very precise in the terminology he used.' In his second year Yeang visited the Montreal Expo in Canada and was 'excited and inspired by the experimental structures'. Yeang's other early influences included, not surprisingly, Mies van der Rohe and Paul Rudolph, but also the work of the Greater London Council's Architects Department and the ideas of Lord Llewelyn Davies on 'indeterminate architecture'.

Upon finishing his third year in 1969, Yeang briefly returned to Asia to work in the practice of Stanley Leong as one of several site architects on the Singapore Mandarin Hotel, an internship that gave him experience in building practice and drawing. In 1971, he returned to the AA to complete his diploma. His tutors now included Ron Herron, a member of the Archigram group, who together with Cedric Price 'offered the most compelling visions of the future and technological fantasies'.[2] 'Herron had a sharp eye and a gift for succinctly distilling his criticism into two or three sentences', says Yeang. The influence of the Archigram group would later surface in Yeang's own work: the MBf Tower (1993) and the 1998 project for the Expo 2005 Nagoya Hyper-Tower have distinct echoes of the Archigram ethos.

The vibrancy of the AA staff in the 1960s and early 1970s, and the investigative nature of the school, left a lasting impact on Yeang. The diversity of the students who later became significant architects in their own right produced a studio environment with a high level of creativity and energy. 'My fifth year under Peter Cook was memorable. He taught us how to design by making lyrical machines. We all grew and developed under him. His was an alternative view of the world as an architectural boffin. This was a view that somehow stuck', recalls Yeang. 'Rem Koolhaas was a contemporary for a while. My other contemporaries include Piers Gough, Roger Zogolovich, Mark Fisher and Janet Street-Porter. We visited Paris with Bernard Tschumi and Colin Fournier, both teaching under Peter.' Another of Yeang's fellow-students was Suha Özkan, who was then at the AA Graduate School and who later, as the secretary-general of the Aga Khan Award for Architecture (AKAA), involved Yeang as a technical reviewer in one of the AKAA cycles.

Yeang also met Leon van Schaik while at the AA and the pair graduated at the same time, but 'in that year Yeang was on the periphery of things I was doing', says van Schaik. 'He became more prominent to me in the years after Cambridge. We met again at an AA function in 1980 and we have not looked back since then.' Some years later, when van Schaik became dean of the Faculty of the Constructed Environment at the Royal Melbourne Institute of Technology, he appointed Yeang as adjunct professor. 'When people ask me now how the practice has made the jump from the purely local milieu onto a "world stage" I attribute it in part to the friendships that I made at the

AA and later at Cambridge: people with whom I have remained in contact for three decades and with whom I have subsequently collaborated professionally', says Yeang.

While still a student, Yeang worked for a short time at the Louis de Soissons Partnership in London. The Partnership, under David Hodge and Nathan Silver, was described as a 'rite of passage' for many AA students. Christine Hawley, later in partnership with Peter Cook and now head of the Bartlett School of Architecture at University College London, and Eva Jirinika both worked there.

Yeang supplemented his student's stipend by doing graphic-design work. He produced posters and designs for the AA, and also drew illustrations for the British magazine *Architectural Design*. The architect and critic Dennis Sharp assigned him a number of design commissions, including the illustrations for a book by the architectural philosopher Henryk Skolimowky.

It was through his graphic work that Yeang developed a friendship with Charles Jencks, for whose book *Le Corbusier and the Tragic View of Architecture* he produced some illustrations. Jencks was completing his doctorate on Le Corbusier, under Reyner Banham, when he commissioned Yeang to produce the analytical axonometric drawings of two of Le Corbusier's houses at Poissy and Pessac.[3] The work of Le Corbusier was to have a significant influence on Yeang's earliest commissions when he set up practice. Early buildings such as the Ulysses House (1980), the Dason House (1983) and a residence built in Kuala Lumpur for his own use, known as the Roof-Roof House (1986), have distinct Corbusien references, as does his first major high-rise building, the Plaza Atrium (1985).

The AA was a tough but enlightening and formative experience for Ken Yeang. A number of acclaimed architects, such as Richard Rogers, Renzo Piano and Norman Foster, were either teachers or visiting critics there. The school 'encouraged students to be "street-wise", creatively opportunistic, and able to convince an often hostile jury of both students and critics to accept provocative ideas and approaches', Yeang recalls. 'We were constantly asked to push frontiers of existing architectural norms. Work was done independently and we had to make things happen for ourselves; a proactive approach rather than a reactive one.' This provided Yeang with exposure and developed his confidence and convictions. Yeang also attributes his lifelong involvement with architectural discourse to his tutors at the AA, in particular Alvin Boyarsky and Roy Landau, who became head of the AA Graduate School. Both had strong influences upon Yeang's various programmes to advance the image of the Malaysian architect and Malaysian architecture when he later became the president of the Malaysian Institute of Architects (Pertubuhan Akitek Malaysia). 'Like many of those for whom Boyarsky was a mentor,' writes van Schaik, 'Yeang fights for the idea of architecture as an intellectual practice.'[4]

Life in London also brought Yeang into contact with students from art schools and expanded his interest in other aspects of design, such as film-making and magazine design. The mood of experimentation had a lasting impact. One of the student projects that he embarked upon at the AA, soon after returning from his short internship in Singapore in 1971, was an entry to the Shinkenchiku Residential Design competition organized by the *Japan Architect* journal. A plug-in, expandable and futuristic McLuhanesque city-planning design called the 'Global Village', Yeang's submission drew inspiration from the work of the Metabolists in Japan and from Archigram. Another student project carried out in 1971 was 'Stylesville', which sought to reshape the built form of a skyscraper. It was published as a postcard by *Architectural Design*.

In 1972, Yeang met Kisho Kurokawa, one of the early exponents of Metabolism, at a London party given by Charles Jencks and Maggie Keswick. By then, Yeang was at Cambridge and already defining the scope of his doctoral thesis on the ecological basis of architecture. The ideas of the Metabolists — of change, the biological analogy and an organic architecture — were, in many respects, compatible with Yeang's own research work. The forces that were to shape his future career were beginning to coalesce. Kurokawa became an important influence upon Yeang, and he was later to write the foreword to the first published monograph on Yeang's work.

CAMBRIDGE AND PENN

Yeang's switch, in 1971, from the AA to Wolfson College, University of Cambridge, was part of an arrangement with the AA to complete his diploma. He joined the Technical Research Division of the Cambridge School of Architecture, led by Alex Pike and John Frazer, and including James Thring (the school was later to merge with the Martin Centre for Land Use and Built Form Studies). Pike and Frazer were studying the feasibility of building an 'autonomous house' (after the ideas of Buckminster Fuller). This was a response to the growing interest during the 1960s and 1970s in environmental issues. The vulnerability of countries to the finite nature of fossil fuels was brought home sharply by the oil crisis of 1973, and there was also a general unease about the proliferation of nuclear power. The idea of the autonomous house project developed from such concerns.

Yeang initially worked as a research assistant investigating the relationship between buildings and environmental ecology, but with the agreement of Frazer he eventually embarked on a separate research programme examining the theoretical aspects of ecological design, which he regarded as a necessary precursor to the design of the systems of the autonomous house. This research was to be the basis of Yeang's doctorate, the eventual title of which was 'A Theoretical Framework for Incorporation of Ecological Considerations in the Design and Planning of the Built Environment'.

The research programme led Yeang to undertake coursework in ecology under Professor J. L. W. Beament at the University's Department of Applied Biology, where he became keenly interested in environmental science and the properties of biological systems. He joined the British Ecological Society, and one of his early research papers was on bionics and the use of biological analogies for design.[5] Throughout Yeang's later work in practice there is a constant reference and refinement of this theme: the concern for the relationship between buildings and the external ecological environment.

Yeang's study of environmental biology and ecology, and their relationship to built form and design, and the lateral thinking that the association of these ideas entailed, brought an increasingly rigorous methodology to his work and provided him with a formal theoretical base from which to argue his ideas. So, too, did his contact with research students and visiting fellows from other disciplines outside architecture. While at Cambridge, he also became aware of general systems theory, which contributed to the development of the ecological design model in his doctoral thesis. In his endeavour to relate ecology to building design in his research work, he would place emphasis on the systemic aspects of architecture and the theoretical basis of building enclosure.

Cambridge also taught Yeang that he should be careful with his use of terminology. This was especially emphasized by

Ronald Lewcock, who was at the time a fellow of Clare Hall – he subsequently became professor of architecture at the Massachusetts Institute of Technology and then at Georgia Tech – and who proofread some of Yeang's research papers. Later, in 1981, Yeang would write the monthly editorial for the newsletter of the Malaysian Institute of Architects and he was its editor for several years. The ideas he expressed show a discernible and consistent pattern of development that can be traced back to his research work at Cambridge.

There remained one more step in Yeang's formal education. While at Cambridge, he took leave from the University to undertake a landscape programme under Professor Ian L. McHarg at the Department of Landscape Architecture and Regional Planning at the University of Pennsylvania. McHarg, the champion of ecologically responsible planning, has undoubtedly been one of the most influential teachers of the twentieth century. His book *Design with Nature* (1969), written in a lyrical poetic prose, is a seminal work which, in the words of Lewis Mumford, 'revives the hope for a better world'. Yeang found McHarg's passion for the protection of the environment overwhelming and he was deeply influenced by his methodology. He has frequently used a modified version of McHarg's 'ecological land-use analysis' for masterplanning projects. The knowledge that Yeang gained in his short affiliation with the landscape and macro-planning course at the University of

Pennsylvania complemented the earlier experience of the AA and the Cambridge School of Architecture. In the process, he acquired what Alan Balfour has referred to as 'the heady vision of the AA, the determinism of Cambridge and the environmental morality of Penn'.[6]

Yeang's doctoral thesis would eventually be published, with substantial updating, in 1995 as *Designing with Nature: The Ecological Basis for Architectural Design*. Yeang has subsequently maintained that this book, particularly the two chapters 'Framework for Ecological Design' and 'External Ecological Interdependencies of the Built Environment', is the fundamental model for all his work.[7] The similarity of Yeang's title to McHarg's was no accident. But Yeang points out that there is a subtle distinction: his book takes 'design with nature' a stage further – it is about the extension of McHarg's ideas into architecture and built form.

RETURN TO ASIA

In 1975, while still at Cambridge, Yeang was offered a job in the office of Akitek Bersekutu in Kuala Lumpur. The firm was unique and somewhat experimental in that it had Malay, Chinese and European partners: Hijjas Kasturi, Nik Yusoff, Tan Toh Hock, Ong Guan Teik and David Joyce. Yeang worked mostly under Hijjas Kasturi, and he retains admiration for Kasturi's strong architectural convictions. However, it was the Cambridge-educated Joyce's interest in a functional modernism that had perhaps the greater impact on Yeang. Joyce was at that time completing the final phases of the Kuala Lumpur General Hospital, the design of which was heavily influenced by Le Corbusier.

Elsewhere, I have referred to the phenomena of the 'returned native'. It is evident that after an education overseas, or after having spent a substantial period working in another country, the Asian architect is able to return to his or her own culture with the confidence to discard or transform those aspects of its tradition that he or she considers no longer relevant. Yeang was one such 'returned native'. He had spent fifteen years in Britain and the United States, and his exposure to the theoretical ideas of some of the most influential teachers of the twentieth century gave him the confidence, just a year after his return to Malaysia, to plunge into private practice.

In 1976, Yeang left Akitek Bersekutu to form a partnership with Tengku Robert Hamzah, a prince of the Kelantan royal family, who had started a small practice operating from a shophouse in Ampang on the outskirts of Kuala Lumpur. Yeang had first met Tengku Robert in 1966, when they were students at the AA. During their middle years at the school, both worked on projects under the same unit master, Nico Diamantis, and both worked on the same site for their RIBA finals. In his final years at the AA, Tengku Robert had studied in the AA's Tropical School

and thus the influence of Otto Koenigsberger infiltrated the work of the new firm, T. R. Hamzah and Yeang.

Yeang's arrival back in Malaysia coincided with a period of extensive Malayanization,[9] the government having introduced policies intended to foster a sense of national identity. Yeang became deeply involved in the discourses on nationalism, identity and critical regionalism that were current in Malaysian architecture at that time. The ecology issue would for a while become overshadowed by these other debates. This intellectual discourse, entwined with the architectural solutions that were then being generated in Southeast Asia, would later lead Yeang to write the book *Tropical Urban Regionalism*.[10]

Yeang always counts himself fortunate to have been in Britain in the 1960s and early 1970s. Many of his friends and acquaintances in London and Cambridge went on to become substantial figures in the world architectural community. The friendships were in several instances to last a lifetime, and many of his contemporaries were subsequently in positions where collaborations with Yeang were to everyone's mutual benefit. Thus the names of fellow-students such as Suha Özkan and Leon van Schaik, and mentors such as John Frazer, Ronald Lewcock and Charles Jencks, will appear again in later chapters of this monograph. And, of course, another AA contemporary, Tengku Robert Hamzah, has remained Yeang's partner for almost two and a half decades.

1 High Aspirations

PRIMARY-LEVEL DESIGN EXPERIMENTS

In his 1992 book *The Architecture of Malaysia*, Yeang discusses the period following his country's independence, a time when there was a strong surge of nationalism and a 'search' for identity. In parallel with the huge political and social changes then under way, some Malaysian architects were beginning to question the validity of Western models. In 1978, in a seminar organized by the Ministry of Youth and Culture, prominent architects, including Hijjas Kasturi, Fawizah Kamal and Ezrin Arbi, spoke out on the issue. At the same time, political pressure was leading some architects to replicate traditional elements such as *Minangkabau* roofs and Islamic arches in their designs. Yeang was uncomfortable with this direct replication of vernacular elements and advocated a reinterpretive approach and the adoption of architectural models that were responsive to Malaysia's climate without trivializing its deep culture, traditional forms and decorative motifs.[1]

In the early 1970s, the Malaysian economy boomed and there was a significant increase in building activity. The network of contacts used to acquire jobs, which until then had been dominated by expatriate firms, ceased to be effective. In the changed climate a new network formed, one increasingly dependent on local contacts to secure commissions, particularly for government-financed projects.

Within this political and social milieu, the fledgling practice of T. R. Hamzah and Yeang sought work. Most of its earliest commissions were small in scale but the Ulysses House, designed for Mr and Mrs Leong Siew Wing in 1976 and completed in 1980, was a strong statement of Yeang's ideas on an architectural identity for an independent Malaysia. It had a fiercely modernist expression, unashamedly Corbusien in its language. The diagrams purporting to show natural ventilation and filtered sunlight are simplistic but the orientation and space-planning respond well to the site and the prevailing wind. There is a conscious attempt to layer the external skin of the house. The unequivocal modern language of the house sends a clear signal of Yeang's position on the identity debate at that time.

In early 1978, the practice achieved a breakthrough with the Taman Sri Ukay project, which included terraced and semi-detached houses, apartments and shophouses. T. R. Hamzah and Yeang eventually acquired one of the three-storey shophouses as their office and relocated there in 1983. Another residence, the Dason House, designed in 1983 and completed in 1986, also exhibited strong Corbusien influences. The language is essentially planar but the form is fragmented and there is a

Opposite

The IBM Plaza in Kuala Lumpur. The principal idea that Yeang explored here was that of vertical landscaping. A diagonal garden climbs one side of the building to the fourteenth storey, where it crosses a landscaped void-deck and then continues its diagonal ascent on the opposite side of the tower. (AL)

serious attempt to create a comfortable microclimate in the open-to-sky central court and the shaded projecting terrace. Yeang's struggle to advance the Corbusien language, acquired during his time in the northern hemisphere, and to adapt it to the tropics is evident at this stage.

In 1984, Yeang completed the now-famous Roof-Roof House, his own residence, which is located less than two hundred metres from his office. This juxtaposition – imitating the cultural practice in Asian cities of 'living-over-the-shop' – has determined Yeang's mode of work for a decade and a half. He arrives in the office early and rarely leaves until seven or eight in the evening, often returning after dinner to work into the early hours of the following morning. The Roof-Roof House is discussed in greater detail in Chapter 5, but its relevance to the identity debate cannot be overlooked at this point. It established Yeang as a radically independent advocate of a critical regional architecture. It developed ideas on designing with climate, as a transitional stage in his ecological agenda, that are directly related to his Cambridge doctoral thesis, and it demonstrated courage, for at the time many in the profession were reluctant to take a position on the identity issue.

In the early 1980s, the practice was commissioned for several high-rise buildings. These were for Yeang essentially single-idea 'Primary-Level Design Experiments' that examined 'one big idea in a single building'.[2] With them, he experimented with the idea of the skyscraper in a tropical context. There were again distinct Corbusien influences in the aesthetics of the earliest of these projects, which Yeang sometimes refers to as the 'Series 1' skyscrapers.

TRANSITIONAL SPACES
Plaza Atrium (1981–1984)

Commissioned in 1981, the twenty-four-storey Plaza Atrium, situated in the commercial area of Kuala Lumpur known as the Golden Triangle, was Yeang's first major opportunity to put into practice his ideas on a climatically appropriate form for the high-rise building type. The challenge was to design a tower suitable for the hot-humid tropical climate. The 'big idea' in this project was the use of a large transitional space located in the building's edge-zone – the space that lies between the inside and the outside of the building – as an 'interstitial atrium'.

Responding to the tropical climate, the multi-storey atrium is topped by a roof of Z-section concrete louvres that filters the rain, permits accumulated hot air to disperse and diffuses sunlight. Various adaptations of this section appear in several of Yeang's buildings in the 1980s, on both the horizontal and the vertical planes. The offices within the atrium are stepped back and are fronted with small terraces that are intended to be landscaped. The external walls of the building have recessed glazing, whereas the walls within the atrium are fully glazed.

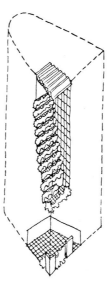

Above

The Plaza Atrium was designed to have an 'interstitial atrium' located at the edge of the building. It was Yeang's intention that vertical landscaping should flourish in the atrium space, though this has not been fully realized. (Ng)

Left

Conceptual sketch of the Plaza Atrium's vertical landscaping.

Far left

The large transitional space located at the edge of the building gives the Plaza Atrium a striking appearance.

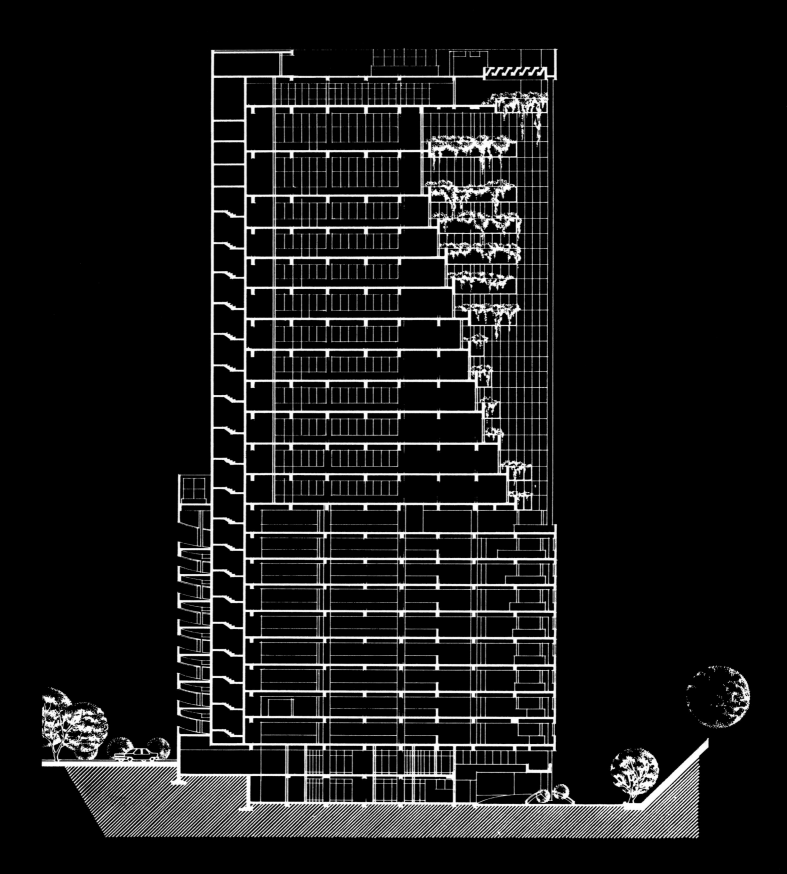

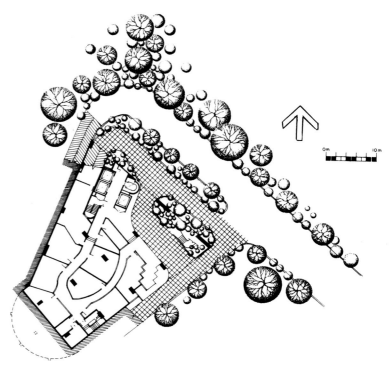

THE BUILDING AS AN ENCLOSURAL VALVE

Plaza Atrium was, for Yeang, an opportunity to develop in a high-rise tower conceptual ideas on buildings as 'enclosural' or 'environmental' valves. In theory, reasons Yeang:

This means the building can be viewed as a series of layers. The enclosure system must not totally exclude the external environment, as say in the case of an aerospace capsule. It should not only filter but also control the entry and the emission of heat, glare, breezes, ventilation, rain, insects, etc. In this sense, the building's openings and 'lids' should be designed and located to operate like working parts of a valve.

Essentially, a valve is a mechanical device for regulating the flow of liquids or gases by movable parts that open, shut or partially obstruct one or more passageways. Viewing the building as an enclosural valve is a useful analogy. In this way, we can articulate various elements in the building as fixed and adjustable 'filter' devices and manipulate them in relation to the internal function, level of external environmental experience, space requirement and comfort required by users.

Some aspects of Plaza Atrium are problematic. Although the notion of the tropical atrium is carried through in a convincing

Opposite

Plaza Atrium, section.

Above

Plaza Atrium, location plan.

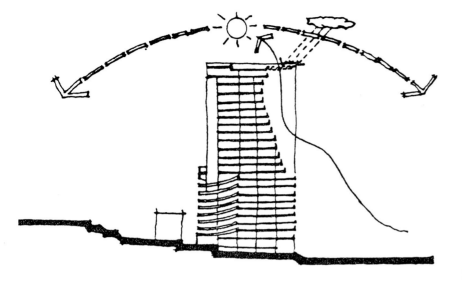

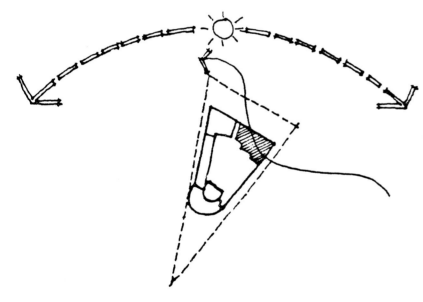

Plaza Atrium, conceptual drawings
showing climatic response.

manner, Yeang's vision of it being a landscaped vertical garden
has never been fulfilled. The balconies are devoid of plants and
in retrospect should have incorporated some form of automatic
watering system for the vertical landscaping to flourish. It is a
fault that Yeang would rectify in the Menara Boustead building
completed three years later, but some of his other subsequent
buildings are also afflicted by the problem. The issue of vertical
landscaping points to a need for public education. Such planting
should ideally become a function of the management of high-rise
buildings, which should involve agreements with contractors so
that they can gain access to private areas in order to carry out
maintenance. Without such agreements the final results can, as
in Plaza Atrium, bear little resemblance to the architect's
conceptual drawings. Plaza Atrium has not been well maintained
and in 1998 looked in need of a major 'make-over'; perhaps the
landscaping could be attended to at the same time.

The site constraints at Plaza Atrium dictated an awkward
geometry. The entrance is an anti-climax, given the strong
impression of the tower from afar. It is constricted: planning is
tight and turning circles are minimal. There is a need in a tropical
high-rise building to give space at ground-floor level 'back to the
people' in the form of areas for social interaction. This is part of
the lifestyle in the tropics: sitting out under trees or upon shaded
verandahs to avoid the heat and to benefit from breezes. The
absence of such an area at Plaza Atrium was particularly

criticized by Lim Chong Keat. Yeang would synthesize this much better in the IBM Plaza, which he completed in 1987.

IDENTITY AND REGIONALISM

In parallel with this environmental focus on the high-rise building, Yeang became closely involved in the discourses on identity and regionalism in architecture. In the 1980s these were issues of increasing concern for architects and intellectuals in Southeast Asia, as they were elsewhere in former colonized countries. This led, in January 1981, to the Malaysian Ministry of Youth and Culture organizing a significant seminar in Kuala Lumpur to discuss the subject of 'Identity in the Arts'. Yeang delivered a paper at the seminar entitled 'Notes on Regional Influences Affecting Design'.[3]

The regionalism and identity issues were intricately connected with the advancement of Malaysian architecture and the Malaysian architectural profession in the 1970s and early 1980s. Upon his return to Malaysia, Yeang had joined the Malaysian Institute of Architects (PAM). First, he became a member of the Institute's Publications Committee, but by 1981 he felt compelled to change what he saw as a bureaucratic institution in which there was rarely any discourse on design. The prevailing mainstream view was that design was subjective and discourse was unnecessary. That year, Yeang stood as an independent candidate for the post of Institute vice-president.

The Council refused to support his nomination but he defeated the Council's own nominee. Two years later, as was the custom, he stepped up to the post of president. The infighting in the profession left some bruises, but Yeang remains philosophical about it: 'You have to stick your neck out,' he says, 'if you are to bring about change.'

Some factions within the Malaysian government were keen to introduce a 'National Style' in architecture and to prescribe guidelines. This was in parallel with similar moves in other countries to renounce the culture of the colonizer and to find an architectural expression that drew its inspiration from the vernacular traditions. There is a now-famous phrase by the French philosopher Paul Ricoeur that sums up succinctly the dilemma faced by Malaysia and other countries in the post-colonial situation:

> In order to get on the road to modernisation, is it necessary to jettison the old cultural past?... On the one hand the nation has to root itself in the soil of its past, forge a national spirit and unfurl this spiritual and cultural revindication of the colonist's personality. But in order to take part in modern civilisation, it is necessary at the same time to take part in scientific, technical and political rationality: something which often requires the pure and simple abandonment of a whole cultural past. There is the

paradox: how to become modern and to return to your sources.[4]

As the president of PAM from 1983 to 1985, Yeang's tactic to deter the precipitous implementation of a national architectural style by these factions was to agree in principle with the broad intention but to insist that such a style needed to be thoroughly discussed and researched. This led to a protracted debate about identity and regionalism in architecture, which coincided with a much wider debate, beyond Malaysia, on critical regionalism, a term that was first used by A. Tzonis and L. Lefaivre in 1981,[5] and one that gained wider currency when used by Kenneth Frampton in 1983 in 'Towards a Critical Regionalism'.[6]

As proposed by Frampton, critical regionalism refers to a measured re-evaluation of specific national characteristics and how historical, social and cultural patterns are manifest in the regional architecture of these countries. The 'critical' part of such an evaluation involves the extent of contemporary interpretation, the degree of literal conformity with and the distance measured from the modern paradigm as a means of comparison. The balance between International Style anonymity and local identity is the key issue in this debate, one that is yet to be resolved since being initiated in the 1980s as a subset of postmodernism. In his own interpretation, Yeang leans more towards modernism than towards an identifiable Malaysian vernacular expression, as

might be expected from his training, but he tempers this with a highly specific climatic response.[7]

In July 1983, the Institute hosted an Aga Khan Regional Seminar in Kuala Lumpur to discuss 'Architecture and Identity'. The seminar was sponsored by the AKAA and the Universiti Teknologi Malaysia. It was attended by delegates from nine countries in Southeast Asia and further afield, including Charles Correa, Tay Kheng Soon, William Lim Siew Wai, Sumet Jumsai, Eric Lye, Hasan-Uddin Khan, Lim Chong Keat, Romi Khosla, and Suha Özkan, then deputy assistant secretary-general of the AKAA.[8] The latter two were Yeang's contemporaries at the AA. In retrospect, Yeang regards the seminar as an important gathering, for it established a number of lasting relationships. It was the first coming together of a number of architects, academics and intellectuals who had previously operated independently within their own spheres of influence. The group represented the cutting edge of architectural discourse in South and Southeast Asia.

All the participants shared 'a common interest in the nature of identity related to cultural change in countries which had been under the influence of colonisation and foreign cultures in the past, and were, in the 1980s, assailed by international multi-national pressures'.[9] Some believed that there was an identity 'crisis'.[10] In Malaysia, this belief seemed well founded in the early 1980s. Anwar bin Ibrahim, then minister of culture and later to become the deputy prime minister of Malaysia, noted in his opening address to the seminar that, as a result, 'There had been attempts to impose *Minangkabau* architecture in Malaysia to represent a national cultural form, and naturally there was some resentment of this amongst architects.'

The seminar was able to agree that: 'Identity is a dynamic evolving process and that it cannot be fabricated, there is a plurality in the many forms that it can take.' The conclusions summed up the general openness of the participants to the notion of change and to a regionalist approach to architecture that is a synthesis of modernity and tradition.[11]

Yeang sees the achievement of his term in office as bringing discussion on design to the fore, but, as he ruefully admits, this lasted for only a decade before other agendas began to dominate. Fifteen years on, he regards the regionalist discourse as being a necessary part of the process of decolonization at the time, but feels that it also had a tendency to pigeon-hole and confine some Asian architects. Concurrently with his term of office as the president of PAM, Yeang served a year – from 1985 to 1986 – as the chairman of the Architects Regional Council of Asia (ARCASIA). His most notable achievement was to bring the Architectural Institute of the People's Republic of China into the Council.

In August 1985, Yeang invited Professor William Porter and his former mentor Professor Ronald Lewcock to participate in a forum on 'Design for High-Intensity Development', held in Kuala Lumpur and organized by the Malaysian Institute of Architects and the Aga Khan Program for Islamic Architecture at Harvard University and the Massachusetts Institute of Technology. Yeang used the forum to present his experimental approach to the design of skyscrapers. In addition to the Plaza Atrium, he illustrated the designs of IBM Plaza and Menara Boustead, which were then under construction in Kuala Lumpur. Singapore architect Tay Kheng Soon posed some searching questions to Yeang:

The ideas of the wind valves and of using the edge of the building as a filter are good ones, but the architectural language used seems to subvert the message of the tropical style it is intended to convey. The Corbusien image, the planar aesthetic, keeps creeping in, even though we profess to want to break the planes and soften the edge of the building. Before we can have a soft-edged building, we have to develop a soft-edged aesthetic by which to convey the idea. Instead we continue using a hard-edged aesthetic and trying to get it to carry the soft-edged message we want to convey. How do we achieve this?

This was a line of enquiry that Tay himself was pursuing and one that would later be articulated in my book *Line Edge and Shade:*

In Search of an Architectural Language for Tropical Asia, a monograph of Tay's work.[12] 'You want to whistle a new song but the same old tune keeps coming up', said Tay. Yeang recalls this remark vividly and he admits that it provoked him and subsequently impacted on his work. He began to develop a new aesthetic, but almost a decade would pass before it would be fully realized in the Menara Mesiniaga (completed in 1992).

The architectural historian William Curtis agreed that the language for the tropical high-rise building had to be developed, and he advised Yeang that: 'It will necessarily have to do with concrete frames and slabs. But it is the grammar that is currently missing. The high-rise buildings underexploit the dialectic between soft and hard. The Plaza Atrium could have gone further with this.' The respected Malaysian architect Lim Chong Keat was critical of another aspect:

> Ken Yeang has not yet addressed the question of context – the relationship of the building to its neighbours. He showed us photographs of the Plaza Atrium that were all taken from a building nearby, but no photograph of that building from the atrium. The outlook, the conflicts, the relationships must be there, but we have not seen them and we are told nothing about them. Experiments in isolation are beautiful in isolation, and can have their own validity. But in context, the final impact can have

disturbing consequences, and we should be more thoughtful about that possibility.

Charles Correa was kinder in his assessment of Yeang's towers and concluded that:

> One reason why high-rise buildings are usually so banal is that intellectually they are so thin. Ken Yeang's buildings are remarkable for the density of intentions he brings to them. It is very easy to build a house that is full of ideas. But most downtown forty-storey office buildings have not an intention to their name. Yeang has taken important steps, both in his own development and in the development of high-rise building more generally.[13]

There was much for Yeang to reflect upon in this critical commentary on his first major high-rise buildings. Nevertheless, the towers generated considerable international interest and were widely published.

VERTICAL LANDSCAPING
IBM Plaza (1983–1987)

The next project in the development of what at this stage Yeang referred to as 'an archetype suited to the tropical climate' was the IBM Plaza, completed in 1987. In this twenty-four-storey tower,

the principal idea explored was that of vertical landscaping in the form of a diagonal garden that climbs one side of the building to the fourteenth storey, where a landscaped void-deck occurs. Traversing this void, the garden emerges and then ascends diagonally, on the opposite side of the tower, to the roof.

IBM Plaza has a hybrid form. The overall massing of the building configuration consists of an office tower linked by a curvilinear bridge to a two-storey crescent-shaped lower block, housing a restaurant and a food court. The two forms are juxtaposed in a plaza to integrate with the adjoining shophouses. The surrounding roads are pedestrianized and paved. The building has a crisp, sharp geometry, with each of the upper floors projecting over the floor below like a slightly displaced pack of cards. This is a development of Yeang's 'filter' ideas, the broken irregular surface and the shading of windows being a reaction against the flat-wall and thin-skin aesthetic of modernist architecture. Here, the aesthetic is derived from the simultaneous resolution of a number of climatic regulatory devices. Yeang explains the principles involved in the following way:

> The building does four things. It sets out to respond by plan and form to the climate. It responds to the requirement for landscaping by introducing planting upwards diagonally across the face of a high-rise built form. It seeks to break away from the conventions of a

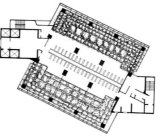

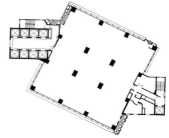

Top

IBM Plaza, with its distinctive silhouette, has quickly become a prominent landmark on the Kuala Lumpur skyline. (AL)

Above left

IBM Plaza, plan of the fourteenth storey.

Above right

IBM Plaza, plan of a typical office floor.

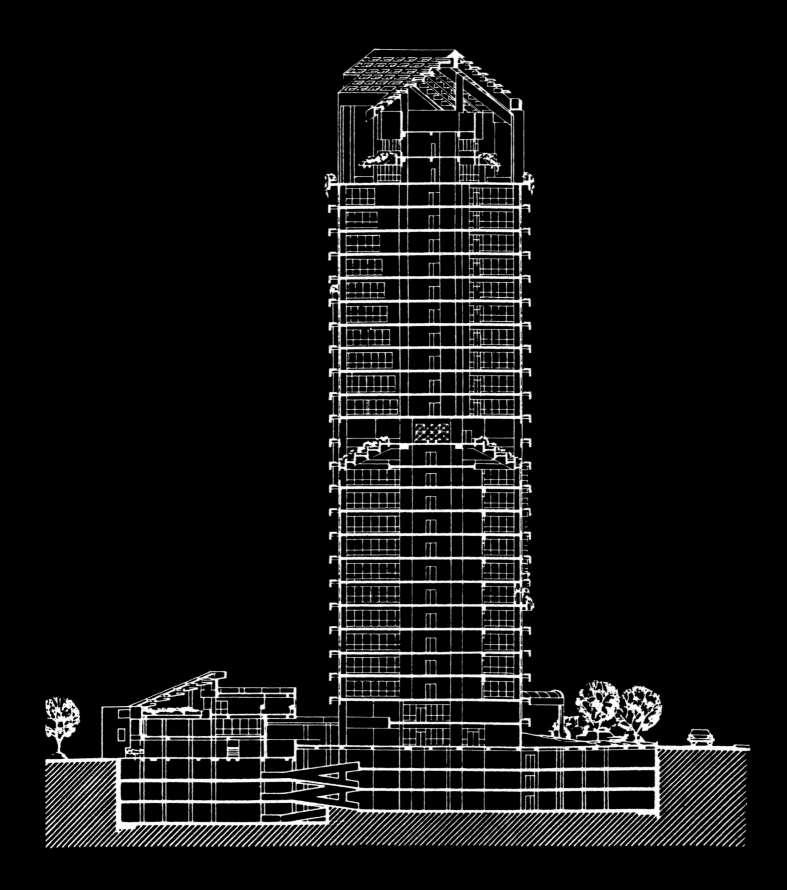

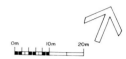

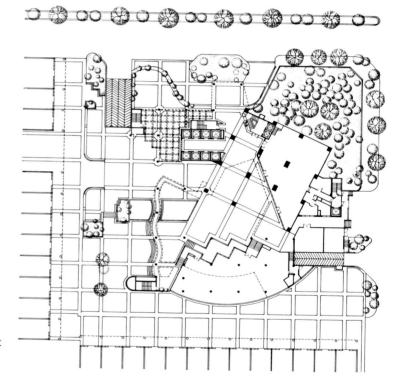

straight plane, curtain-walled modernist tower block. In terms of urban design, it relates and provides linkages to the low-rise commercial shophouses surrounding the base and the pedestrian plaza.

A number of design principles for the tropical urban high-rise prototype are explored in the IBM Plaza. Yeang recognizes that there are two geometries, one being the sun's geometry on its east–west path, and the other being the geometry of the site in relation to the roads, that is, the contextual geometry. The two geometries do not always coincide: the positioning of the building to reduce insolation on the east and west sides also needed to be taken into consideration.

The typical floor plan is orientated towards the north–south axis in relation to the sun's path. The service-cores (lifts, stairs and toilets) are located on the hot sides of the tower (i.e. the east and west sides) – they provide shading. All the lift-cores and staircases are located on the outside of the building (as against central-core positions) so that they receive natural light and ventilation. In this manner, the configuration of the built form responds to the local climate.

At the ground level, the entrance area (including the lift lobby that leads to the plaza) is open to the outside and is naturally ventilated. Precast and pretiled spandrel panels project beyond the edge of each floor to give sun-shading to the glazing. The

Opposite

IBM Plaza, section.

Top

IBM Plaza, sun-path diagram.

Above

IBM Plaza, location plan.

Above

Precast and pretiled spandrel panels project beyond the edge of each floor to give sun-shading to the glazing.

Opposite

The tower is linked by a curvilinear bridge to a two-storey block housing a restaurant and a food court.

upper floors are extended in an asymmetrical pattern resulting in the wedge-shaped projection of the upper floors. This generates an overall form that is irregular and thereby deviates from the conventional tower block.

The top of the tower is pitched as an abstraction of the traditional Malay house form. A version of the Z-beam that Yeang employed for the roof of the Plaza Atrium is adapted and used here as a double roof. Glass-reinforced concrete precast fins shade the roof garden and mechanical rooms on the twenty-fourth floor and create the pitched-roof form. The pitched *attap* roof of the traditional *kampong* house is transformed into a filter device, but retains a symbolic value in addition to its new functional purpose. The sectional profile of these beams differs from that of the Z-beams in the Plaza Atrium in that the former are laid at an incline to create a different filtering effect. Yeang is at this stage gradually evolving a range of filter devices for different locations and situations.

The potential of an open foyer at ground level to receive cooling breezes is exploited. The essence of the tropical high-rise building is to free the ground floor to allow the penetration of prevailing winds. Here, Yeang resolves some of the criticisms of the Plaza Atrium's ground floor made two years earlier by Lim Chong Keat. The potential of the area is recognized and a public plaza creates a behavioural setting for the street life and outdoor dining that one sees throughout Malaysia.

The impact of planting upon Menara
Boustead is to create a soft edge to the
façade – a reaction against the smooth-
skinned modernist aesthetic. (AL)

IBM Plaza is thus a fusion of modernism and the vernacular;
an abstraction of cultural patterns and forms welded to climatic
responses.[14] It is an elegant tower – the form is equally engaging
from all angles, but especially so when glimpsed above the trees
on the main highway from Kuala Lumpur city centre to Taman
Tun Dr Ismail (TTDI) – and has become a significant landmark
on the city skyline. The project was initiated and executed by
Ken Yeang over a period of five years. Learning that IBM rarely
invested in their own offices outside the United States, Yeang
brought the multinational corporation and the developer of the
building together and arranged a deal between the two. IBM
would commit to a long lease of the building prior to
construction, and in return the developer would build to meet
IBM's specifications. Yeang's role highlights a side of the
profession that is often neglected: an architect must have
commissions and opportunities to produce architecture, and if
necessary he or she must create these opportunities. This
demonstrates an entrepreneurial facet of Yeang's character,
something he attributes to the pedagogy at the AA, which
'encouraged me to be proactive in the creation of a project'.

Menara Boustead (1983–1987)

Designed and constructed concurrently with IBM Plaza, Menara
Boustead is a thirty-two-storey office tower connected by an
overhead bridge to a twelve-storey car-parking annex. The site is
located in Kuala Lumpur's Golden Triangle, not far from the
Plaza Atrium. Structurally, it uses prestressed beams to provide
clear spans and column-free office floor spaces. There are
banking halls on the ground and first floors, a helipad on the
thirty-second floor, and in the annex there are spaces for four
hundred cars, a food court and sports facilities.

Completed in 1987, the cladding system uses a double-
ventilated heat-sink shield to reduce the heat load on the
building – in effect, a double wall. It builds upon the idea of
cooling fins, first introduced by Yeang in a smaller, low-rise
project, the Wisma Hong Leong Yamaha (1983), which drew
inspiration from the cooling fins on the engine of a Yamaha
motorcycle. The overall concept of the building significantly
advances Yeang's exploration of the high-rise prototype. All
glazing is recessed unless facing exactly north or south. The
cladding of the building uses a ventilated lightweight composite
aluminium material that enables the heat to be dissipated before
it can be transmitted to the structure. In this building, instead of
a peripheral atrium, the sky-courts are given greater emphasis. It
develops the idea of a tropical building language being soft
edged, ambiguous and multi-layered, as opposed to the

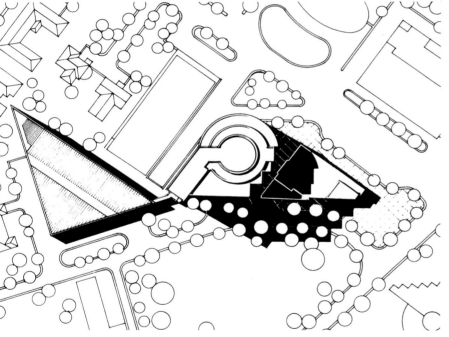

Top

Menara Boustead is the first of Yeang's so-called 'hairy' buildings. (AL)

Above

Menara Boustead, location plan.

Opposite, left

Menara Boustead, section.

Opposite, top right

Menara Boustead, plan of the first storey.

Opposite, bottom right

Menara Boustead, plan of a typical office floor.

Corbusien language of Plaza Atrium, and thus it goes some way to answering Tay Kheng Soon's criticism in 1985. The key idea here is the positioning of the lift-cores and escape-stair-cores on the east and west sides to serve as passive low-energy solar thermal buffers. Secondary ideas explored are the location of well-vegetated corner balconies or 'sky-terraces' at the edges of the building and the incorporation of vertical landscaping on the façade.

THE SOFT-EDGED AESTHETIC

The sky-terraces of Menara Boustead permit the introduction of local planting and landscaping on the upper floors of the building. They provide adequate sun-shading to allow for full-height glazing to enhance the quality of light in the office work space, and they have the potential for the location of supplementary air-conditioning units. The edges of the balconies in Menara Boustead have planter-boxes fed by an automatic fertilizing and watering system, a substantial improvement on the manual watering required in the Plaza Atrium project. The impact of the planting on the elevation is a 'hairiness' that gives a soft edge to the façade. Menara Boustead does not interact with the public domain as well as the IBM building, but in other ways the planting that shrouds the elevations conveys a strong symbolic message about the 'green skyscraper'.

As mentioned above, Yeang refers to the three towers

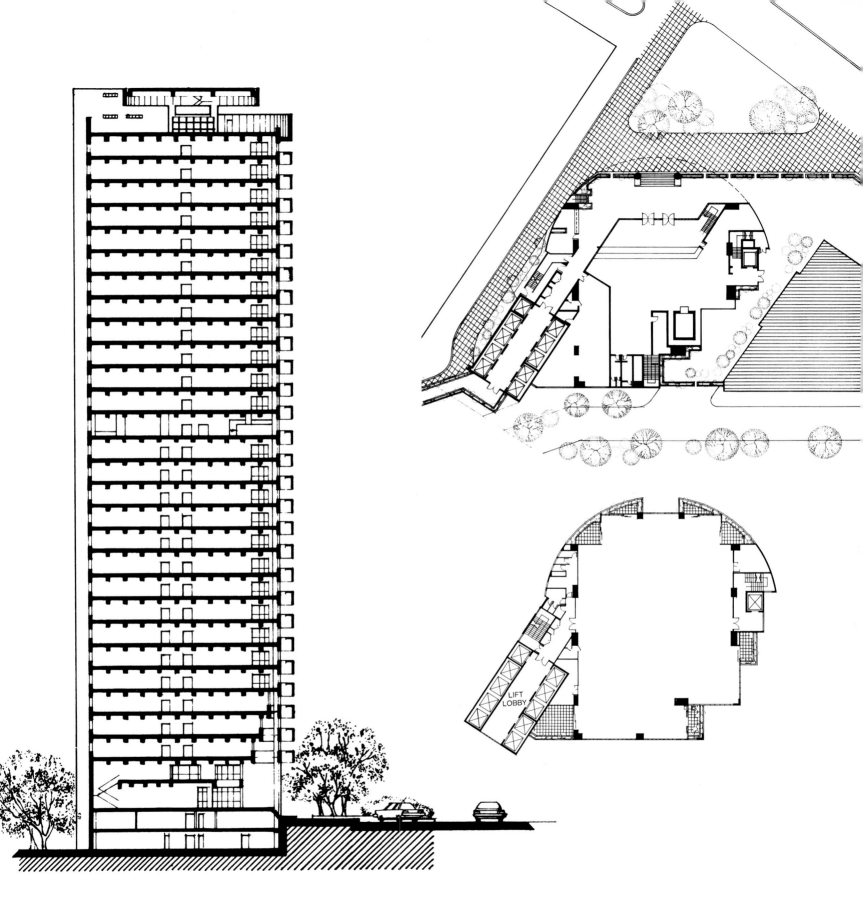

LIFT LOBBY

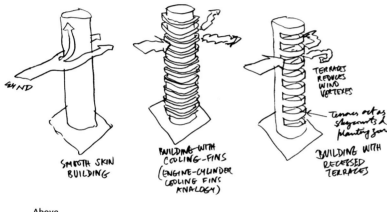

SMOOTH SKIN BUILDING

BUILDING WITH COOLING-FINS (ENGINE-CYLINDER COOLING FINS ANALOGY)

BUILDING WITH RECESSED TERRACES

WIND

TERRACES REDUCES WIND VORTEXES

Terraces act as skycourts & planting zones

Above

Menara Boustead, conceptual sketches of climatic responses.

completed between 1984 and 1987 as the 'Series 1' towers or as 'Primary-Level Design Experiments', each driven by a single 'big idea'. In the next cycle of exploration, Yeang would seek to combine these ideas and to create prototypes for different site conditions. However, in the middle of the 1980s the Malaysian economy, which was still largely dependent on the export of commodities such as rubber and palm oil, was hit hard by a worldwide recession. It would be some years before economic recovery and diversification into high technology and heavy industry would provide the impetus for another spate of high-rise buildings.

Tropical Urban Regionalism (1987)

When Yeang met Kisho Kurokawa in London in 1973, Kurokawa had urged the young student to write a book, remarking that his own first book on Metabolism was written when he was just twenty-four years of age. The downturn in the Malaysian economy in the mid-1980s provided Yeang with an opportunity to commit his ideas to print and he wrote two books, *The Tropical Verandah City*, in 1986, and *Tropical Urban Regionalism*, in 1987. As Kurokawa had predicted, the discipline of writing forced Yeang to organize ideas. It helped to disseminate his experiences and at the same time revealed gaps in his knowledge. Yeang is one of a small but erudite group of practising Asian architects outside academia who publish. Other members of this loosely linked fraternity, which regularly meets through ARCASIA, Asia Design Forum (ADF) and AA Asia, include William Lim Siew Wai, Tay Kheng Soon, Charles Correa, Sumet Jumsai and Tao Ho. They are all contributors, along with younger architects/practitioners such as Tan Hock Beng, Rahul Mehrotra and C. Anjalendran, to an intensifying architectural discourse in South and Southeast Asia.

Tropical Urban Regionalism examines Yeang's ideas on building in the context of Kuala Lumpur. It articulates the need of the newly industrialized and developing countries for an architecture and urban form that reflects cultural and climatic influences in a way that International Modernism has often failed to do.[15] The book is divided into four sections: 'On Building and Thinking', 'Regionalist Design Intentions', 'An Armature for Interpretations' and 'Consequences'.

'On Building and Thinking' is a reflection by Yeang upon the state of architecture in the tropical context, specifically in Malaysia and Singapore. He laments the fact that Asia is in an 'architectural backwater of debate'. This was true in the mid-1980s, for few schools of architecture in the region were then doing research into building in the tropics, and their graduates usually headed for universities in Europe, Australia and the United States – that is, in temperate latitudes – to study problems encountered at first hand in their home countries. Yeang goes on to detail the idea of the building as an 'environmental filter', stressing that his intention was not to provide a prescriptive manual, but simply to give an analogy that could be used for design synthesis and analysis.

'The emergent regionalist architecture', he writes, 'seeks its architectural significance through relating its built configuration, aesthetics, organisation and technical assembly and materials to a certain place and time.' This is a vital connection that links technology with culture. Indeed, there are several connections:

Firstly, a *direct connection* which involves the creative adaptation for contemporary uses of an existing range of built forms; secondly, an *indirect (abstract) connection*, through the interpretation into form, by design, of the general principle derived from an analysis of architectural heritage and cultural traditions; thirdly, an *inclusive contemporary connection* in design through the selective use of current technology, forms and ideas; fourthly, a *landscape connection* that integrates the building with the physical context and natural history; and, fifthly, and perhaps most importantly, a *forward connection* in which design considerations include an anticipation of the likely consequences of the building.

The last two 'connections' foreshadow Yeang's later focus upon ecologically sustainable architecture.[16]

Yeang recognized that architectural regionalism was an evolving enquiry, and he expressed the view that the search for a national identity in architecture was an urgent necessity since the globalization of economic practices was increasingly leading to a submergence of local, regional and national characteristics in architecture.

In the second section of the book, 'Regionalist Design Intentions', Yeang places himself in the heart of the debate on regionalist architecture. He argues that an appropriate regional urban architecture should embody a sense of continuity and place. He deplores the banal appearance of contemporary imported models and calls for an exploration of the abstract and direct links between architectural and cultural heritage.

In the third section, entitled 'An Armature for Interpretations', Yeang illustrated how his own architectural practice attempted to develop an appropriate architecture for the region. This section of the book includes the three major towers completed in Kuala Lumpur up to 1987, together with the Roof-Roof House. Yeang again proposes the building enclosure as an environmental filter, an idea that would be articulated more precisely in a 1989 publication by the present author, *Ken Yeang: Rethinking the Environmental Filter.*[17]

The 'Consequences' of this approach on architectural form are the subject of the fourth section of the book. 'By regarding the building enclosure as an *environmental filter*,' writes Yeang, 'this provokes a critical questioning of the way we perceive the functions of the parts of the building enclosure; attention is brought to the role of components of the enclosure as modifiers of the internal built environment.'

'In the process of giving form to the regionalist connections,' Yeang concludes, 'the results that emerge might appear visually unfamiliar despite the intentions and sources. We must be prepared for this if a new architecture is to emerge.'

A decade later Yeang would shift significantly from the views he held on regionalism and identity in 1987; views that, in retrospect, he would regard as being too reactive and thereby limiting the scope and ambitions of an architect in the Third World. In order to propel his practice onto a world stage, in the mid-1990s he would encompass more generic issues and an agenda, based on his Cambridge doctoral thesis, that is not tied specifically to a location in the tropics.

BUSINESS SKILLS

During the downturn in the Malaysian economy in the late 1970s, one of Yeang's cousins who was also a successful businessman had advised him to do a course in marketing. Impressed by the course, Yeang signed up in 1979 to take a further course in management, and later another in financial control, none of which is part of the training in schools of architecture. Some years later Yeang wrote:

> Architects are not properly taught about business in their education. Few schools of architecture are prepared to teach their students how to set up practice or how to be successful in their professional practices. Architects have to learn their business acumen on the ground. They are expected to acquire business knowledge, skills and attitudes during their mandatory apprenticeship before professional registration. Ethically, I believe an architect must be financially solvent in his business. A financially unstable architect is an instant liability to his clients. He

may be too busy fending off his overdue creditors, at his business as well as his home, to do his work or to manage his practice properly. Some architects openly express the view that they enjoy their work regardless of whether they are paid or not. This is a horrendous attitude that is detrimental to the whole profession.

'There are three essential aspects of an architectural practice,' Yeang believes, 'getting the business, doing the business and running the business':

Getting the business is the marketing function of the practice. If an architect is not able to market his business well then he will not get any commissions. If the architect does not get any commissions, then no matter how talented, how well staffed or equipped the company may be, the business will have no business to conduct. Marketing is more than just getting sales, it has to pervade the whole organization.

Doing the business is the actual performing of the scope of work of an architect – design, design development, documentation, contract administration, etc. If the architect does not do this well, he might be sued by his client or be subject to disciplinary action by the professional institute.

Running the business is the internal management, administration, personnel management, financial planning, accounting and fee collection. These are usually the most neglected aspects of practice by many architects, but if they are not done well the firm will fall apart.

Yeang sees it as equally important to exhibit his work. This was emphasized to him by Roy Landau at the AA in the early 1970s. In 1985, Yeang and six other architects from Kuala Lumpur held a joint exhibition of their work entitled 'Houses – 7 KL Architects' at Tokyo's Ginza Pocket Park Gallery. The show was organized by another of Yeang's mentors, Dr Takekuni Ikeda of Nihon Sekkei.

Yeang brings to the functions of marketing, management and financial control the same disciplined approach that pervades every aspect of his investigation of the skyscraper. It is a feature of his work that gets little recognition, but it has not come about without rigorous application and continuing education.[18]

'Everything is to do with focus', says Yeang. 'You must decide what you do best and concentrate upon that.' There is an *aide-mémoire* alongside Yeang's desk in the T. R. Hamzah and Yeang office; it reads simply:

Focus: The Future of Your Company Depends on It.

2 Focus on Towers

In 1989, in *Ken Yeang: Rethinking the Environmental Filter,*[1]
I looked at Yeang's work in the context of the discourse on
regionalism and identity with which societies in the Third World
had been grappling throughout the 1980s. It was an important
issue for many developing countries in the aftermath of
colonization. They were simultaneously confronted with the
tasks of modernizing their economies and overcoming a
perceived conflict with traditional values. In the monograph,
I situated Yeang's work within a taxonomy of regionalism,
offering assessments of the significance of the Roof-Roof House,
Plaza Atrium, IBM Plaza and Menara Boustead, while an
introductory essay built upon the notion of critical regionalism
as articulated by Kenneth Frampton, Hasan-Uddin Khan and
Peter Davey. The taxonomy was a useful tool for analysing and
reviewing the spectrum of approaches to regionalism in
architecture. In relation to Yeang, *Rethinking the Environmental
Filter* highlighted the lack, at that time, of a concise theoretical
framework for his work. It was apparent that Yeang, too, was
conscious of a need to define in more empirical terms the
ecological agenda. The monograph enabled him to assess

the progress that he had made from 1976 to 1989.[3] As a result
of the book's publication, in August 1989 Yeang was invited by
Ho Pak Toe, then the director of the School of Architecture at the
National University of Singapore, to conduct a workshop on the
tropical skyscraper. (He later repeated this workshop with
variations at universities in Hong Kong, Malaysia, the United
States, Australia and Britain.[2]) Initial exploration of the tropical
high-rise building subsequently gave way to the bioclimatic
skyscraper ideas, and then to the green skyscraper agenda.[3]

CRITICAL DISCOURSE: THE ASIA DESIGN FORUM

Yeang completed IBM Plaza and Menara Boustead with
the intention of immediately continuing the exploration
of the tropical skyscraper, and had two projects already at the
conceptual stage: the Northam City Tower in Penang and
the Kinta Apartments in Kuala Lumpur. But the Malaysian
economy nose-dived into recession and both projects were
swiftly abandoned. The economic downturn prompted Yeang
to review his commercial (and discursive) position.

Yeang saw that Asia, apart from Japan, was isolated from the
energetic debates on design that he had enjoyed at the AA.
It prompted him to seek ways of stimulating critical discourse
about both his own and other architects' projects in Asia. In
1989, he had the idea of creating 'a network of communications
between progressive-minded Asian architects and designers'.[4]

In April 1990 he convened a meeting, at Cherating in Malaysia, of twelve architects from India, South Korea, Malaysia, Singapore and Taiwan. The group called itself the Asia Design Forum (ADF). The proceedings of the meeting were recorded, as were those of a second forum held one year later in the Sorak Mountains of South Korea. In due course these were edited and published by the chairman of the inaugural meeting, Dr P. G. Raman, under the title *Criticism and the Growth of Architectural Ideas*.[5] Yeang, the founder of the Forum, participated as one of the architects who presented their schemes for critical review by their peers. Yeang's paper that accompanied the presentation of his skyscrapers outlined the state-of-the-art in tropical-skyscraper design. The criticism he received was forthright but constructive. Raman's own critical comments, for instance, reinforced the need for quantification to give credibility to Yeang's work:

> Some of the elements used by Ken Yeang appeared to many of us to be aesthetic as opposed to functional. Planting appeared rather two-dimensional. Is it worth looking at it more three-dimensionally, perhaps growing trees several storeys high through holes in floors? Perhaps the idea of covering the building with plants should be looked at on the cityscape level rather than on the basis of individual buildings. Energy auditing of Ken Yeang's

buildings ought to be done to determine the real benefits of some of the devices proposed. Otherwise most of the ideas will continue to remain tentative and not challenge the conventional approaches to the design of tall buildings in the tropics. Tall buildings are here to stay, as cities will be constrained to remain compact for ecological reasons, and the idea of conceiving buildings as landscape elements (e.g. tall buildings as mountains covered in greenery) is one idea which goes beyond being a simple gesture towards tropicality.[6]

Yeang readily admits that for two years (1987–9) he had temporarily 'lost his way' and that he needed to refocus. His three completed towers in Kuala Lumpur had achieved international interest but he was aware that more-intensive thought had to be given to the next generation of skyscrapers. Raman's remarks suggested a strictly ecological approach. This was significant, for the idea of measuring the inputs and outputs of buildings was a key factor in Yeang's essay 'Framework for Ecological Design', which had formed part of his doctoral thesis at Cambridge. Elsewhere, Lam Khee Poh has also written of the need to establish the validity of Yeang's ideas by conducting audits on designed and completed buildings. It is a view shared by Professor Tunney Lee of the Chinese University of Hong Kong. Critics will continue to be cautious in their acceptance of ideas and propositions until the results of independent building audits are disseminated.[7]

FOCUS ON SKYSCRAPERS

After the period of uncertainty in the late 1980s, Yeang's focus sharpened and his *modus operandi* changed. Admitting that the earlier towers were 'rather intuitive interpretations of bioclimatic principles',[8] he set himself the task of 'rethinking the skyscraper' from very first principles. The fundamental agenda for this task had already been laid out in his doctoral thesis. By adopting a more quantitative approach, future towers would have a more precise resolution. Not in the least modest about his intentions, he confided: 'I want to be able to do the best designs for skyscrapers in the world. The concept of the "bioclimatic skyscraper" has to become synonymous with the name Hamzah and Yeang.' The intensity of this desire is palpable. Yeang rationalizes it in this way: 'Architects often ask me how Hamzah and Yeang has managed to "leap-frog" from the local milieu onto the "world stage". My reply is that you must first identify what is your single most important asset, your strength as an architect, then you must concentrate on it. I would say to any aspiring young architect that you must focus.'[9] Yeang is given to telling apocryphal stories when advising young architects. He will often tell the story of an international tennis player whose strength was his left forearm volley and who eventually became Wimbledon Champion by concentrating on the power of this stroke. In 1989, Yeang essentially identified his strength as ecologically responsive large buildings, and that has been the focus of the practice for the last decade.

THE TURNING-POINT

The 'turning-point' for Yeang was an exhibition of his work entitled 'Tropical Skyscrapers' that was held in the Tokyo Designers' Space Gallery in the Axis Building, Tokyo, in January 1990 and was coordinated by Hidenori Seguchi. The positive response from the Japanese critics convinced Yeang that it was towards the skyscraper that his energies should be directed. He returned to Kuala Lumpur with a renewed sense of purpose and vigorously sought new commissions to explore the possibilities. Fortunately the economy was reviving and there was an air of confidence in Malaysian financial institutions. He began work on a new series of skyscrapers in which he attempted to integrate all his research and to develop a series of prototypical solutions. Yeang's work shifted from the 'aesthetic' to the 'scientific', from being a single 'big idea' to a more technical orientation, or, as he describes it, from a 'divergent' to a 'convergent' viewpoint.

Menara Mesiniaga (completed 1992)

Menara Mesiniaga is the headquarters building of an IBM franchise located in Subang Jaya, near Kuala Lumpur. The client

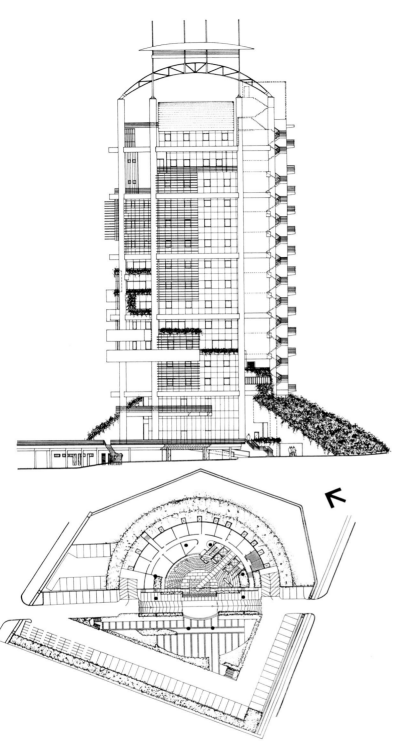

Top

Menara Mesiniaga, south-west elevation.

Opposite

Menara Mesiniaga. 'The total effect is
of a pure cylindrical form, radically

Above

Menara Mesiniaga, plan of the first storey.

corrupted by irregular recesses and
projects' (Abel 1994). (Ng)

commissioned Yeang to build a high-tech corporate showcase.
A site with high visibility was selected, and the building plans
were approved in 1989. The fifteen-storey tower, modest by
recent standards in Kuala Lumpur, nevertheless stands out from
its immediate context. It has become a landmark on the road
from the Subang domestic airport (formerly the international
airport) to the city.

The circular building has a tripartite structure that consists of
a sloping landscaped base, a spiralling body with landscaped
sky-courts and external louvres that shade the offices, and an
upper floor (or fifth façade) that houses recreational facilities, a
swimming pool and a sun-roof. The structure of the building is
exposed and the tubular-steel structure that crowns the tower is
intended for the future installation of solar panels to further
reduce energy consumption. Building automation systems (BAS),
an active 'intelligent building' (IB) feature, are used in the building
for saving energy.

The interstitial spaces in the Menara Mesiniaga high-rise
tower are a dramatic improvement on Yeang's earlier projects.
The landscaping of the sky-courts and terraces is well established
and receives regular maintenance. The idea of landscape
spiralling up the outside of the tower and linking with the sloping
base creates physical continuity and encourages species
diversity. The sky-courts provide visual relief for the office worker
and are used by some employees for brief respites from the

Above

Menara Mesiniaga, the entrance vestibule and reception area. (Ng)

Right

Menara Mesiniaga, the entrance canopy and drop-off point for visitors arriving by car or taxi. (Ng)

Opposite, top

Menara Mesiniaga has become a landmark on the way from the domestic airport to the city. (Ng)

Opposite, bottom

Menara Mesiniaga, conceptual drawings.

Opposite

A variety of sun-shading devices are used on Menara Mesiniaga, combined with deeply inset sky-courts. (RP)

Left

Menara Mesiniaga's roof-top pool, deserted during the week, is a focus of family activity at the weekend. (Ng)

Below

The sky-courts are used by a number of the building's occupants for brief respites from office routine. There is a need to relate the activities within the spaces adjoining the sky-courts to the open-to-sky space. (Ng)

stress of staring at a computer screen, though the numbers are disappointingly few. Perhaps others will come to recognize these benefits in time – the architect has provided the opportunity.

The façade of the building is designed to be an environmentally responsive 'sievelike' filter and not a 'hermetically sealed skin'. Louvres of varying configuration relate to the orientation of the building to the sun and reduce solar gain. Deep insets in the façade permit the use of full-height clear glazed curtain walls on the north- and south-facing façades. The planar Corbusien image of Plaza Atrium and IBM Plaza is abandoned: Menara Mesiniaga looks distinctly high-tech, the external cladding being steel and glass curtain walling. The placement of the core functions on the hottest (east) side of the tower contributes to the ecological sensitivity. Local taxi-drivers refer to it as 'the rocket', and it does indeed look as if it is poised for take-off.

Menara Mesiniaga is a seminal building that integrates all of Yeang's previous research into the principles of the design of tall buildings in tropical climates. It is the first of what he terms the 'Series 2' towers. It heralds the arrival of an original, new type of skyscraper, the form of which is derived from the application of ecological principles.

In 1995, the Menara Mesiniaga building received an Aga Khan Award for Architecture; the selection process is recorded in the book *Architecture Beyond Architecture*.[10] Charles Jencks, one of

the members of the jury that awarded the prize, explaining
the reason for the tower's selection, says: 'This striking
interpretation of the corporate "landmark" skyscraper explores
a new direction for an often pompous building type. Instead
of a typically authoritarian and introverted statement of a
multinational corporation, the tower is a robust, informal and
open expression of emerging technology'.[11]

'The result', Jencks concludes, 'recalls the climatic
architecture of the 1950s and Frank Lloyd Wright's skyscraper
projects, in a move towards a new architecture for the 1990s. It is
a striking alternative to the reigning mode of corporate towers
and a new synthesis for contemporary architecture that is
responsive to the climate of a particular place and finds

inspiration for a new architectural language from forces that
are ultimately cosmic.'[12]

Peter Eisenmann, another member of the jury, has no doubts
about its relevance: 'Menara Mesiniaga', he asserts, 'is one of
the few projects that contributes new thinking to the general
culture of architecture.'[13] In 1996, underlining this critical
acclaim, the building was awarded the International Architecture
Award of the Royal Australian Institute of Architects.

Menara Mesiniaga is not problem-free, however. Due to high
levels of humidity, some rusting can be observed, and some of
the insulation material on the underside of the roof has proven
not to be durable in the Malaysia context. It points to the need
for life-cycle costing of the materials used in skyscraper
construction; in Yeang's later ecological agenda such
information on the inputs and outputs of a building is accorded
much greater priority.

MBf Tower (completed 1994)

The architectural language of the MBf Tower on the island of
Penang, completed two years later, is in sharp contrast with that
of the Menara Mesiniaga. The MBf project had a chequered
history. Originally known as the Northam City Tower, the
building was shelved in the 1986–9 recession. Revived in the
early 1990s, it has a Metabolist image with overtones of the spirit
of Archigram. It forms a 'bridge' between the Corbusien

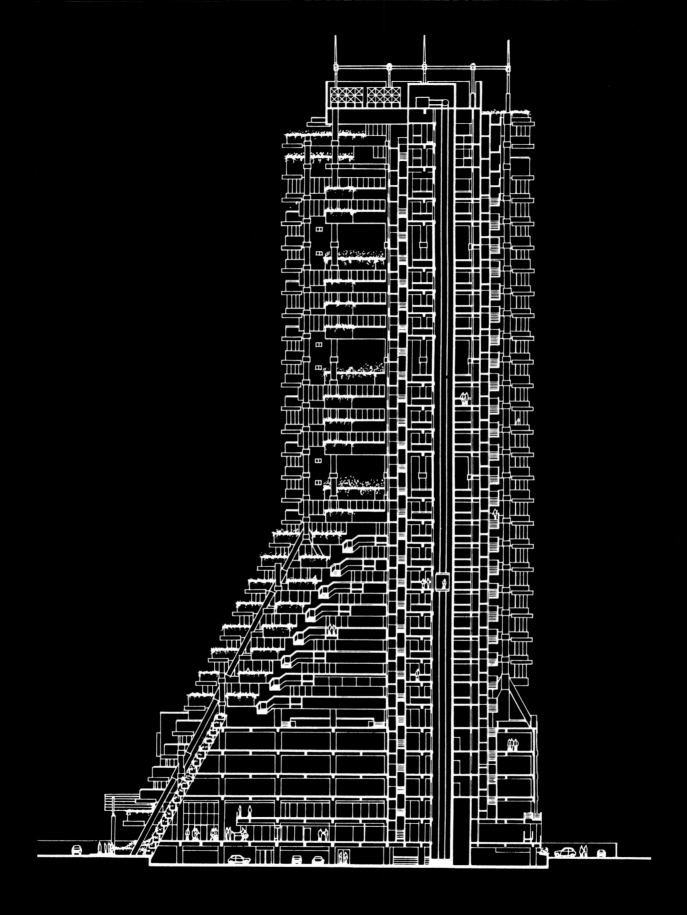

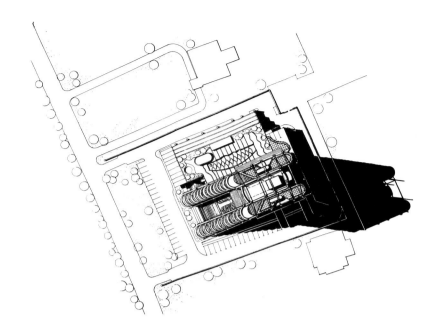

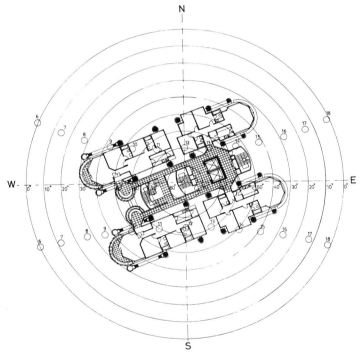

language of Yeang's early towers and the new generation of 'Series 2' towers. It also looks ahead to schemes undertaken in the late 1990s, such as the Expo 2005 Nagoya Hyper-Tower (designed 1998).

MBf Tower is a thirty-one-storey building that comprises a six-storey podium containing offices, retail spaces and a banking hall, above which are sixty-eight apartment units. The reinforced concrete frame is in the form of two separate rectangular towers with curved ends: each is one apartment wide and two deep, linked together by a central, open-air circulation core. The towers flank shared, double-height sky-courts, that provide natural ventilation and 'places-in-the-sky' for planting. The lift lobbies are naturally ventilated with bridgelike walkways leading to the apartment units. Floors are designed to be column-free, the tower columns being located at the periphery of the apartment units and the load being transferred via transfer beams at the podium. The office floors are cooled with central water-cooled package air-conditioning units with variable air-volume control.

The structure has a dramatically inclined south-western façade, which steps back halfway up the building with landscaped planter-boxes and open terraces overlooking the sea to the south and west. The enlarged bottom half accommodates larger apartments and office spaces and also gives the building a striking profile reminiscent of the A-frame structures of Paul Rudolph or the work of the Japanese Metabolists.

Above

MBf Tower, sun-path diagram.

Opposite

MBf Tower, section.

Top

MBf Tower, site plan.

Left

Inhabitants of MBf Tower can enjoy wonderful views and experience bracing sea breezes. (RP)

Above

The tower is tough and muscular in appearance. (RP)

Above

Buildings like MBf Tower's neighbours, with blue-tinted glass to the left and brown-tinted glass to the right, can be found anywhere in the world. (RP)

Opposite, left

MBf Tower, plan of the first storey.

Opposite, right

MBf Tower, plan of the sixth storey.

If the spirit of Archigram is also present in this work it is hardly surprising, for 'Cedric Price and the emergent Archigram figures were among the influences that Yeang experienced as a student, together with the Tropical Studies School'.[14] Yeang continues to maintain strong links with London. 'All these influences', says Professor Alan Balfour, 'are still present in his work and the imagination, yet a transmutation has occurred in the desire to form a response to the nature of a Malaysian and Asian reality through the forces of climate'.[15]

The MBf project examined the insertion of transitional spaces in the upper parts of the building and the placement of residential apartment units into the structure as 'detached bungalows' in the sky. Penang enjoys prevailing winds from the north-east and south-west and the orientation of the tower is ideal to maximize their effectiveness. Each apartment unit is designed to have maximum external wall surfaces to increase its natural- and cross-ventilation opportunities but the apartments do have the option of air-conditioning. There are panoramic views from the balconies of the apartments and the bridges that connect to the central lift lobby. Regrettably, once again, as in Plaza Atrium, the landscaping is inadequate. The balconies were conceptualized as planted gardens-in-the-sky but very few of the building's residents have provided the symbolic greenery to accompany the ecologically responsive features of the tower.

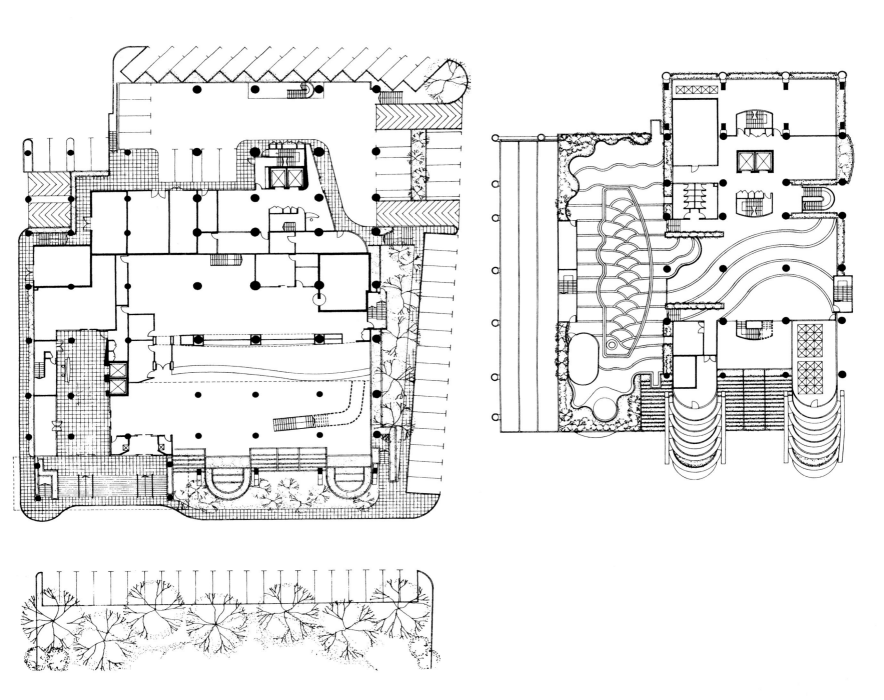

In spite of this, the MBf Tower is impressive. It is a building with 'attitude' which, though smaller than the two high-rise towers that flank it, stands out. It is a muscular, tough and assertive advocate of Yeang's ecological agenda. It is particularly striking in that its immediate neighbours, one clad in blue-tinted glass and the other in brown-tinted glass, are almost offensive for their bland international corporate imagery.

Central Plaza (completed 1996)

The twenty-nine-storey Central Plaza tower is located on a long narrow site in Kuala Lumpur. It has an east–west axis with the narrow west façade facing a main street, Jalan Sultan Ismail, thereby demanding views out. It is far from the ideal configuration for a building that is intended to be responsive to climate.

Office floors are column-free. To achieve this, structural cross-bracing is provided to the end columns on the east and west façades. The structure is projected above the roof and creates a distinctive silhouette on the city skyline. Sun-shading to the west façade is created by expressing the structure and deeply recessing the façade glazing. Similarly, the east façade has wide balconies as sun-shading.

Planter-boxes ascend diagonally up the north face of the building, terminating at the poolside terrace on the roof. But the landscaping is disappointing, for the same reasons

Opposite, left

Central Plaza, section.

Opposite, right

Vertical planting ascends diagonally up the north-facing façade of Central Plaza, terminating at the poolside terrace on the roof of the building. This façade does not receive direct insolation. (Ng)

Above

The potential of Central Plaza's interstitial space is demonstrated by the cafeteria on the twenty-eighth storey. (RP)

Right

Central Plaza, typical floor plan (twelfth to twenty-third storeys).

Below right

Central Plaza, section.

Below

Central Plaza, north elevation.

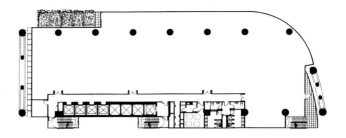

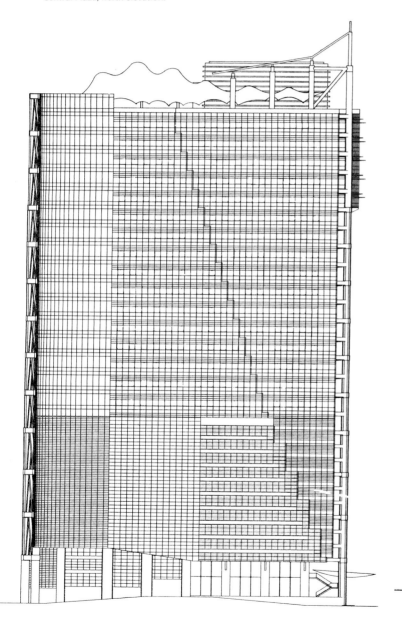

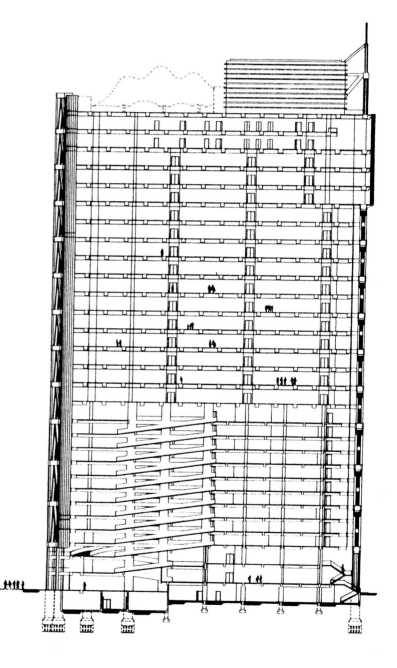

that the Plaza Atrium and MBf Tower landscaping fails to impress. The planter-boxes, which, in theory, should create a contiguous 'staircase' of greenery and assist in biodiversity, have sparse vegetation and are ineffective. But the roof-top swimming pool is a delightful surprise, an oasis in the city with surreal views of the neighbouring towers. The fully glazed curtain wall on the north façade gives an uninterrupted view of the distant hills beyond Ampang. This façade does not receive direct insolation, so it has a sun-shade-free elevation.

The main staircase is naturally ventilated, as is the ground-floor lobby, while the lift lobbies are naturally ventilated in part. The core, which consists of the lift lobby, stairways and toilets, has both natural ventilation and natural lighting. The escape staircase is 'open-to-sky'.

Climatically responsive features, such as the deeply recessed balconies and the stepped planter-boxes, give the tower a strong identity, and it has attracted a coterie of small companies in search of a prestigious building from which to operate. A number of the occupants express genuine pleasure at the environmental features. A business centre on the twenty-eighth storey has a cafeteria with a generously landscaped garden on the east-facing sky-terrace. The management has provided seating and tables for staff who wish to use the space. It is a demonstration of the potential of the sky-court when used by a sensitive tenant.

Above

Central Plaza's roof-top swimming pool is an oasis in the city, with surreal views of the neighbouring towers. (RP)

Right

The thirty-seven-storey Menara TA1 can be seen here in the foreground. (Ng)

Opposite, top

The TA1 tower is a well-detailed addition to the city skyline with a number of climate-responsive features. (RP)

Opposite, middle

The roof-top level of Menara TA1 is utilized as a communal space. A tensile membrane structure protects an entertainment area. (RP)

Opposite, bottom

Menara TA1, sun-path diagram.

Menara TA1 (completed 1996)

Menara TA1 occupies another narrow rectangular site in Kuala Lumpur. Work on the thirty-seven-storey skyscraper commenced in 1994 and was completed in 1996. Viewed along one of the city's principal boulevards, Menara TA1 appears in the foreground beneath the twin towers of Cesar Pelli's Petronas Building, but it is by no means overawed by its lofty neighbour. The site conditions here are such that the geometry of the tower and the geometry of the sun's path do not coincide. The building is orientated diagonally north-west–south-east, which is far from ideal for buildings near the Equator.

The typical internal office floors are column-free. The external skin is glazed with tempered float glass and there are a variety of sun-shading devices on the west- and south-west-facing façades. The north and south corners do not have louvres since there is minimum insolation on these surfaces.

The service-core, which consists of the lift lobby, toilets, fire stairs, and mechanical and electrical (M. & E.) rooms, is located on the east side of the structure. It acts as a barrier or shield, keeping the morning sun out of the offices, while allowing natural lighting and natural ventilation into the core areas.

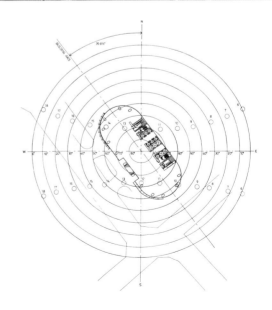

The roof-top level is used as a communal space, and a tensile membrane structure provides protection to an entertainment area. This structure is largely decorative, rather than fulfilling any strict ecological function, but it does provide a recognizable

feature on the city skyline. It has been designed to withstand maximum gusts of 42m/sec. Another tensile canopy is used at the entrance to the building to give protection to visitors arriving by vehicle. The ground-floor entrance lobby is naturally ventilated.

The opportunities to make significant advances on this project, in terms of the bioclimatic aspects, were minimal compared with the Menara Mesiniaga. The site orientation and configuration severely limited the geometric options. But the tower is nevertheless a well-detailed and sophisticated addition to the city skyline, with a number of modest climate-responsive features. It would be instructive to know if the various sun-shading measures provided do in fact have a significant effect on the energy consumption of the building.

Casa-Del-Sol Apartments (completed 1996)

The Casa-Del-Sol Apartments are situated at Bukit Antarabangsa, on the outskirts of Kuala Lumpur. The eleven-storey residential tower has a semicircular form incorporating 160 apartments. The apartment units face east with a view into a lushly wooded valley. The central open space, embraced by the tower, has a swimming pool and a communal clubhouse.

West-facing, single-loaded access corridors serve as a buffer and as sun-shading to the west side of the building. The corridors are separated from the curved residential slab

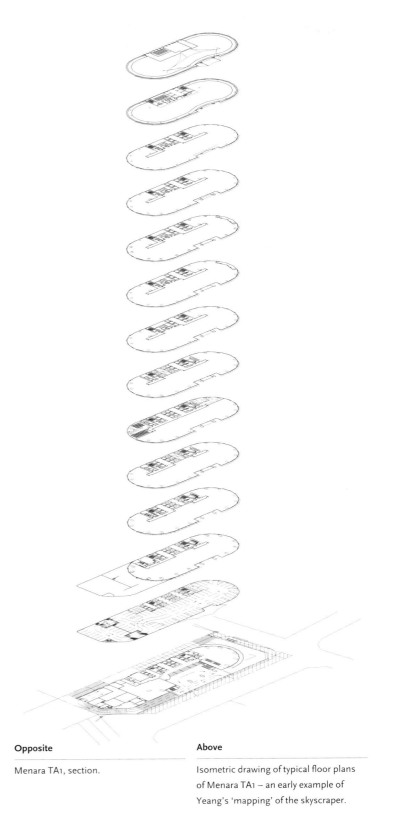

Opposite

Menara TA1, section.

Above

Isometric drawing of typical floor plans of Menara TA1 – an early example of Yeang's 'mapping' of the skyscraper.

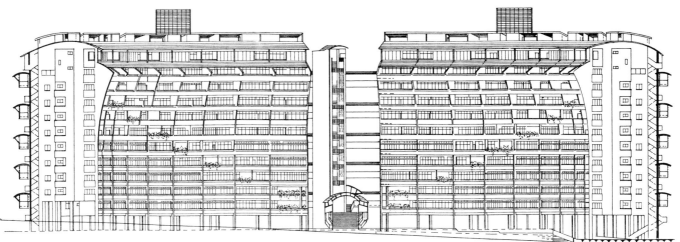

Opposite, top

A swimming pool and a communal clubhouse occupy the central open space of the Casa-Del-Sol Apartments. (Ng)

Opposite, bottom

Casa-Del-Sol Apartments, east elevation.

Above left

The main lift lobby and staircases that separate the two halves of the curved Casa-Del-Sol Apartments tower block are naturally ventilated. (RP)

Above right

On the west side of the tower, a single-loaded access corridor serves as a buffer and as a shading device from the afternoon sun. (RP)

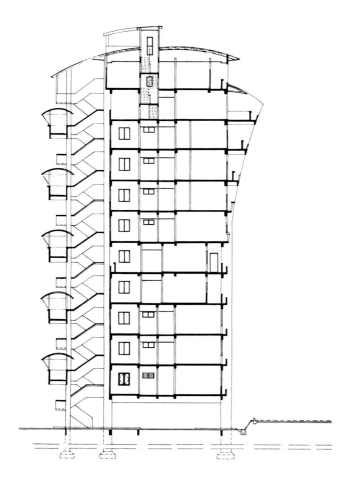

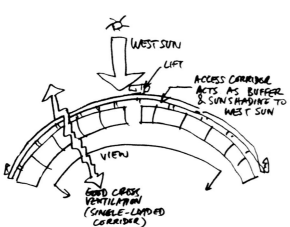

WEST SUN

LIFT

ACCESS CORRIDOR ACTS AS BUFFER & SUN SHADING TO WEST SUN

VIEW

GOOD CROSS VENTILATION (SINGLE-LOADED CORRIDOR)

Top

Casa-Del-Sol Apartments, section.

Above

Casa-Del-Sol Apartments, conceptual sketch showing shading and ventilation.

block by a gap that gives privacy to the apartments and also increases cross-ventilation. This element reminds one vividly of Ralph Erskine's designs for the Byker Wall in the north of England. The open-to-sky access verandah is sensible in the tropics, and its separation from the slab block gives a strong articulation of the building's elements. There is an openness and a permeability in the section, qualities that cannot be appreciated from drawings alone. All the apartments are designed with natural ventilation.

The main lift lobby and staircases that separate the two halves of the curved tower block are naturally lit and ventilated. The project has a number of planted and terraced sky-courts that are spatially interconnected. These sky-courts provide terraces for the adjoining residential units.

As with the MBf Tower in Penang, the most impressive feature of the Casa-del-Sol Apartments is the effectiveness of the passive energy-conservation measures. It is the initial configuration that is the main factor underpinning a genuine low-energy building. 'Sixty percent of the energy used in a building in its entire life-cycle is in the mechanical devices used for heating or cooling and ventilating or air-conditioning etc.,' says Yeang emphatically, 'so if you want to reduce the energy used ... you should design a building which is low-energy in a passive way. If you don't configure the building properly in the first place through bioclimatic principles, then some of the electromechanical devices you put in will have to correct the mistakes you made in the first place, and that makes total nonsense of a low-energy building'.[16]

TOWARDS THE BIOCLIMATIC SKYSCRAPER

The four high-rise buildings in this chapter represent what Yeang retrospectively terms the Series 2 towers. All were designed between 1989 and 1993 and essentially they reassemble the 'single big ideas' inherent in the Series 1 towers into a new series of buildings that are increasingly holistic in their approach. Ivor Richards refers to projects such as Menara Mesiniaga as the 'Sun-Path' projects, and others such as the MBf Tower as the 'Wind-Rose' projects.[17] Yeang disagrees with this taxonomic labelling of the towers, for it suggests that as with the earlier buildings their design is centred around one 'big idea', whereas they embody all the expertise previously acquired. He also sees the Series 2 towers as progressive developments of prototypes for different situations.

Yeang's discursive position shifted substantially in this period of refocusing. He had become increasingly uncomfortable with the strident tones of the identity debate and the limitations that he perceived in the regionalist position. There was a gradual change in Yeang's terminology from the 'tropical skyscraper' of the 1980s to the 'bioclimatic skyscraper' of the early 1990s. This reflected an acceptance of the coexistence of local identities and global identities and the universal applicability of his ecological agenda.

The fact that Yeang has received so many commissions to build towers in tropical Asia is in some measure due to the boom in Asian economies in the early 1990s – more towers were being built in Asia than any other part of the world. However, much of the expertise in skyscraper design is in the United States, Europe and Japan. This expertise is not willingly 'given away' for it ensures that a large share of the international demand is directed to the profession in these countries. For an architect in Southeast Asia to acquire expertise in this building type is therefore not easy, so Yeang's decision in 1990 to focus on high-rise architecture was courageous. Some Asian architects were content simply to be the production office for towers designed by architects from developed countries, but Yeang set about questioning every premise on which the skyscraper was founded. Gradually, his focus on tall buildings in the tropics was extended to enable the principles of designing with climate to be applied to skyscrapers in both temperate and subtropical locations.

3 Globalizing the Discourse

THE BIOCLIMATIC SKYSCRAPER

The 1992 United Nations 'Earth Summit' in Rio de Janeiro led to the publication of the influential *Agenda 21*. Issues of sustainability and of sustainable development were accepted as key concerns of national and city governments. The International Union of Architects (UIA) Conference in Chicago in 1993 underlined the concern of the international architectural community about the future of the world's environment and its resources. Energy consumption, global warming and pollution are significant factors but the key issue is how to cope with rapid urbanization and the management of cities. This is where the most intense environmental damage is taking place. If cities in the developing world achieve the unsustainable level of resource use that is currently 'enjoyed' by the richest cities in the developed world, we may 'soon experience large-scale ecosystem collapse'.[1] It is the densely populated cities that hold the key to a sustainable future.

The proposition that Yeang makes for the skyscraper as an ecologically responsive building is regarded by most architects and laymen with acute suspicion, and by some with derision. The skyscraper is arguably the city's most intensive building type. Skyscrapers, in comparison with small ecologically responsive buildings, are by no means low-energy, nor are they self-evidently ecological building types, for by virtue of their enormous size they are high consumers of energy and materials.

But as Yeang points out, 'it is a building type that will not just simply go away'. The skyscraper will continue to be built in the foreseeable future, in order to accommodate ever-increasing populations, particularly in the rapidly growing cities of Asia. This condition will remain until radical changes are effected in political policy and planning practice to reverse the current trend of high rural-to-urban migration.[2]

Yeang argues that the design of this massive building type as an ecologically responsive building has to be urgently addressed, for the alternative is a situation where an ever-increasing number of high-energy-consuming, polluting, waste-producing tall buildings will be constructed in the rapidly developing cities of the world, particularly those of the developing world. 'Research efforts must be directed to developing strategies for the design of ecologically responsive skyscrapers. The immediate benefit will be the reduction of their impact on the biosphere.'[3]

By the early 1990s the 'regionalism in architecture' debate had moved on. Even today, it remains a subject of seminars as architects in the least-developed countries struggle to resist the pressures created by the movement of international capital.

Opposite

Menara UMNO in Penang is a conscious rupture with the past, emerging, as it thrusts skywards, through the previous layers of the old urban morphology. (RP)

Architects in industrialized countries or developed countries have their own concerns about this phenomena. But for many architects in the developing world who live simultaneously in two cultures, the paradox that Ricoeur referred to in 1965 (*see Chapter 1*) is no longer so apparent. William Lim Siew Wai and Tan Hock Beng, in their 1997 publication *The Contemporary Vernacular*, illustrated several recent architectural expressions in Asia that demonstrate a successful synthesis of modernity and tradition.[4]

Yeang concluded that the term 'tropical skyscraper' had become too restrictive. The terminology had to become more generic, and so he adopted the term 'bioclimatic skyscraper' instead. In 1994 the term was used as the title of a new publication, *Bioclimatic Skyscrapers: Ken Yeang*.[5] The book reviews the output of the T. R. Hamzah and Yeang practice from 1989 to 1993. In an introductory essay, Alan Balfour perceptively identifies the post-colonial agenda in Malaysia and Southeast Asia as 'how to inflect architecture with modernist reason while detaching it from Europe's tendency to symbolic abstraction; how to frame an architectural language which, while showing an understanding of traditional values, would express the economic ambitions of the new nation'.[6] 'Yeang's towers', writes Balfour, 'seem, in their paradoxical mix of orders and desires, to achieve a synthesis exactly appropriate to the cultural promise of Southeast Asia, their warrior-like stance ready for the economic revolution of the new century.'[7]

In another introductory essay, Ivor Richards locates Yeang among a number of architects who 'are developing an ecological architecture in different regions of the world'. He identifies Nicholas Grimshaw, Richard Rogers, Norman Foster and Renzo Piano as architects who have had 'a long involvement with an ecological evolutionary process that generates new buildings like new species in nature'.[8]

Bioclimatic Skyscrapers illustrates a collection of projects that apply Yeang's ideas on bioclimatic design to a variety of towers in China, Vietnam and Europe, as well as several towers in Malaysia that were subsequently completed. Most of the sun-path diagrams in the book relate to projects designed for locations in the tropics, but some of the new towers are designed for subtropical or temperate climatic zones (a sun-path diagram indicates the cardinal points of the compass and the path of the sun, with its seasonal variations in the latitude in which the building is located, superimposed upon a plan of the building correctly orientated). Wind turbines are considered in China Tower No. 1, with accompanying sketches by the innovative environmental engineers Battle McCarthy. China Tower No. 2 has a 'clover-leaf' plan form intended to bring natural ventilation to the internal lift-core. There are generators on the roof, and movable wind shields to give protection in the typhoon season. Sadly, many of the towers, specifically those in China, were not realized.

Yeang contributed to the book an essay entitled 'Theory and Practice', which draws together the various strands of his design agenda. He speculates that future studies will inevitably be directed towards lifestyle changes arising from low-environmental-impact design. In an appendix entitled 'Climate and Design', he analyses the architectural response to varying conditions in the four major climatic zones in the world – tropical, arid, temperate and cool – and systematically explains their influences on built form. Yeang's design guide for the skyscraper was subsequently republished in the book *The Technology of Ecological Building* by the German engineer Klaus Daniel.[9]

PASSIVE LOW-ENERGY DESIGN

For Yeang, the first step in passive design is 'to configure the skyscraper's built form in relation to the ambient environment of the locality in order that it can function in a low-energy way without supplementary "active" devices'. Yeang terms it the 'bioclimatic' design approach.[10]

In the bioclimatic approach, the designer has to respond inventively to the climate of a specific location in terms of site, orientation, configuration, layout, construction and mechanical and electrical systems. 'The natural climatic energies of the location should be employed to their fullest', Yeang emphasizes. 'A design solution engineered in this way does not inhibit creative interpretation. The bioclimatic approach is not one

consisting of a hard-and-fast set of design rules that result in a deterministic set of built forms. Variations will be the natural outcome of responding to different site geometries and to the meteorological data. Inventive methods of compensating for deviations from the ideal configuration will result.'[11] With regard to energy conservation in the tall building, Yeang looks at:

- the skyscraper's configuration and the relationship of this with the ambient environment (passive systems);
- its energy-management system (efficiency systems);
- and its M. & E. engineering systems (active systems).

The last of these three has the biggest effect on the overall energy consumption in any building project, but in order to be effective in achieving real energy conservation, all three aspects must be implemented. This has to be done at the planning stage and will not be effective if done later.

DESIGNING WITH NATURE

In 1995, McGraw-Hill published Yeang's *Designing with Nature: The Ecological Basis for Architectural Design*. The book is essentially Yeang's updated doctoral thesis,[12] and it provides the theoretical framework for his designs. The title pays quiet homage to the pioneering work of the influential Scottish-born landscape architect, planner, teacher and writer Professor Ian L. McHarg, who headed the Department of Landscape Architecture and Regional Planning at the University of Pennsylvania, where Yeang studied for a semester in the early 1970s.

The content of Yeang's book 'takes off from where McHarg finished. McHarg is not an architect so his book took ecological design up to the planning level, whereas my book takes ecological design up to the level of architecture.'[13] Yeang frequently refers to *Designing with Nature* as defining the fundamental agenda for all his subsequent work.[14]

ECOLOGICAL DESIGN PRINCIPLES

Ecological design, for Yeang, involves 'the holistic consideration, of the sustainable use of energy and materials over the life-cycle of a building "system", from source of materials to their inevitable disposal and/or subsequent recycling'. His intention is to reduce the impact of buildings upon the natural environment. Yeang's strategy for the ecological design of a skyscraper begins by first considering its design in terms of energy conservation.

Yeang structures these considerations within the framework of a set of interactions between the built environment and the ecological environment. His model is expressed as follows:

Given a designed system and its environment, let suffix 1 denote the system under consideration and suffix 2, the environment around that system. Further, let letter L be the interdependent connections within the framework. It follows that four types of interactions can be identified in the analysis: L_{11}, L_{12}, L_{21} and L_{22}. This can be further represented in the form of a partitioned matrix (LP):

$$(LP) = \begin{array}{c|c} L_{11} & L_{12} \\ \hline L_{21} & L_{22} \end{array}$$

'**L_{11}**' refers to the process and activities that take place within the system or the area of internal interdependencies.

'**L_{22}**' refers to the process and activities that take place in the environment of the system, or the external interdependencies.

'**L_{12}**' refers to the exchanges of the systems with its environment, or the transactional interdependencies of the system/environment.

'**L_{21}**' refers to the exchanges of the environment with the system, or the transactional interdependencies of the environment/system.

In the ecological approach to design, Yeang suggests that we must simultaneously consider all four of these aspects as well as their interrelationships with each other.[15]

The difference, as Yeang sees it, between his approach, with its pursuit of ecological goals, and the approach of other designers who are less motivated by concerns of sustainability is illustrated in the following table.[16]

	DESIGN MODE		
	Bioclimatic	Ecological	Others
Built-form Configuration	Climate Influenced	Environment Influenced	Other Influences
Building Orientation	Crucial	Crucial	Relatively Unimportant
Façade and Windows	Climate Responsive	Environmental Responsive	Other Influences
Energy Source	Generated/Ambient	Generated/Ambient/Local	Generated
Energy Loss	Crucial	Crucial/Reused	Relatively Unimportant
Environment Control	Electro-Mech/Manual	Electro-Mech/Manual	Electro-Mech
	Artificial/Natural	Artificial/Natural	Artificial
Comfort Level	Variable/Consistent	Variable/Consistent	Consistent
Low-Energy Response	Passive/Electro-Mech	Passive/Electro-Mech	Electro-Mech
Energy Consumption	Low Energy	Low Energy	Generally High Energy
Materials Source	Relatively Unimportant	Low Environmental Impact	Relatively Unimportant
Materials Output	Relatively Unimportant	Reuse/Recycle/Reintegrate	Relatively Unimportant
Site Output	Important	Crucial	Relatively Unimportant

Yeang is almost unique in that there are few other practising architects who have his background in ecology – and possibly none who have built on the scale that he has – in order to verify his theoretical propositions. To quote Leon van Schaik, 'Yeang has created a significant body of architectural designs from knowledge that elsewhere, alas, seems to inhibit all design ambition'.[17] The fact that Yeang has built his own theoretical agenda has earned him the respect of other practising architects. William Lim Siew Wai notes that Yeang is perhaps the first Asian architect outside Japan to have been accepted by the 'metropolitan architectural elite on their turf'.[18]

From 1994, a new series of towers emerged that were now, with Yeang's increasing collaboration with engineers, material scientists and environmental scientists, executed with more precision and greater technical understanding. Yeang occasionally refers to these new towers as the 'Series 3' skyscrapers. The towers begin to consider the low environmental impact of material sourcing, and the reuse and recycling of materials. The inputs and the outputs in the matrix of ecological interactions are given greater attention, though it will be some time before the built results are evident.

Menara Lam Son Square (1994 – unbuilt)

The twenty-six-storey Menara Lam Son Square in Ho Chi Minh City, Vietnam, is circular in plan, rising from a four-storey podium that has a rectangular extension housing a car park. The programme called for a 'landmark commercial tower'; Yeang's response was conceptually a 'boulevard in the sky'. He reinterpreted the tree-lined boulevards of the French-influenced Ho Chi Minh City in a 'vertical' high-rise built form. Glass-sided elevators pass through sky-courts, alongside trellises that have

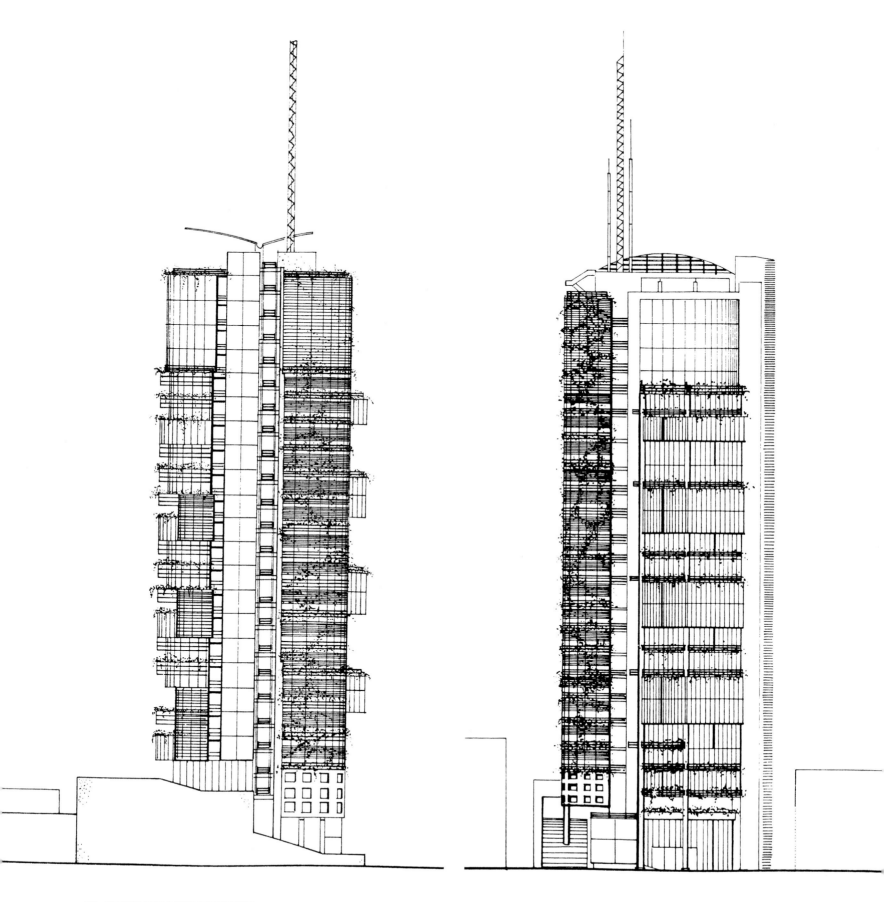

vertical landscaping. There are exhilarating vistas of the city, and the penthouse floor has more planting to create a special place analogous with the termination of the boulevard.

The sun-path and the wind-rose determine the configuration of the floor-plates (a wind-rose is a diagram indicating the predominant wind direction with the speed and frequency related to the cardinal points of the compass). The east side of the tower has a variety of sun-shading devices, while the west side has deeply cut-out sky-terraces. The terraces have clear glazing and sliding glazed doors, which give the option of natural ventilation in the event of the shutdown of mechanical and electrical services due to localized power failure in the city, a situation not infrequently experienced. The lift lobbies, staircases and toilets are all naturally ventilated. The result is a building that recognizes the reality that on occasions the building will have to function without air-conditioning: energy is not cheap and it is not always available. The overall form of Menara Lam Son Square is a sophisticated, ecologically sustainable solution to these realities.

Opposite

Menara Lam Son Square,
two elevation views.

Above

Menara Lam Son Square,
aerial view of the model from the west.

Top

Menara Lam Son Square,
model of the urban context.

Hitechniaga HQ (1995 – unbuilt)

The nineteen-storey Hitechniaga HQ tower is to be the corporate headquarters of Hitechniaga, a Malaysian company dealing in data communication. The tower rises from a six-storey podium housing the reception area, a computer-data centre, an

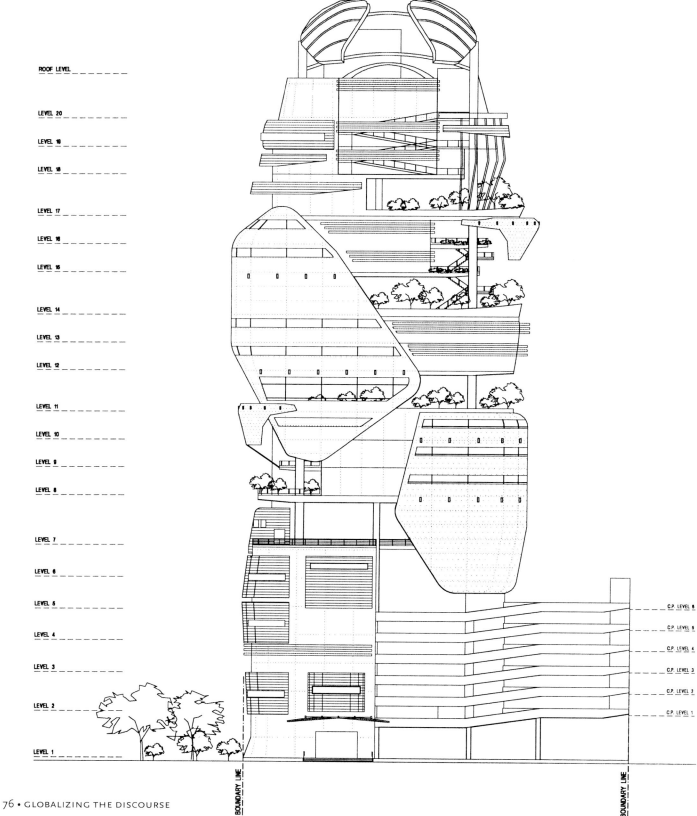

ROOF LEVEL

LEVEL 20

LEVEL 19

LEVEL 18

LEVEL 17

LEVEL 16

LEVEL 15

LEVEL 14

LEVEL 13

LEVEL 12

LEVEL 11

LEVEL 10

LEVEL 9

LEVEL 8

LEVEL 7

LEVEL 6

LEVEL 5

LEVEL 4

LEVEL 3

LEVEL 2

LEVEL 1

C.P. LEVEL 6

C.P. LEVEL 5

C.P. LEVEL 4

C.P. LEVEL 3

C.P. LEVEL 2

C.P. LEVEL 1

BOUNDARY LINE

BOUNDARY LINE

auditorium and meeting rooms. The plan form above the podium level is an elongated oval with the longer 'sides' orientated north-west and south-east. Pods of accommodation are inserted into the skeletal structure. Gaps between the individual pods and the structure ensure that they are visually articulated; these gaps also separate the different accommodation within the building. Terraces are not created by subtraction but use the gaps, and metaphorically they represent the lungs of the building, allowing their users to 'breathe' despite their apparent enclosure. The intention is that the interior should be shaded from solar gain. In some cases – where the floor-plates overlap – the form of the building provides enough shading; however on the east and west elevations sun-shading devices are employed. Perforated metal shields add layers to the basic form. They are carefully designed and positioned so that they give maximum shading, but they have a curious *ad hoc* appearance, almost like parasols spontaneously opening, or like foliage turning in a reactive manner to the sun. They give an organic appearance to the façade. They can also be read as the façades' loose-fitting 'clothing', an analogy that seems entirely appropriate in this humid tropical location.

All the lift lobbies, staircases and toilets, which are located on the north-west façade of the building, have natural sunlight and ventilation, making it a low-energy building and safe to use and operate (i.e. naturally lit stairs and lobbies are unquestionably

Opposite

Hitechniaga HQ tower, elevation.

Above

A trellis protects the tower's roof garden.

Top

Perforated metal shields add layers to the basic form of the tower. They can be read as the façades' loose-fitting 'clothing'.

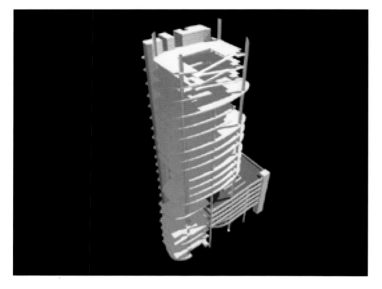
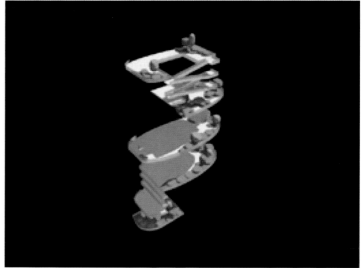
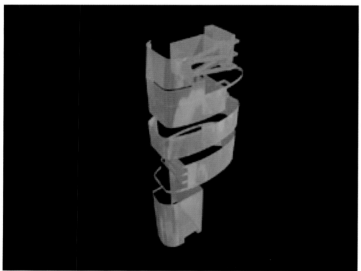
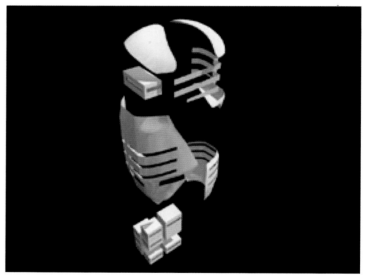

Above

Computer-aided modelling of Hitechniaga HQ illustrating the building's elements. Clockwise from top left: basic structure; sky-courts and roof garden with connecting ramps; external layer of sun-shading devices; building cladding.

safer in the event of power failure or other emergencies). Sky-courts and 'ventilating zones' are located on the tenth, thirteenth and sixteenth floors, with a roof garden on the nineteenth floor – the tower's fifth façade. Additional staircases and ramps increase the accessibility of these sky-courts.

The plans do not appear to be highly efficient in purely commercial terms, but one might reasonably question whether commercially leasable floor space is the most important criterion. It has resulted in millions of square metres of floor space being constructed elsewhere in tropical Asia that

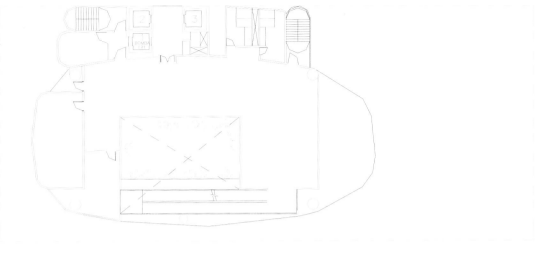

Left

Hitechniaga HQ, nineteenth-storey plan.

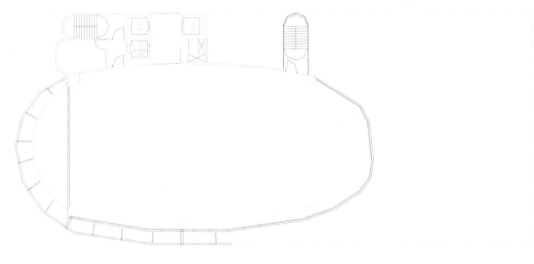

Left

Hitechniaga HQ, tenth-storey plan.

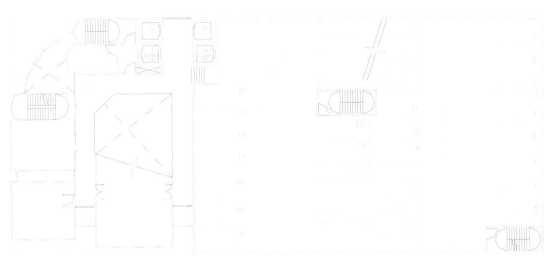

Left

Hitechniaga HQ, second-storey plan.

PLECTRUM
SHAPED
FLOOR PLATES
ROTATED
ALTERNATE
FLOOR

Roof-top
garden

Intermediate
garden

STEPPED
TERRACES
&
PLANTERS

(GARDENS
&
SKY-COURTS)

SERVICE
TRACK
THAT
SPIRALS
UP THE
BUILDING
WITH
MOBILE
"CHERRY-
PICKERS"

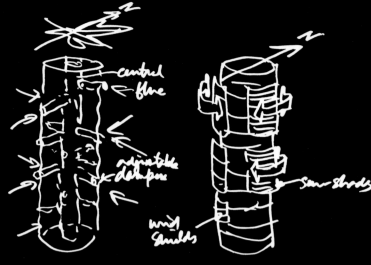

central
flue

adjustable
dampers

wind
shields

sun-shades

WIND FLUES
TO BRING
WIND TO
INNER PARTS
OF THE
BUILDING
WITH
ADJUSTABLE
DAMPERS

ROTATING
MOVEABLE
SUN-SHADES
& WIND-SHIELDS

Above

Tokyo-Nara Tower, Yeang's
conceptual sketches.

Right

Tokyo-Nara Tower, typical floor plans.

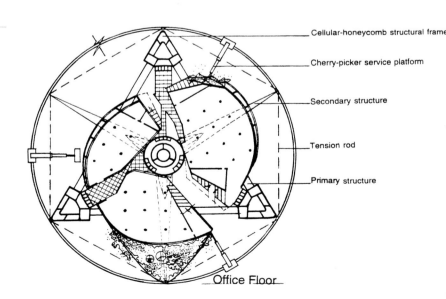

Cellular-honeycomb structural frame

Cherry-picker service platform

Secondary structure

Tension rod

Primary structure

Office Floor

would be virtually uninhabitable in the event of a power failure, whereas Yeang's tower would fare comparatively better in such a situation.

The design for the Hitechniaga HQ explored variations on the idea of the 'bioclimatic skyscraper' and of 'urban design in the sky', of which more will be mentioned in subsequent chapters. The latter reflects Yeang's tentative exploration of the skyscraper as a 'vertical city' and the notion of the 'mapping of the skyscraper', both of which are attempts to increase the connectivity of movement systems in a building. The genesis of such ideas lies undoubtedly in the Archigram and Metabolist projects that had enthralled Yeang as a student at the AA.

Tokyo-Nara Tower (1995)

The eighty-storey Tokyo-Nara Tower, a conceptual project prepared for the 1995 World Architecture Exposition in Japan, is an experiment in configuring and rotating the floor-plate to serve as sun-shading to the floor below. The service-cores of the building are orientated according to the solar conditions. Positioned on the east–west axis, the lift- and service-cores absorb a significant percentage of heat gain. The cooler façades on the north–south axis are left open with clear glazing and atrial voids. The north–south axis can be identified by the open louvres, tiered sun-shades and clear glazing, which are all used as a consequence of lower solar exposure.

The shielding and glazing systems are orientated to minimize solar gain. Those sides of the building along the east–west axis are more solidly glazed, with cast- and perforated-metal cladding, a preferred material because of its heat reflection, its light weight and its structural strength.

But the principal idea behind the tower is the use of vertical landscaping that spirals around, through and within the built form. This element performs several important functions. Firstly, the foliage acts to cool the building, both by way of shading and by chemical photosynthesis. Secondly, planting to the fringe of floors and atrium spaces controls air movements within the built structure. Thirdly, the mass of planting relative to the built structure ensures that the biosystem is acting symbiotically with mechanical systems to provide a balanced built environment.

The maintenance of the vertical landscaping, as well as the upkeep of external fixtures, glazing and cladding panels is ensured by specialized mechanical devices, an important advance on earlier towers: the landscaping of Plaza Atrium and Central Plaza, as mentioned earlier, fell short of expectations due to lack of subsequent maintenance. These devices, constructed in the form of multi-purpose 'robot-arms' or 'cherry-pickers', travel along an external track that spirals and circles around the tower.

The radial/spiral movement of the floor-plates creates a particular built form that allows each floor to shade the one below as they spiral upward. There is a constantly changing

atrium space, articulated by terraces, hanging gardens, internal courts and private gardens. Located at regular intervals, the sky-courts provide the building's inhabitants with green parks, suspended high above the city, which benefit from fresh air. Winding within the atrium spaces of Tokyo-Nara Tower are the arterial routes that are intended to create behavioural settings to assist in residents' interaction. The atria, bridged by walkways and flanked by stairwells, constitute a microcosm of the city within the tower, which, while open to the environment, is insulated from noise and pollution.

Menara UMNO (completed 1998)

The twenty-one-storey Menara UMNO is located on the island of Penang. The tower contains two banking halls on the first floor, and on the eighth floor is an auditorium for meetings and assemblies. The auditorium is accessible by a separate lift (away from the main tower lifts) and its own staircase.

Like Yeang's earlier towers, the form of Menara UMNO arises out of a conflict between the geometry of the site and the geometry of the climate (the specific and the general environments). The building exhibits what Alan Balfour terms 'the ingenious and aggressive body language of [Yeang's] work as it struggles to reconcile the discontinuity between form and climate'.[19]

The site determines the orientation of the tower. It 'faces' west with a variety of sun-shading devices to control sunlight

Opposite

The Menara UMNO tower has been likened to a raked-back ship's funnel – the sky-courts simulate decks around the leading edge. (Ng)

Above

Menara UMNO exhibits what Balfour terms 'the ingenious and aggressive language of Yeang's work as it seeks to reconcile the discontinuity between form and climate'. (RP)

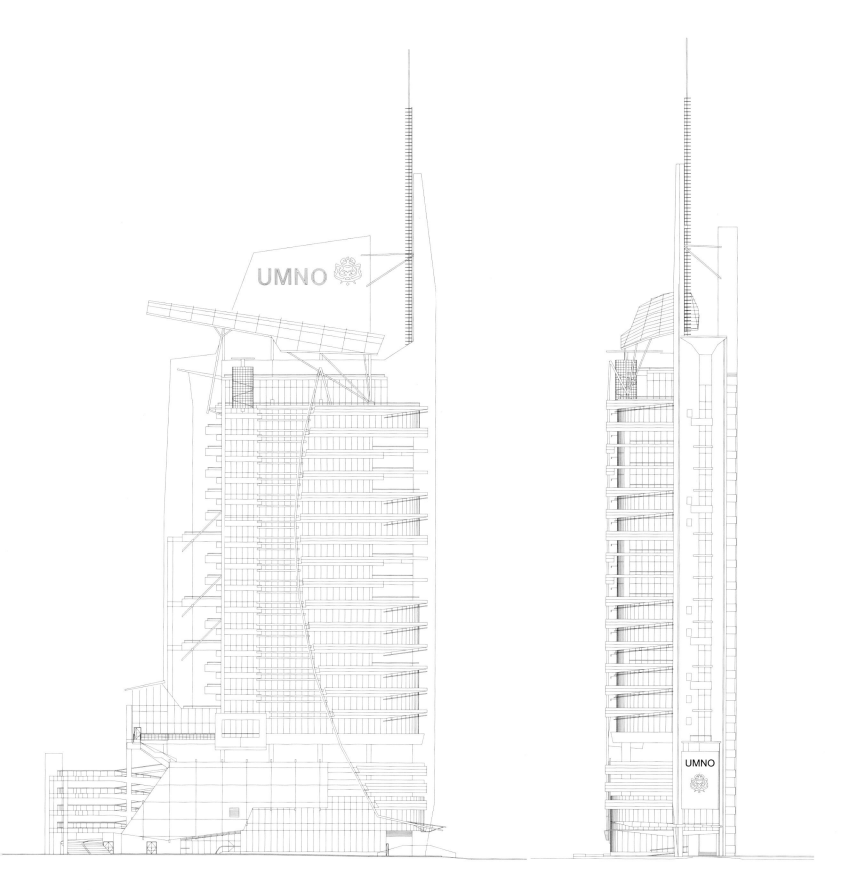

penetration at various times of the year. A twenty-one-storey-high solid wall faces east, shielding the building from sunlight until noon. There is a duality in the construction of the building's walls: the west-facing façade is constructed of high-tech steel, glass and aluminium; the east-facing façade – a party wall – is utilitarian concrete.

The UMNO building was initially designed to be naturally ventilated. The intention was to generate natural ventilation with a high air-change rate, which creates comfort conditions in the interior through air movement and temperature control. This is a major advance upon the more common use of natural ventilation to provide fresh air supply only.

Above left

Menara UMNO's wing-walls are combined with variable transitional zones as ventilators. (Ng)

Opposite

Menara UMNO, north-west and south-west elevations.

Above right

Metal shading devices fit like 'loose-clothing' on the structure of the tower. (RP)

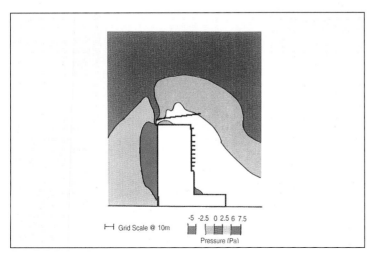

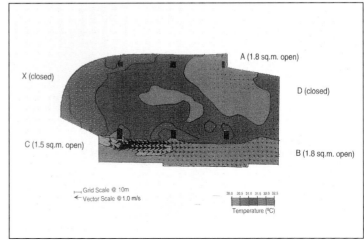

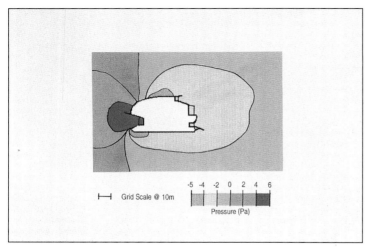

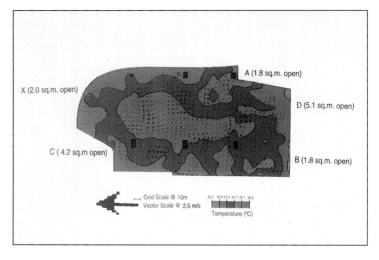

Top left

Air-pressure contours show wind-flow around Menara UMNO (vertical section). (Ng)

Bottom left

Air-pressure contours show wind-flow around the tower at level 12. (Ng)

Top right

Internal temperature distribution and air-speed vectors at 1.2 metres height (south-westerly wind @ 2.5m/s). (Ng)

Bottom right

Internal temperature distribution and air-speed vectors at 1.2 metres height (ventilation by stack forces only). (Ng)

Opposite

Menara UMNO, isometric drawing of the roof plan, the roof terrace and a typical office-floor plan.

The principle of the wing-wall or wind-wing-wall is used here. Vertical walls the full height of the building protrude from the north-east and south-west elevations. The prevailing winds are channelled into the building from the windward side and pressure zones are created on the leeward side. The use of 'wing-walls' is combined with variable transitional zones as ventilators. The principle of wing-walls is not new but in the past their use has been confined to low-rise buildings. As far as is known this is the first application of the technique in a high-rise building, although its principles were indicated by the performance characteristics of the MBf Tower in Penang, completed just over four years earlier.

At the design stage, careful analysis was made of the wind

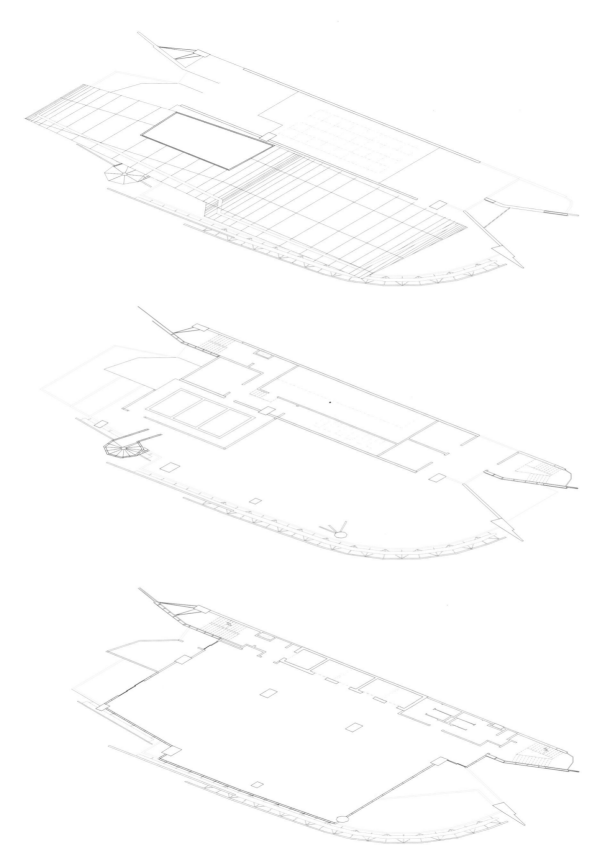

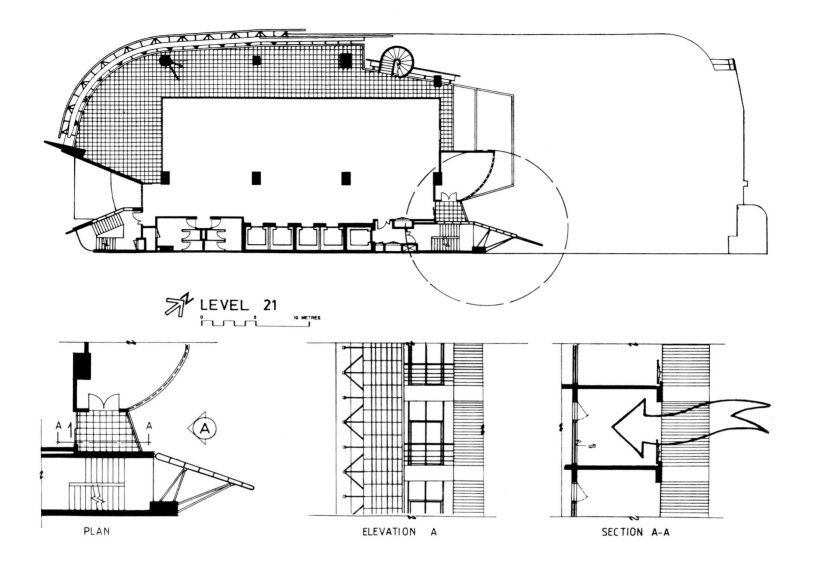

LEVEL 21

0 5 10 METRES

PLAN

ELEVATION A

SECTION A-A

movement around the building.[20] The air-flow model DFS-AIR was used to simulate wind-flow and to obtain values of the surface pressures at each window and balcony door opening. The simulation indicated the effectiveness of the wing-walls and balconies in establishing clear high- and low-pressure areas.

Ventilation strategies were then evolved after simulating the internal air-movement patterns in order to diffuse the incoming air 'jets' and to avoid short-circulating air between supply and exhaust openings: Yeang is now looking at the incorporation of 'spoilers' or 'deflectors' located near the openings. Although air-conditioning was subsequently added to the building for commercial reasons (at the client's request), Menara UMNO represents an important breakthrough and provides a concept for developing energy-efficient, naturally ventilated 'green' skyscrapers.

Within a typical floor, no desk location is more than six metres away from an openable window, to enable users to receive natural daylight. The lift lobbies, staircases and toilets all have natural sunlight and ventilation.

The sky-courts and roof-top spaces are much more generous than on previous Yeang towers and they have a sense of enclosure, missing in earlier buildings, which is a crucial psychological factor in ensuring their use. The twenty-first-storey reception pavilion looks out to sea and inland to Bukit Pinang. Sky-courts at the south-west corner have magnificent views to the distant hills. Metal shards shade the west façade of the building. They work well: at 5.30 in the afternoon the penetration of sunlight is tolerable.

What could be more significant than the fact that UMNO is Malaysia's ruling political party? Menara UMNO, the 'upstart' child of a Western building type, thumbs its nose at the West, but it also, perhaps, sends a political message to Malaysia's opposition parties that with UMNO Penang will progress. The building expresses self-reliance and is symbolic of Malaysia's emergence, under Prime Minister Datuk Seri Dr Mahathir Mohamad, onto a world stage.

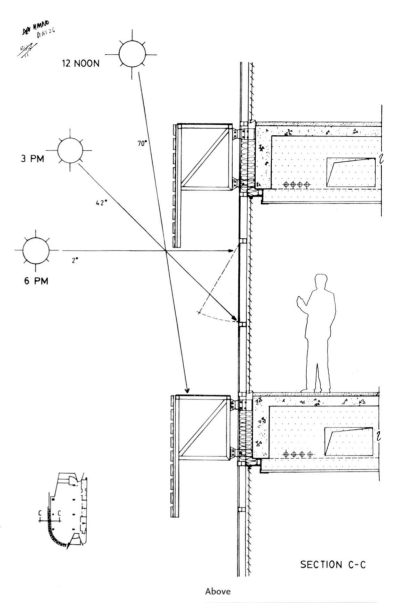

Above

Menara UMNO, detail of a shading device on the north-west elevation.

The building is also an expression of the contradictions of urbanization in nations that are experiencing rapid development. The Neo-classical façades of two-storey shophouses, timber and tiled dwellings and open drains are juxtaposed alongside the sleek symbols of modernity. To protest that the scale is 'wrong', that the resolution is non-contextual, is to ignore the political and commercial forces acting upon architecture and the overspill of the globalization of economies.

The building does not by site amalgamation disrupt the existing street pattern, though it has a significant impact on the 'texture' of the urban morphology; this is a conscious and deliberate impact, a rupture with the past emerging through the previous layers of morphology. The vertical city grows out of the horizontal layers of the old city, sucking in and dispersing kinetic forces: a centripetal and centrifugal force, like an igneous eruption from the core of the earth thrusting through the crust of history, fighting to escape its earthbound existence. Strands of glass and metal reflect and refract the sunlight. The sky is impaled upon the tower's razor-sharp edge(s) and at the summit (point) there is an impressive blood-red sign proclaiming 'UMNO'!

Leon van Schaik sees in the form of Menara UMNO various references to marine architecture: the tower itself, for instance, is perceived as a raked-back ship's funnel, while the sky-courts simulate decks around the leading edge, 'rather like the bridge of an immensely tall cruise liner'. 'At penthouse level', writes van Schaik, 'a set of executive function rooms are housed under an over-sailing roof, canted to suggest that this is indeed a ship of state steaming inland.'

'I suspect', he concludes, 'that this is rather more expressive than Yeang would like, but I also suspect he has not worked out how to escape from the *gestalt* of certain machines. The next development in the aesthetic of the bioclimatic skyscraper needs to engage more directly with the industrial design of this very impressive bioclimatic system.'[21]

Menara MISC Headquarters (1997)

This eighteen-storey tower for the Malaysia International Shipping Corporation Berhad (MISC) is located in Shah Alam town centre, Malaysia. The elliptically shaped skyscraper (*see page 93*) rises alongside a four-storey common-facilities wing of rectangular configuration, built over a three-storey basement car park. Aluminium louvred sun-shading is wrapped around the building. It has a distinctive wave form that is an exact response to the movement pattern of the sun, thus reducing solar gain in the office area. There is a landscaped roof garden, and landscaped sky-courts are incorporated at each floor of the office tower, providing the building's occupants with the opportunity to relax. The project was temporarily 'put on hold' in the wake of 1997 economic crisis in Asia.

GROUND CONNECTIONS

The proceedings of the third, fourth and fifth Asia Design Forums were not recorded, but in March 1995 the sixth forum (ADF No. 6) assembled on Hokkaido Island, Japan. On this occasion Leon van Schaik recorded and published the proceedings.[22] Yeang's presentation described the latest developments in the design of bioclimatic high-rise buildings. He focused on the relationship of the buildings to the ground plane. Van Schaik wrote of the presentation:

> Year by year, the buildings have developed a growing fluidity and sculptural vigour, a process that Yeang is not willing to discuss. The Asia Design Forum felt that this growing aesthetic assurance was evident, but differed on whether it should be dissected consciously or be left to develop silently as a consequence of the gradually increasing layering of sophistication through the parametric process. The work does demonstrate a marked aesthetic evolution, and it seems perverse not to acknowledge the drivers of the formal development. Pressed to suggest the next area for parametric improvement, the Forum suggested that a deliberate mapping of the social programme of the tropical high-rise might advance some of the aspects of the designs which were still relatively generalised in their conception.[23]

MAPPING THE SKYSCRAPER

In August 1997, ADF No. 7 convened in Bali. On this occasion, Yeang presented the latest design for Hitechniaga HQ, mapped as a land-use diagram. Architectural critic Rowan Moore applauded Yeang's determination to invent a new approach, but the chairman of the AA, Mohsen Mostafavi, argued that for all the technical determinism of Yeang's presentation, there is an aesthetic that he manipulates to a desired effect. He wondered what conditions other than optimization obtained in the design, because the design is 'also clearly determined by an evolving look'. 'It is time', said Mostafavi, 'for Yeang to look more seriously at the quality of the internal spaces being produced. It was important that dressing the façades should not take the place of a continuing investigation of inhabitation and its pleasures.'[24] The conclusions of both meetings underlined the need for the consideration of the behavioural settings created in the high-rise building.

Shanghai Armoury Tower (1997 – unbuilt)

Some of the ideas that Yeang explored in the Tokyo-Nara Tower subsequently found their way into the Shanghai Armoury Tower, which is located in the Pudong district of Shanghai. The design is intended to create a modern urban icon for the client, the Northern Pudong Open Economy Company, and its 'progressive and valiant march into the twenty-first century'. It is a multi-use

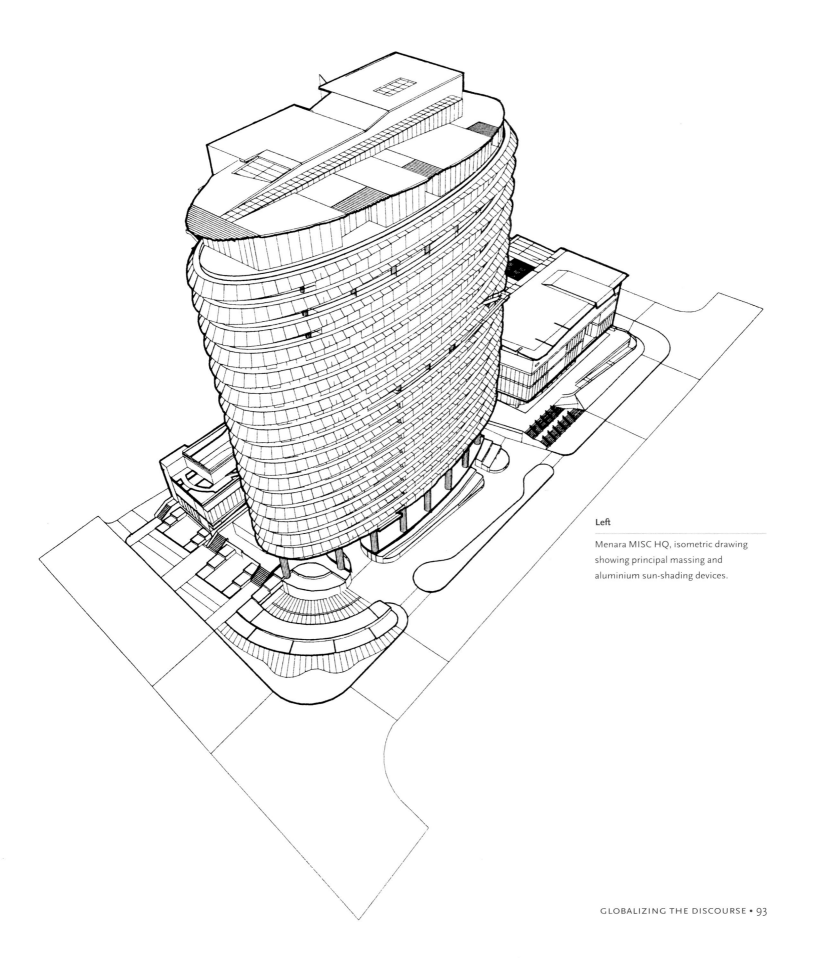

Above left

The Shanghai Armoury Tower is intended to create a modern urban icon for its client and its 'progressive and valiant march into the twenty-first century'. It is a symbolic interpretation of components found in military armaments. (Ng)

Above right

The circular Shanghai Armoury Tower has a void in the centre of the floor-plates that extends through the full height of building. It is combined with sky-courts to create cross-ventilation. (Ng)

Opposite

Computer-generated 'wire' diagrams showing form and massing of the Shanghai Armoury Tower.

building, the lowest third of the floors in the building being a hotel, and the upper two-thirds, commercial offices.

The thirty-six-storey circular tower is a symbolic interpretation of components found in military armaments. The sweeping panels of metallic screens on the exterior allude to the armour of the Chinese warrior; the curved solar panel atop the building depicts the helmet; the topmost extension of the tower is said to depict the 'victorious torch'; and the stair plan suggests the trigger of a gun. The iconography is similar to, but not as physically aggressive as, the samurai-inspired buildings of Shin Takamatsu, such as Origin III and Pharaoh Dental Clinic in Japan.

The Shanghai Armoury Tower is located in a temperate climatic zone and the design, in addition to the explicit symbolism, adopts seasonal passive low-energy concepts.

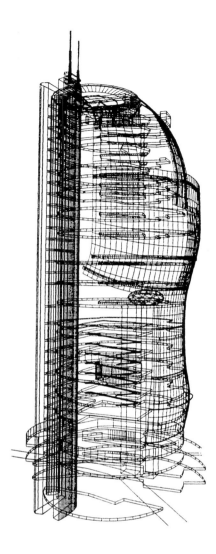

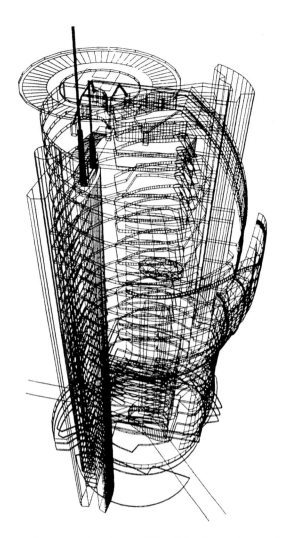

The external and internal design features use a bioclimatic approach to produce an operationally energy-efficient building that optimizes the coastal climatic conditions of Shanghai and allows the occupants to experience, and be aware of, the changing seasons of the year.

Landscaped sky-terraces placed strategically in the tower create buffer zones between the inside and outside. They act as 'green lungs' that improve the microclimate at the building's periphery. The external weather-screen performs as a multi-functional filter against extreme climatic conditions, while allowing generous views of the surrounding urban space. The lift- and stair-core is located on the east-facing façade, with balconies to most rooms facing west. An auditorium is located on the eighteenth storey, together with a two-storey roof garden.

The tower has a void in the middle of the floor-plates. This central atrium extends through the full height of the building. It is combined with the sky-courts and is intended to create cross-ventilation in summer, which can be enhanced in mid-season by the thermal stack effect and wind suction. In winter, the louvres in the double-skin façade of the building are closed with the intention of insulating the building with an air cavity.

GLOBALIZATION OF PRACTICE
In a 1998 paper, 'Notes on Practice and Architecture', Yeang situated his practice firmly within a global discourse:

> I am constantly plagued by questions about the issue of 'identity' in architecture. This seems to be an almost

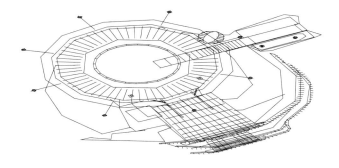

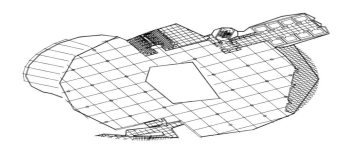

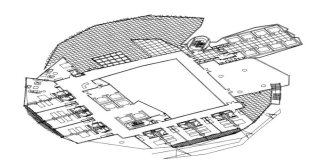

Shanghai Armoury Tower, isometric drawings of a typical office-floor plan, a sky-terrace and the roof plan. The tower represents a continuation of Yeang's exploratory mapping of the skyscraper.

obsessive-compulsive preoccupation of some Asian architects. I cannot think of architects anywhere else in the world who are similarly as overtly worried about this issue of architectural identity.

We need to recognise that we are neither 100% east nor 100% west in our modes. Furthermore, we are on the threshold of the 21st century and not living a way of life that existed a hundred years ago. The way we dress today and the way we behave is a composite. This is the context that we are in.

Having a British upbringing and coming from Asia, I cannot say that I am entirely east or west in my outlook. I think in English but count in Cantonese, although I cannot explain this. I speak Malay sometimes to my children, English mostly to my wife, Cantonese to my mother and English to my colleagues and staff. I read French. I know my home town Penang well, but I know certain districts of several major cities in the world virtually like my own backyard: Tokyo, London, Berlin, New York. I have offices in Kuala Lumpur, London, Australia, Singapore and China. I lead a global lifestyle in that every weekend, my work takes me often to the other side of the globe, only to return back to my office in Kuala Lumpur before the following week starts.

I cannot regard myself as a Malaysian architect doing work internationally, but rather as an international architect with my headquarters based in Kuala Lumpur. Our staffing has become international, and so must be the standards of our design work, presentation, production drawings and delivery. There is a blurring of the distinction between the metropolis and the province for us. The world becomes for us simply a linked set of nodes differentiated spatially by time zones and travel distances. I am sure this similarly applies to many of my colleagues from those nodes elsewhere. At the end of the day, our architecture reflects the inevitable global mental outlook and lifestyle.[25]

ABOUT BEING WORLD CLASS

'It is all about being best in the world or about achieving world-class standards', says Yeang, a term he attributes to Rosbeth Kantner, a Harvard professor and author of the book *World Class*:

I used to say I want to be as good as those in the developed world, but now I realize that that is not good enough. If we in the Third World only want to be as good as those in the First World, we forever condemn ourselves to a 'subaltern mentality' in post-colonial terminology. We have to overachieve.

We must first find out what it is we do best. What we do best we need to make top class and be absolutely unbeatable. It means the tenacious perseverance and all-consuming desire to push performance to the highest level. There must be a commitment to constant practice and constant improvement. We have to seek to be the best in the world in our endeavours.[26]

'In marketing terms this is termed "differentiating" your product', says Yeang. 'The product, in our case the skyscraper, has to be identifiable, unique and differentiated.' Yeang uses the term 'differentiating the product' not in the sense of the commodification and objectification of architecture, with the obvious connections that this would have with inbuilt obsolescence and consumer trend cycles, but to mean refining the skyscraper, so that it is identifiable by its ecologically sustainable features and attributes – a skyscraper that would nevertheless render obsolete energy-guzzling, highly polluting and waste-producing models, which would gradually be phased out. The next stage in Yeang's development would be a new cycle of primary-level explorations of ecologically sustainable large buildings.

4 Refining Typologies

ON RAPID-PROTOTYPING AND PRODUCT DEVELOPMENT

'To fully understand our design work,' says Yeang, 'it is crucial to delve beyond simply an understanding of the physical planning, aesthetics and technical features. More important than understanding these aspects is the *modus operandi* and the underlying set of attitudes that has directed the design and built works completed over the last two decades.'[1] Yeang's approach regards architectural design as being a research-based activity that requires subsequent verification by simulation and prototyping. It is an approach that can be traced back to his studies at Cambridge. He describes the process as 'rapid-prototyping' or 'rapid product development'.

The terminology and methods are borrowed from the business of automobile design and manufacturing. He sees the design of skyscrapers as a similar process in which both invention and the generation of new technology and ideas leading to a new production model take place at once. Innovations and the subsequent refinements occur simultaneously in an interactive, parallel process to produce an operational prototype, rather than through a sequential linear set of activities. A later stage of refinement improves the

product and fine-tunes its performance. The traditional step-by-step flow of activities in product development is generally a linear one in which all aspects of the design are fully refined in a sequential process before the final stage of production of the marketable product. This linear process takes a considerably longer time than the parallel one.

Yeang believes that the rapid-prototyping process is suited to the design professions in those economic environments where fast-track and fast-design-and-build developments are taking place, as was the case in the rapidly growing Asian economies until the latter half of 1997, and as will probably be the case in the future. In such environments, appropriate designs that work have to be produced extremely quickly to meet the rapidly changing market conditions and to fulfil the instant demands of the entrepreneur-type of client that is predominant in the emerging market-place.

Yeang gives the example of the wing-wall device described earlier in reference to the Menara UMNO project. It has previously been used with considerable success in low-rise buildings and medium-rise buildings, while various cross-ventilation devices in the high-rise building type have been extensively used by many architects (e.g. Le Corbusier in his *Unité d'Habitation*). But the wing-wall with the adjustable orifice-opening is novel in the high-rise building as a device to concentrate wind in order to generate internal conditions of comfort.

Opposite

The Gamuda Headquarters in Shah Alam, Selangor. The focus of the office tower is an elliptical atrium created by the building's two curved wings. Sunscreens and solar filters are strategically incorporated into the design. (Ng)

99

By rapid-prototyping the wing-wall idea, investigative work in natural ventilation in high-rise buildings is advanced, although it remains a fundamentally crude prototype, requiring subsequent technical refinements. Nevertheless, the wing-wall has been shown to be a viable proposition in the high-rise building. Future refinements will be in developing more-analytical methods for locating the wing-walls on the floor-plate, based on more-reliable wind data. The wing-wall components in the future may be capable of orientating to variable angles to follow shifts in the wind direction. The location of the wing-walls need not be at the edges of the orifice but can be relocated at the centre of the opening to be more effective, and horizontal spoilers can be added to adjust the wind throughflow under extremely windy conditions. This process of rapid-prototyping is typical of Yeang's building projects.

In applying the concept of rapid product development to the professional practice, Yeang contends that an architectural firm's extensive experiences in skyscraper design are difficult to share, or are useless to others, unless they are converted into 'transferable expertise'. Doing this is a process that requires the preparation of design guides and primers (*see below*). Yeang's frequent publications are his contribution to this transfer of knowledge.

The next activity in the cycle of advanced product development is equally important. Yeang concludes that a firm's tangible expertise must be translated into 'customer benefits'. The practice needs to use its accumulated knowledge to benefit the clients so that they receive 'added-value' features. Its expertise has then to be converted into 'marketable products or marketable features'. Finally, the last stage for the architectural firm is the conversion of the entire set of activities into a profitable proposition. If the firm itself, as an enterprise, is not profitable, then it will not survive, nor will it have opportunities to repeat the cycle with new projects. Yeang calls this method of work 'Research, Design and Development' (R. D. & D.). The process thus involves not just research and development but also design, which he sees as essential part of the cycle and as the poetic interpretation of his research work.

NEW RESEARCH DIRECTION

In early 1997, Academy Editions published a primer by Ken Yeang on the principles of designing high-rise buildings entitled *The Skyscraper Bioclimatically Considered: A Design Primer*.[2] In Yeang's view, 'the book establishes an alternative approach to skyscraper design which, if adopted, will affect the development of the ubiquitous skyscraper away from the central-core location in the floor-plate, from high-energy performances, and from prismatic gratuitous forms that are sprouting up everywhere'. It differentiates Yeang's skyscrapers from those of his competitors.

'If one accepts', says Associate Professor Lam Khee Poh, Dean of the Faculty of Architecture, Building and Real Estate at the National University of Singapore, 'that the skyscraper is the inevitable typological solution to modern city habitation, then the design issues raised by Dr Yeang in this book are very pertinent to the important aspiration to create sustainable built environments for the future.'[3] Professor Lam continues:

> The fundamental concerns of the 'bioclimatic' approach which seeks to achieve a low-energy, passive building and better occupant comfort are not new, but attempts to apply the bioclimatic principles to skyscraper design in the manner that Yeang does is unconventional. It has resulted in a distinctly recognisable architecture that has caught the attention of the architectural community worldwide. The strength and authority of Yeang in championing the cause for a bioclimatic approach to skyscraper design lies in the fact that he has implemented several such schemes.

Lam, an architect with a background in building science, suggests that Yeang should seize the unique opportunity to conduct post-occupancy evaluation to study the actual performance of the buildings and to compare it with the behaviour envisaged at the design stage. 'This', says Lam, 'will provide invaluable insights to derive lessons to be learnt in a systematic way.'

It is a point that Yeang is acutely aware of, but setting up research projects is difficult in a busy architectural practice: 'Many of the design propositions have to evolve through a discontinuous process. It is inevitably intermittent and in most instances evolved "on the run". The whole fragile framework for simultaneous "professional work-cum-R. & D." is fraught with practical obstructions that must be constantly overcome.'[4]

One of Yeang's collaborators, the engineer Christopher McCarthy, is also one of his staunchest supporters. McCarthy believes that, 'Yeang has already made a significant contribution to the built environment. His work reconsiders environmental values and illustrates the potential for an improved understanding of moderating climatic forces away from the traditional sealed building.'[5]

By 1997, Yeang's work had progressively advanced, and the practice had acquired precise data on natural ventilation. Laboratory-standard computational fluid dynamics (CFD) studies had been done to verify some of the propositions. Energy-performance calculations and design criteria extended beyond simple overall thermal transmittance value (OTTV) comparisons. Sun-shading design methods were further developed. Calculations on embodied energy in the projects on the drawing board were proceeding and some post-occupancy studies on Menara UMNO were completed. Yeang's ideas on the morphology of the skyscraper had also moved forward.

But propositions can only advance and be tested in-use when conceptual projects get the go-ahead from the client to be built. Inevitably, the state of the economy is a major determinant. Likewise, post-occupancy evaluation depends largely on the interest shown by academic institutions and manufacturers to verify the design propositions. Consequently, research is not carried out in a satisfactory continuum but progresses only when these organizations become part of the ongoing work in practice.

In a similar manner, Yeang is often criticized for the apparent disparity between his theoretical writing and his buildings: it is difficult to juxtapose the theory alongside the built work. And yet this is understandable. Chronologically, it is impossible for buildings, particularly skyscrapers, which are designed several years before they are completed, to be synchronized with the theoretical ideas that may have advanced in the interim. The disparity between the publication of these works and the current state of theoretical and technical development is inevitable. Leon van Schaik puts it this way: 'Like John Frazer [Yeang's PhD supervisor and now head of the School of Design at The Hong Kong Polytechnic University], I think Ken Yeang is very important, if sometimes running ahead of himself.'[6]

Yeang readily agrees that he post-rationalizes his actions. He contends that, 'design is indeed an a posteriori process, consisting of speculation and field search followed by a process of interrogation, post-rationalization and advancement (of ideas,

inventions or theory development)'. Decisions that are quite often based on intuition and 'gut feeling' are later embraced by theory. Ecological design in relation to high-rise buildings is in its infancy and many of the technical solutions proposed by Yeang, as he is the first to admit, are not totally rigorous or predictable.

A NEW CYCLE BEGINS

Yeang frequently uses the word 'kaizen' to explain how T. R. Hamzah and Yeang operates. It is a Japanese word that means literally a method of working that stresses continuous improvement: so that when, in 1997, Yeang returned to primary-level investigations of several aspects of skyscraper design, it was a logical step in this process. A new cycle of 'Primary-Level Design Experiments' then began, which Yeang has referred to elsewhere as the 'Series 4' skyscrapers.[7] These included investigations into several aspects of ecological sustainability:

The cladding and the skin

Buildings need to be detailed in order to enable materials used in the construction to be easily recyclable. The structure of a building has a long life but cladding may have a relatively short life. Yeang began investigating how a building can be detailed in such a manner that the secondary elements of the superstructure can be speedily and effectively replaced when they reach the end of their effective life, while the redundant components are recycled.

Greening the skyscraper

Yeang initiated more-rigorous investigations into the green façade and the creation of an interactive biosphere in which plants, humans and animal life exist in harmony. A 1998 experimental project for a three-storey building on the Permasteelisa Technological Campus in Italy gave the opportunity to demonstrate this approach, which if proven successful will be incorporated in future skyscraper projects.

Wing-walls

Menara UMNO, completed in 1998, proved the effectiveness of wing-walls (i.e. vertical walls, constructed as an integral part of the building fabric, that 'close-haul' to the wind, maximizing its cooling and ventilation effect). The principle will now be further refined and will eventually find its way into other projects on the drawing board. Yeang is currently investigating wing-walls with variable 'settings' in response to shifts in wind direction.

Source-to-sink analysis

All materials embody energy; it is used in their production, manufacture and erection. Yeang began to look at detail design in terms of energy-embodiment consequences, potential for reuse and the ecological impact of materials as the basis for design development.

A number of new towers exploring these principles were commissioned and designed in the latter half of 1997 and in early 1998. But almost simultaneously the buoyant economies of Southeast Asia plummeted into recession: the devaluation of the Thai baht, and the subsequent fall in value of the Indonesian and Malaysian currencies, means that many of the projects are unlikely to progress on site until the early part of the twenty-first century. Meanwhile, Yeang is using the 'space' created by the delay to refine rigorously various aspects of the ecological agenda.

Gamuda Headquarters (1998)

The focus of the ten-storey Gamuda Headquarters building in the Kota Kemuning Business Park, Shah Alam, is an elliptical atrium created by the two curved wings of the office tower: a central space visible from all floors. The office floors are raised twelve metres above the ground plane to allow the public atrium space to blend into the extensive landscaping throughout the business park. The landscape of the park is carried up the façade of the building in the form of planted terraces and balconies.

Top

The Gamuda Headquarters is set within the Kota Kemuning Business Park. The building is raised twelve metres above the ground to permit the central atrium space to blend into the landscaping that extends throughout the park. (Ng)

Above

The central space in the Gamuda Headquarters office tower is visible from all floors. (Ng)

Opposite

Gamuda Headquarters, isometric drawings showing typical floor plans.

The building is designed as a passive low-energy structure. The orientation is intended to minimize insolation. The building incorporates lift-cores as east–west solar buffers, a strategy favoured by Yeang for buildings in this latitude. A simple geometrical method for calculating sun-shading is devised for the elliptically shaped structure. This is based on different cross-sectional designs for the eight façade segments of the building (i.e. N, NE, E, SE, S, SW, W, NW), each of which is drawn geometrically. Analysis of sun-shading and OTTV has been carried out, together with predictions of cost savings that will accrue as a result of these measures.

The design of the building takes advantage of the prevailing winds to naturally ventilate the atrium space. Wind-tunnel tests were carried out on the design by a laboratory at the National University of Singapore, and have been analysed for the natural ventilation of the public areas. Energy-embodiment studies (EES) were carried out on the materials to be used in the building and are currently being analysed to assess the ecological 'input'.

The idea of vertical mapping is explored in the form of a conceptual vertical land-use plan and building programme. The vertical-mapping technique encompasses service zones, communal zones, open space, circulation zones and climatic buffer zones. Transportation and movement is integrated into the plan with a hierarchy of systems including pedestrian movement (horizontal and vertical), main-line elevators, branch-line

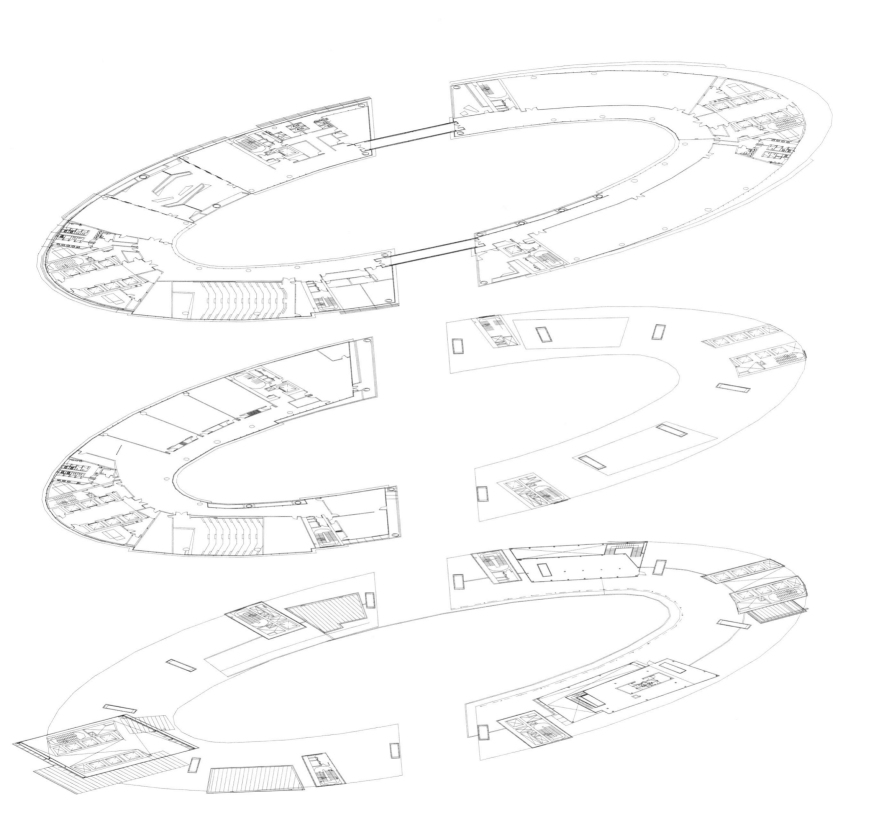

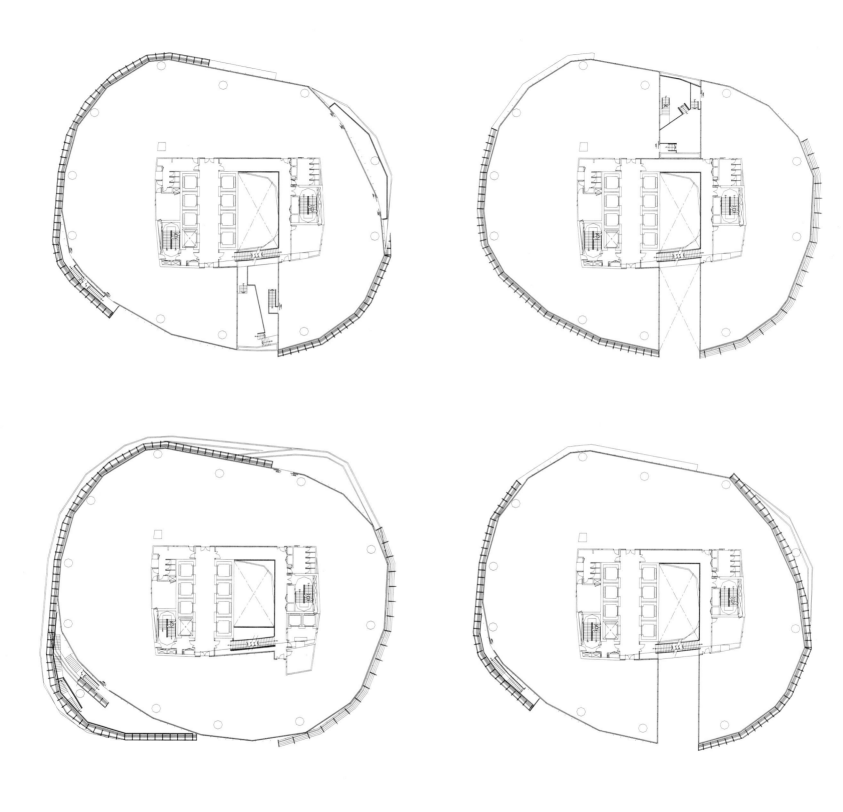

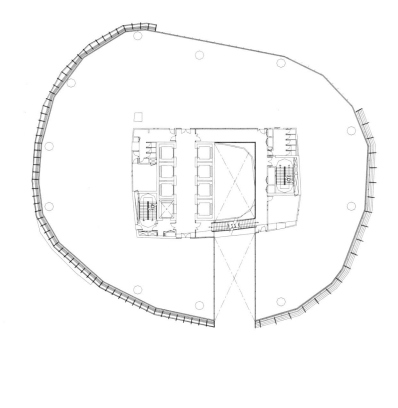

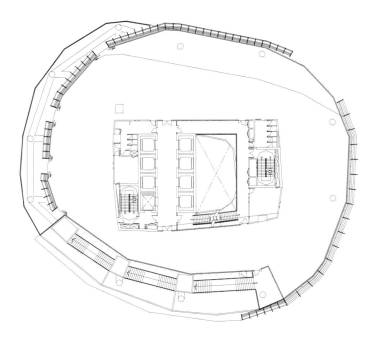

Left and opposite

FACB HQ, typical floor plans indicating a variety of shading devices.

Following pages

The FACB HQ project explores the total greening of the building with vegetation that spirals upwards.

elevators, service elevators and emergency elevators. These ideas are developed with even greater sophistication in the later conceptual design for Expo 2005 Nagoya Hyper-Tower (1998).

FACB HQ (1997)

FACB HQ in Selangor is a twenty-nine-storey hemispherical tower with a central atrium that brings natural ventilation into the inner parts of the building. Designed in 1997, the project explores the total greening of the building with vegetation that spirals upwards. The façade is designed with an interstitial space and an extensive outer layer of planting that protects an inner, glazed surface. Within this transitional space there are, in some situations, ramps giving the building's occupants the experience of moving outside the building to ascend or descend between floors. This is a development of the detached walkways used in the earlier Casa-Del-Sol project (1996) and Hitechniaga HQ (1995). There are sky-courts on floors 10, 19 and 20.

The greening of the external façade is combined with a variety of shading devices designed in relation to the sun-path. Extensive landscaping of the roof, the fifth façade, completes the green 'enclosure'. The roof garden is accessed by an external stair that ascends from floor 23 to floor 29. There are deep vertical 'gouges' or 'chimneys' in the south elevation from floors 12 to 18 and in the north elevation from floors 19 to 23 that bring natural light and ventilation into the central atrium space.

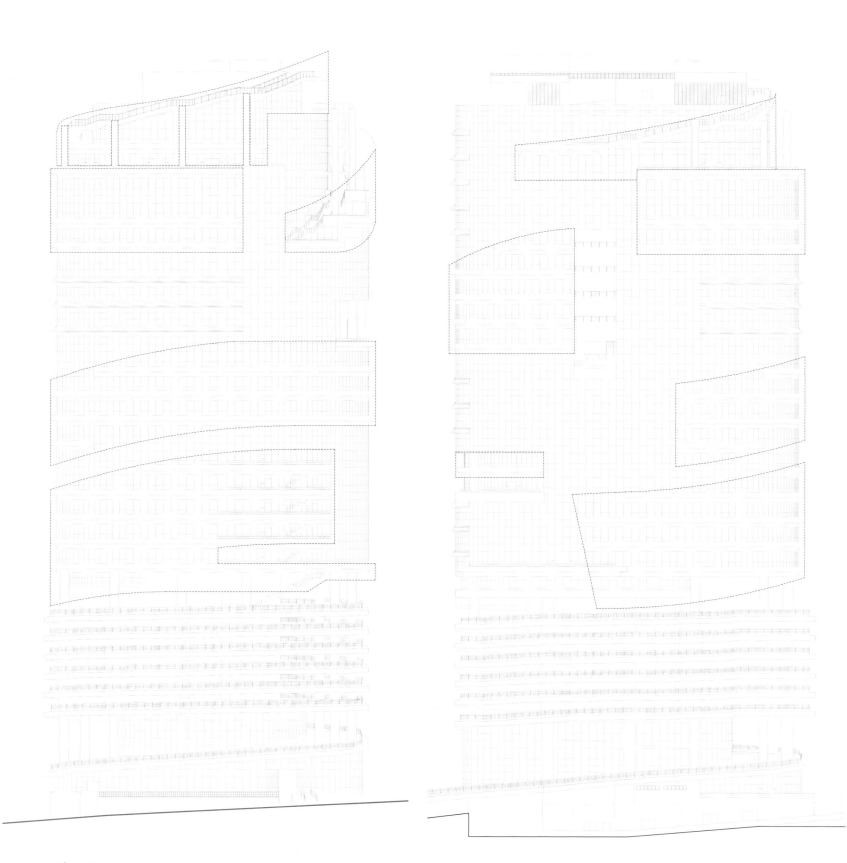

Above

The central atrium of the TA2 tower is topped with a translucent roof with a gap, which allows the atrium to 'breathe'. (Ng)

In this project, the 'greening' of the façade and the addition of organic mass into built form takes precedence. The service-cores are no longer at the periphery of the façade: they are located inside an internal atrium but are still naturally ventilated and lit by the sun. Yeang's intention is that the building should express both literally and metaphorically the notion of the 'green skyscraper'.

TA2 *Service Apartments (1997)*

The TA2 tower, also designed in 1997, explores the central atrium concept, with access to residential units via connected passageways, ramps and bridges. The mixed condominium and service apartment tower is intended to accommodate a high-end residential lifestyle. Located within the financial district of Kuala Lumpur, the tower is designed for a young corporate market. It is relevant to the discourse on the 'compact city' and the proximity of workplace and residence. People want to live in cities for the convenience and access to services; and such a lifestyle reduces the high energy costs of daily commuting. But the high-density environment has to offer security and privacy in addition to providing opportunities for communal interaction and casual encounters. Included within the TA2 tower are fibre-optic connections to every room, a business centre, an indoor and outdoor gym, a multi-function sports park, a members' 'sky-club', courtyard terraces and squash courts.

The form of TA2 is intended to provide maximum views from the perimeter to the distant jungle-clad terrain. The plan of the tower is split in two to allow cross-ventilation as well as stack-ventilation. The smaller of the two blocks houses single-level apartments with 3.1-metre-high ceilings. In the larger of the two blocks, the apartments have 6.1-metre-high ceilings, with mezzanine floors and double-height living rooms. All the apartments have external balconies linked to the principal living space and the master bedroom. The apartments are naturally ventilated but have the option of installing air-conditioning. There is also a naturally ventilated central atrium space and service-core. Inside the atrium are column-free corridors at each level linking apartment units to the lift lobby. The access corridor is another development of the detached access walkway used successfully in the Casa-Del-Sol Apartments (1996). The central atrium is topped with a translucent roof with a gap that allows the atrium to 'breathe'. Heavy planting is planned for the access corridors, and garden voids are created at various levels to encourage cross-ventilation.

The idea of vertical urban design is advanced further with communal facilities strategically located at various levels. At the base of the tower, within the internal void, is a multi-purpose park that provides recreational courts. On levels 12 and 13 is a racquet club connected to a high-level park. On levels 30 to 32, a clubhouse with a lounge, a restaurant, and a large roof garden

has a panoramic view of downtown Kuala Lumpur. On the same floor is the gymnasium with indoor and outdoor activities. On the thirty-first floor is a health spa with a swimming pool and garden, and two floors higher is a business centre with multimedia facilities. The dispersal of these functions throughout the building and their connection to adjoining landscaped sky-courts and sky-plazas is a tentative step towards a new theory of vertical urban design.

Taman Tun Dr Ismail-6D (TTDI-6D) (1997)

TTDI-6D is a residential development consisting of 320 units of apartments in two twenty-eight-storey towers. The project is in Kuala Lumpur, located close to the IBM Tower that Yeang designed in 1987. The two TTDI-6D towers are visually related, being placed at right angles to each other and in close proximity. The east–west axis bisects the angle between the two blocks. Each block has a roughly H-shaped configuration, the precedence for which is the MBf Tower in Penang, completed in 1993, where the configuration encouraged natural ventilation. TTDI-6D examines a similar use of sky-bridges to those employed in the MBf Tower.

The project extends the suburban concept of the detached bungalow vertically into the high-rise condition. In a typical suburban street, residential dwellings are physically separated from one another, providing a high level of privacy. This layout

Above

The two twenty-eight-storey towers of the TTDI-6D residential development are placed in close proximity and at ninety degrees to one another. In each block, and at every level, a central, naturally ventilated access corridor, or sky-bridge, serves the apartments, which are conceptually detached units.

Opposite

Conceptual drawings show TTDI-6D's detached units served by sky-bridges.

permits good cross-ventilation and cooling to occur around each house unit as the external walls of each dwelling unit are not shared party walls.

In each block at TTDI-6D, a central, naturally ventilated access corridor at each level serves six units, three disposed on either side of the corridor. The apartments are conceptually detached dwelling units. At each end of the central corridor, there are open-to-sky escape stairs. The spine wall of these stairs

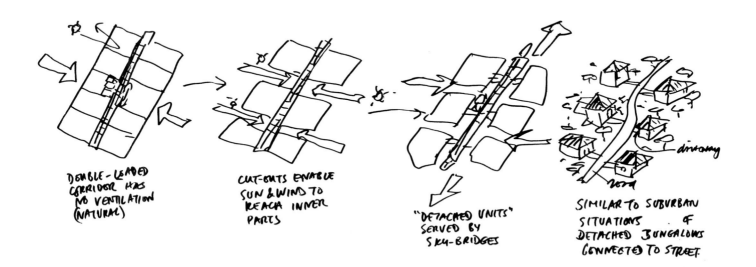

DOUBLE-LEADED CORRIDOR HAS NO VENTILATION (NATURAL)

CUT-OUTS ENABLE SUN & WIND TO REACH INNER PARTS

"DETACHED UNITS" SERVED BY SKY-BRIDGES

SIMILAR TO SUBURBAN SITUATIONS OF DETACHED BUNGALOWS CONNECTED TO STREET

serves the function of a wing-wall directing natural breezes through the central space. Wind-tunnel tests have been carried out to evaluate the effectiveness of the wing-walls, which serve a similar function to those in Menara UMNO (1998). The lift shaft is also naturally ventilated.

Each unit has an external balcony. Another climatically responsive device is the introduction of large sky-courts within the towers. These are cut out from the façades at levels 4, 11 and 20 to give two- or three-storey communal green 'spaces-in-the-sky'. They are used for planting and enable sunlight to penetrate to the internal bridges and walkways. The end walls of the towers that are exposed to the west sun have sun-shading devices. Connecting the two blocks at second-storey level, above the sub-basement car parks, is a communal deck with a swimming pool, changing rooms and squash courts.

The floor-slab design introduces ceiling plenums between floors to channel wind. These are controlled internally by adjustable shutters. The overall effect is to increase natural ventilation and to provide greater fresh air supply to the apartment units. The bioclimatic applications also extend to the façade design, where the external wall treatment varies depending on the building's orientation in relation to the sun. Various louvred screens and sun-shade configurations have been devised.

In the preceding chapters we have traced Ken Yeang's continuous rethinking of the skyscraper. This has formed the core of T. R. Hamzah and Yeang's work from the early 1980s. But in parallel with the development of tall buildings, Yeang has also used the evolving ecological design approach for a number of low-rise buildings. The lessons learned have then been selectively applied to the high-rise projects. In Chapter 5 we shall digress from the examination of Yeang's high-rise agenda to look in detail at some of his most important low-rise projects, and in Chapter 6 we will consider Yeang's urbanistic propositions.

5 Research by Design

Research by design is a critical factor in the continuous improvement of Yeang's 'differentiated product'. Smaller projects that come to the practice are used to test ideas that are then selectively applied to skyscrapers and other large building types.

THE FIFTH FAÇADE
Roof-Roof House (completed 1984)

Perhaps the most widely known, most photogenic and consequently best publicized of Yeang's earliest buildings, the Roof-Roof House was one of Yeang's earliest experiments in the application of bioclimatic principles to residential design. In particular, it explored the roof as the fifth façade.

The two-storey house was an attempt to put all his early ideas into practice and to test their viability. The form is undeniably modern, the language, Corbusien. Yeang's developing ideas on sun-shading, the double roof and 'filter' architecture are all examined here. He sees building enclosures as environmental filters and interprets this idea into built form. The outer curved roof acts as a solar filter to the rest of the house and the movable internal glass partitions and panels become the adjustable parts that can be manipulated to control wind-flow and consequently the microclimate. The ground-floor living room looks out to a shaded swimming pool. Yeang attempted to break down the distinction between inside and outside spaces, and the pool area is therefore seen as an extension of the living space.

Opposite

The Roof-Roof House looks magical in the early evening. The language of the building is distinctly Corbusien. (AL)

Above

In theory, the prevailing wind blows over the shaded pool, which assists in creating comfort conditions in the house. (AL)

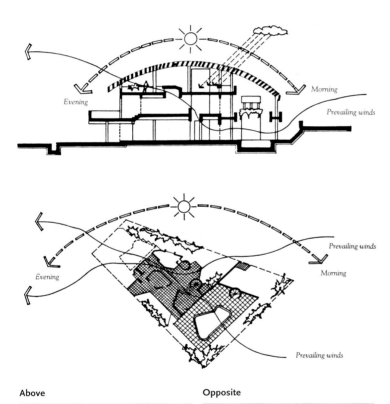

Above

The orientation of the Roof-Roof House in relation to the sun and wind.

Opposite

Roof-Roof House, plan of the first storey.

There is poetry in the building. The play of light as the sun moves across the louvred roof and the secondary forms is delightful. The mood of technical experimentation that was nurtured in Yeang in his AA days is fully expressed here. Indeed, there are so many ideas incorporated in this building that Haig Beck, the Australian architectural critic, was moved to exclaim that, 'the house lacks the scale to adequately carry all the experimentalism packed into it'.[1]

The Roof-Roof House is now ageing and losing a little of its lustre. But it still looks magical in the morning sunlight, the juxtaposition of one element over another is breathtaking, as is the clarity of edges, shadow lines and dark recesses.

The premise was to reinterpret architecture as an enclosure system that operates analogously to a filter, or an 'environmental filter', between the enclosed internal spaces and the external landscape. The name of the house comes from the secondary roof that soars above the building. This sweeps over the flat terraced roof of the second storey as well as the pool-terrace area, shading both. The sectional design of the 'louvred' roof is angled and shaped to reduce as much as possible the insolation of the west and midday sun while letting in the morning sun. The angled configuration works together with the north–south orientation of the building, with the ground-floor living spaces facing the east and the space that opens out to the poolside taking advantage of the prevailing winds. The wind is cooled as it

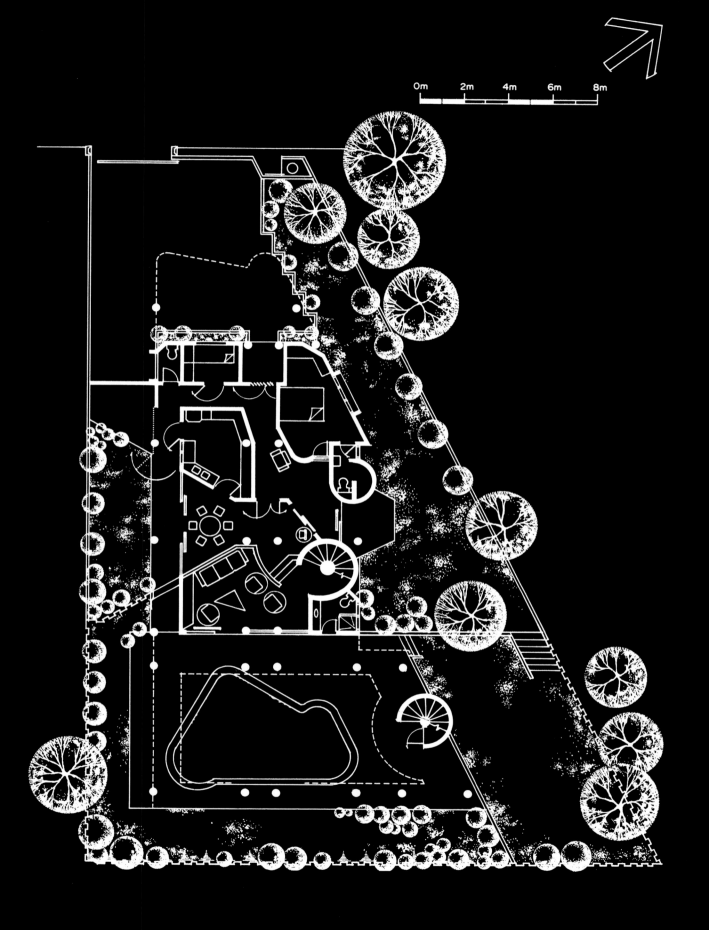

Left

The Roof-Roof House was an attempt to put into practice all of Yeang's early ideas on sun-shading, the double-roof and the wall as an environmental filter. (AL)

traverses over the pool water (by evaporation) before entering the living spaces. Three layers of movable parts (i.e. sliding grilles, glazed panels and adjustable blinds) are adjusted to control the microclimate of the living spaces. Their adjustment permits individual levels of environmental articulation, modulating choices in privacy, ventilation, natural lighting, space usage, security and comfort, depending upon the time of day, the household activity, the prevailing wind direction and wind intensity. The house has been intentionally designed to function as a 'system of working parts', allowing greater microclimatic control based on the users' experience of the local climate.

However, the Roof-Roof House is not without faults, and some of the 'valve' devices that Yeang has incorporated require considerable effort to balance. The house was designed by Yeang when he was a bachelor. Now that he is married, and with children and domestic staff sharing the accommodation, some of the climatic control devices do not work as well as intended, for they have to cater for the multiple activities of a family.

The house is at the edge of the city and the desire for openness is confronted with a requirement for security and for the exclusion of mosquitoes and other 'wildlife' from the adjoining rubber estate. The openness of a Malay *kampong* house, it seems, is not possible in an urban situation and the need to install extensive security devices is the price to be paid for a low-technology solution. Air-conditioning is now essential

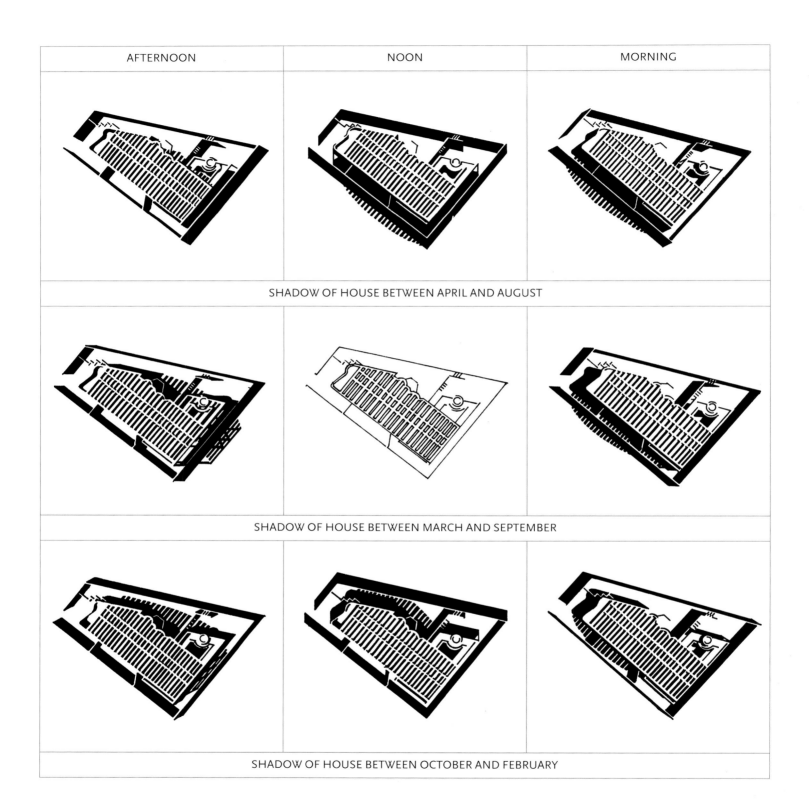

AFTERNOON	NOON	MORNING

SHADOW OF HOUSE BETWEEN APRIL AND AUGUST

SHADOW OF HOUSE BETWEEN MARCH AND SEPTEMBER

SHADOW OF HOUSE BETWEEN OCTOBER AND FEBRUARY

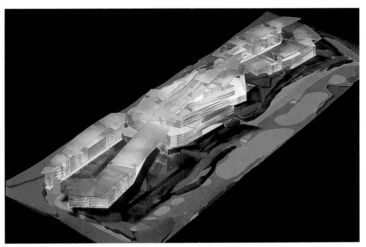

in the bedrooms. The interior configuration has been altered, but nevertheless it is a seminal building in the tropics and perhaps one day it will be retrofitted to its original condition.

The completion of the house confirmed Ken Yeang as an architect of serious intent and poetic sensitivity; an architect with an intellectual rigour behind his work. It was this intellectual content that Yeang found lacking in much of Malaysian architecture in the 1980s. Writing a review of Malaysian architecture from 1957 to 1987, he noted that 'there is insufficient thought given (by many Malaysian architects) to designing buildings to give them a didactic role beyond the demonstration of competence'. Yeang brought the architect to the edge of the political arena when he stated in 1984 that 'the fight for independence in this country, must be matched by a fight for an independent architecture based on independent thought'.[2]

SD HQ and Condominium Competition (1997 – unplaced)

This conceptual competition project is a gigantic version of the filter roof used in the Roof-Roof House. Designed more than a decade later in 1997, it is a series of large overlapping trellises spanning various medium-rise, two- to six-storey office and condominium apartment blocks below. The roof is designed to act as an environmental filter. The intention is to create cool outdoor spaces within which people are able to meet, eat and socialize. This is an intuitive response to the Malaysian lifestyle,

Opposite

The effectiveness of the Roof-Roof House's upper roof is indicated on this series of drawings.

Above

Conceptually, the SD HQ and Condominium is a series of super-large trellises spanning medium-rise buildings and acting as an environmental filter to the spaces below. (Ng)

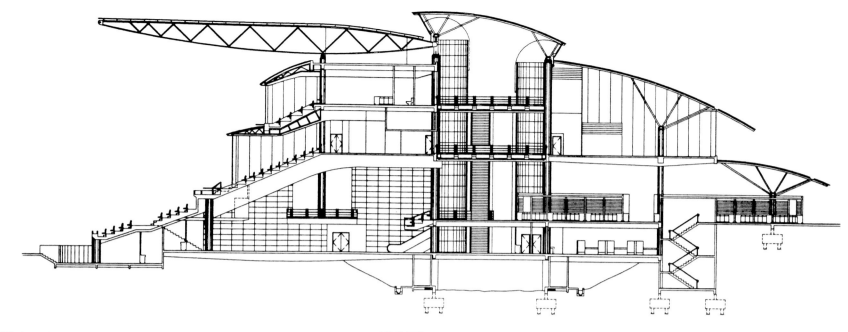

which favours outdoor activities from early evening until late at night. A promenade connects the two condominium parcels and passes through the office complex. The separation of the condominiums and offices is achieved by changes in the landscape. The use of the trellis roof structure is intended to reduce the amount of insolation the buildings will receive, thereby achieving a low-energy solution.

COMPUTATIONAL FLUID DYNAMICS
Selangor Turf Club (completed 1992)

The large-span roof design over the grandstand of the Selangor Turf Club in Kuala Lumpur has a central atrium. Computational fluid dynamics (CFD) simulation studies of the temperature and air-flow through the central atrium were carried out with Professor Phil Jones from the University of Wales, Cardiff. This methodology later assisted in the examination of natural ventilation opportunities in the Menara Mesiniaga tower and in Menara UMNO.

The emphasis was on providing the client with a building that would primarily be naturally ventilated, without resorting to expensive mechanical controls. The roofs are designed with substantial overhangs, to block out the west sun, but are split

Top

Selangor Turf Club, section.

Above

Computational fluid dynamics simulation studies were carried out on the roof of the Selangor Turf Club grandstand. The methodology was later applied to Menara Mesiniaga and Menara UMNO. (Ng)

Permasteelisa Technological Campus, conceptual office plan (*below*) and elevation (*right*), indicating the use of planting as a component in the building's façade.

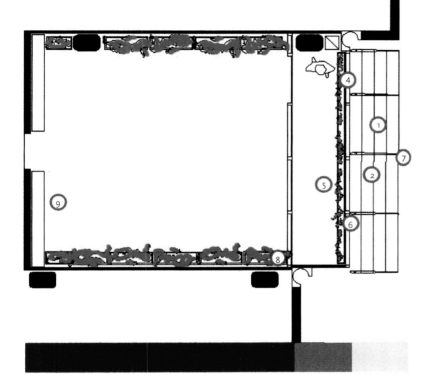

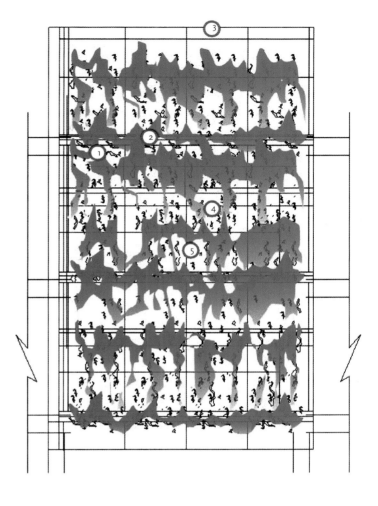

into a number of 'leaves' to encourage cross-ventilation. Louvres are incorporated into the roofs, to allow hot air to escape, while excluding the rain.

GREEN FAÇADES
Permasteelisa Technological Campus (1998)

The Permasteelisa Technological Campus project in San Vendemiano, Italy, is a test-bed for the application of experimental façades on high-rise buildings. A research programme has been set up to test the possible configurations of various façade systems. Yeang's proposal blends the existing Quaternario ABS façade concept with the innovative use of planting in a hybrid system.

ZONE 1 – Shading
1 • Annual creepers begin to defoliate in tandem with the requirement of increased sunlight penetration.
2 • External catwalk provided to ease maintenance and servicing of planted sun-shading.
3 • Extent of sun-shading decreases as exposure to sunlight falls.

ZONE 2 – Acclimatization
4 • Perennial plants to help in convectional cooling of air through heat absorption during transpiration.
5 • Thermal flue improves convectional air-flow acts as thermal buffer.
6 • Plants, microbes and protozoa in the soil help in the removal of airborne toxins.

ZONE 3 – Purification
7 • Cooling and heating system configured to avoid conflict with the moderation of internal environment through passive infiltration of ambient air.
8 • Microbes and protozoa in the soil complements perennial plants in the absorption of airborne toxins.
9 • Gravi-wall or equivalent cooling and heating system.

The main design feature is the use of planting and vegetation as a crucial component of the building's façade. Planting is used in three zones:

- **Zone 1** uses external planting as sun-shading (passive).
- **Zone 2** uses planting as acclimatization and thermal buffer (passive).
- **Zone 3** uses indoor planting for air-purification (active).

The passive environmental control system works in tandem with an active heating and cooling system, i.e. mechanical and electrical systems, to regulate the internal temperature in order to achieve a comfortable level throughout the year. The passive system helps to reduce the energy consumption of the active system and enhances the energy efficiency of the building. This leads to a lower-energy-consuming building, a further development of a 'green' architectural philosophy.

The hybrid façade incorporates a rainwater collection-and-filtration device, a glazing system, planter-boxes with self-irrigation and hydroponic planting, and an external planted trellis. The design creates a thermal flue in summer and a thermal buffer in winter. Plants are selected and incorporated precisely for their ability to provide shade, to remove heat by transpiration, and to absorb toxins and microbes emitted from the building's occupants and equipment.

COOLING AND THE ECOLOGICAL BENEFITS OF VERTICAL LANDSCAPING

The technology developed in the Permasteelisa Technological Campus project will, if it proves successful in field trials, have several applications in the 'green skyscraper'. It could enable a breakthrough in the development of the interactive wall.

In any ecosystem, Yeang writes, 'the climate is held to be the predominant influence even though other biotic factors such as flora and fauna and their interaction with the soils have an influence on the system. In most urban locations, all that remains of the site's ecosystem components is the upper geological strata, with a much simplified and reduced flora and fauna component. In any new built system, the fundamental ecological value of increasing the site's biological diversity should be recognized. Vertical landscaping in the skyscraper introduces organic matter into an otherwise high concentration of inorganic mass on a small site.'[3]

Quoting A. H. Rosenfield, Yeang notes that, 'Plants have aesthetic, ecological and energy-conservation benefits as well as providing effective climatic shields to sun, wind and rain. Planting can shade the internal spaces and the external wall, and can minimise external heat reflection and glare into the building. Plant evaporation processes can be effective cooling devices on the façade, affecting the façade's microclimate.'[4]

Plant leaves can be 1°C lower than the ambient air temperature and damp surfaces such as grass, soil or vegetation-covered concrete can be 2°C or more below, and can contribute significantly to a cooler and healthier building. Façade planting can lower ambient temperatures in the tropics (and summer temperatures in temperate climates) at street level by as much as 5°C . Heat loss in winter can be reduced by as much as thirty per cent in temperate climates.[5]

Biologically, the leaf is an efficient solar collector. In summer in temperate climates, the leaves take advantage of solar radiation, permitting air to circulate between plants and the building. This provides cooling by means of a 'chimney effect' and through transpiration. In winter, the overlapping leaves form an insulating layer of stationary air around the building. Even in regions too cold for evergreens to grow, summer cooling may still be an important factor, lending an energy-saving and biological validity to planting. The skyscraper's façade area can be up to four or five times the site area. If the façade is covered with planting in entirety, the increase in cooling can be significant. The complete covering of the façade can even contribute to reducing urban heat-island effect. Externally, vegetation can also lower urban temperatures in the boundary layer by 1°C, while tree canopies may lower external ambient temperatures by an additional 2°C beneath the canopy.[6] Plants also process internally generated carbon dioxide and release oxygen into the air, and remove formaldehyde, benzene and airborne microbes, thereby contributing to a healthier internal environment. Yeang gives the example of the Boston fern, which removes ninety per cent of the chemicals that cause allergic reactions.[7]

Roof-top vegetation functions in the same way as at ground level and can have a role in climate control. Certain plants can grow on just 7cm of soil consisting of pea gravel and silt-sand. Hardy plants can adapt to environments with minimum soil depth or humus content. Landscaping at roof or sky-court level can contribute beneficially to the climatic conditions of the city by reducing heat absorption. Roof gardens can also be used for urban agriculture: most vegetables need no more than 20cm of soil.

Plants evaporate water through the metabolic process of evapotranspiration. The water is carried from the soil through the plant and evaporated from the leaves as part of the photosynthesis process. Transpiration by plants helps to control and regulate humidity and temperature. Yeang points out that:

A single large tree can transpire 450 litres of water a day, equivalent to 230,000 kilocalories of energy in evaporation. The mechanical equivalent to the tree transpiring 450 litres a day is five average room air-conditioners, each at 2,500 kilocalories per hour, running for nineteen hours a day.

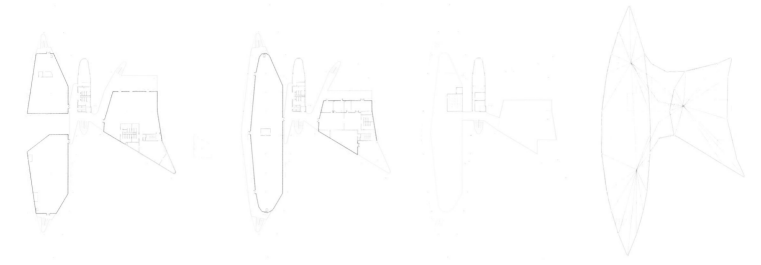

Above (left to right)

Guthrie Pavilion, plans of the first storey, the second storey, the roof terrace and the roof.

Opposite

The Guthrie Pavilion looks like a huge airship about to take flight. At night, the pavilion takes on the appearance of a giant firefly. (Ng)

Air-conditioners only shift heat from indoors to outdoors, and they also use electric power. The heat is therefore still present to increase urban air temperatures and in the process contributes to the urban heat-island effect. But not so with the tree, which has transpiration to eliminate this.[8]

Physical continuity between planting is important for encouraging species diversity. To achieve physical continuity in 'vertical landscaping' in the skyscraper, the system should be aligned (e.g. using stepped planter-boxes organized as 'continuous planting zones' up the face of the building). This permits some species interaction and migration and can be linked to the ecosystem at the ground level. The alternative is to separate the planting into unconnected boxes. However, this can lead to species homogeneity, which necessitates regular maintenance if the vegetation is to remain ecologically stable.[9] The green façade is taking on an important role in Yeang's evolving ecological agenda.

TENSILE STRUCTURES

Guthrie Pavilion (completed 1998)

The Guthrie Pavilion is a three-storey structure designed for Guthrie Property Development Holding (GPDH) Malaysia. It has a dual programme as an office and a golf clubhouse. The project explores the use of an inflated fabric roof canopy providing sun-shading and rain protection for a low-rise structure beneath. The high-tech Teflon-coated fibreglass roof, suspended on cables from tall steel masts, hovers above a lower pavilion. It is an astonishingly beautiful object: seen from afar it is almost incomprehensible. At night, it takes on the appearance of a giant firefly, the lighting beneath the canopy creating a jewel-like ambience. It is a dramatic building that has a presence far in excess of its size.

The secondary roof structure serves the practical purpose of shielding the building from the elements. Calculations were carried out to determine the optimum configuration of the roof to provide sun-shading at different times of the year and at different times of the day. The orientation was also calculated with reference to the wind-rose of the locality. The provision of the shading device has enabled Yeang to be freer with the design of the pavilion beneath. The office and clubhouse are enclosed in glass curtain walling, using clear glass to maximize the occupants' experience of the external environment. Beneath the vast sun-shade, the roof of the office-and-clubhouse complex

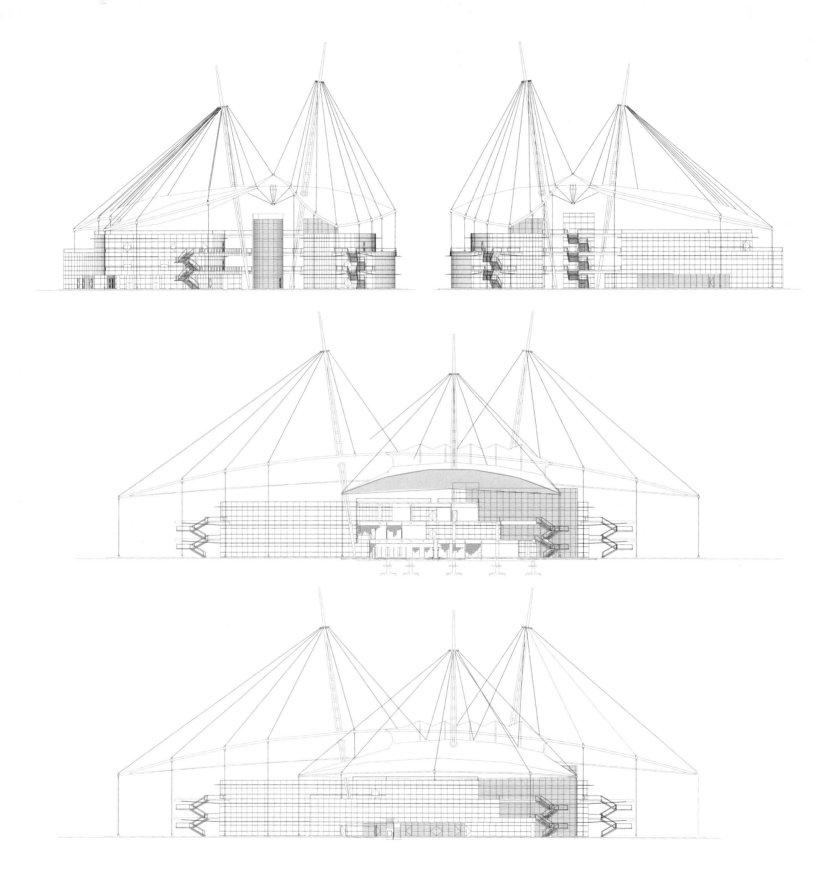

Above

The Guthrie Pavilion overlooks a golf course owned by the Guthrie Property Development Holding. The course is fringed by palm trees, a commodity upon which the company built its considerable wealth. (Ng)

Opposite

Guthrie Pavilion, typical elevations.

serves as a terrace that affords a breezy vantage point overlooking the company-owned golf course, which is fringed by palm trees, symbolic of the Guthrie organization's plantation origins. It provides its clients with 'a notable and memorable statement'[10] that is quite unique in the Malaysian context. For Yeang, it is a test-bed for tensile structures, which might, in future projects, cover large urban complexes.

It is to urban investigations that we now turn, for in parallel with Yeang's 'research by design' programme, the large-scale implications of the bioclimatic and green agenda have been applied to a number of masterplanning projects. Chapter 6 examines these large-scale investigations.

Opposite

The configuration of the Guthrie Pavilion's secondary roof structure has been carefully calculated to provide optimum sun-shading at all times. (Ng)

Above

The Guthrie Pavilion explores the use of an inflated fabric roof canopy to provide sun-shading and rain protection for a low-rise structure beneath. (Ng)

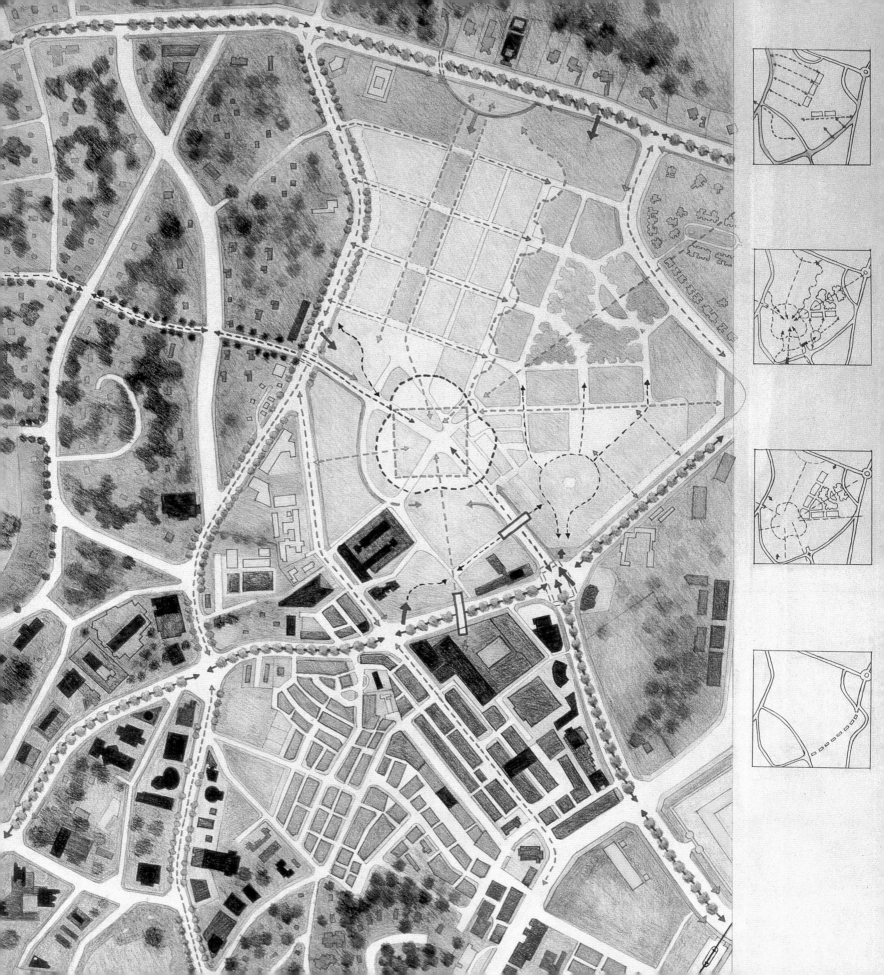

6 Urban Investigations

The larger-scale implications of the bioclimatic and ecological approach to design are explored by Yeang in a number of urban planning and urban design projects. They are carried out concurrently with the skyscraper explorations. In these projects Yeang frequently applies a methodology that he acquired during his brief attachment to the University of Pennsylvania in the 1970s. The influence of the 'ecological land-use analysis' and 'sieve-mapping' methods devised by Professor Ian L. McHarg, is evident in several T. R. Hamzah and Yeang urban design projects.

Kuala Lumpur Golden Triangle Urban Design Competition (1985)

In the early 1980s Yeang began to look closely at the built results of the economic boom of the 1970s and the disruption of the urban fabric of Kuala Lumpur. Historically, the old city had an intimate, organizing device – the 'five-foot way' or verandah – that responded to the Malaysian climate by providing pedestrians with a semi-covered shelter from sun and rain within the traditional shophouse typology. It provided a transitional 'space': a layering of the outer skin of the building.

In the 1970s, the International Style made inroads in Kuala Lumpur and the result was that major parts of the city were transformed 'into rows of glass, steel and concrete boxes, set back from the street behind plazas which threatened to design out of the city the critical element of "cityness" – the streets, sheltered walkways and buildings with memorable façades'. Yeang's competition entry for the Golden Triangle area of Kuala Lumpur was for a 'linked city'. The concept used the verandah as a generic urban design device for providing links between buildings.

The Tropical Verandah City (1986)

In 1986, Yeang's first book, *The Tropical Verandah City*, was published.[1] The title originated from a challenging remark made at the conclusion of a conference organized in 1985 by the Malaysian Institute of Architects and the Aga Khan Program for Islamic Architecture at Harvard University and the Massachusetts Institute of Technology. Professor Julien Beinhart pointed out that the West has a tradition of designing city forms, especially in the late nineteenth and early twentieth centuries. Le Corbusier's *Une Ville Contemporaine* and Ebenezer Howard's Garden City are two examples that have been used selectively all over the world. There was no such model for the tropical city and Beinhart suggested that a research task should be undertaken, and that the generative metaphor could be that of an 'urban garden'.[2]

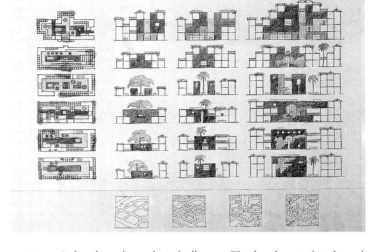

Opposite

Bandar Sunway Competition, conceptual drawing.

Right and below

The Tropical Verandah City examined in detail the 'in-between' spaces around a building and concluded that the edges of a building in the tropics must, by virtue of its many layers, become softer.

Yeang's book took up this challenge. The book was developed from the submission, in the preceding year, to an urban design competition for the area of Kuala Lumpur adjacent to the Golden Triangle. The book delved into Malaysian architectural heritage and cultural and symbolic influences. It developed the concept of Kuala Lumpur as a 'tropical urban garden' with landscaping, connected by a system of covered and open walkways. An urban design plan was evolved in schematic terms for the city, employing a network of such walkways. Major pedestrian routes were designated alongside the Klang River to provide historic linkages and to connect civic nodes.

The publication was timely, for it implicitly criticized the proliferation of insensitive development with the segregation of functions and zoning laws based on imported models. The criticism was directed particularly at the pattern of development in many Asian cities where individual buildings are separated by car-park access roads, thus stressing the convenience of car owners rather than pedestrians. Yeang called for a bold contextual experiment to make the tropical verandah city a reality. It was a call for an urban design that is integrative rather than divisive.

The book examined the idea of what Kisho Kurokawa refers to as the 'in-between' spaces around a building. Yeang looked at the permeable edges of traditional tropical buildings and the layering of façades and concluded that the edges of a tropical building must, by virtue of their many layers, become 'softer'.

He thus expounded a 'soft-edge' tropical architecture and the idea of ecologically responsive urban planning.

THE METAPHOR AS A DESIGN MODEL

The 'tropical urban garden' metaphor provides the designer with a concept for the urban design and planning of cities. It encourages low-energy consumption and an ecologically sustainable approach. It encourages, too, the maintenance of biodiversity. The use of energy in a city and the environmental comfort are essentially dependent upon, and achieved by, the choices and decisions that architects, urban designers and planners make.

The concept of the urban garden might lead to the development of a distinctive local identity for the tropical city. For a city to have an identity, its places must have a clear perceptual framework that is recognizable, memorable, vivid, engaging of attention, and different from other locations. These are the objective basis for one's perception. The test of a place's identity is the degree to which it is vividly remembered, used and identified by its inhabitants.[3] This is the aesthetic justification for the tropical garden city.

Bandar Sunway Competition (1987 – unplaced)

In the Bandar Sunway Competition organized by the Malaysian Institute of Architects in 1987, the entry from T. R. Hamzah and

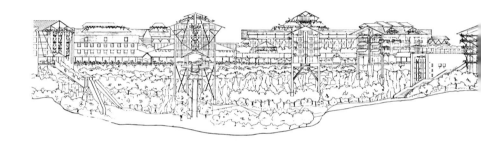

Yeang explored ideas for an ideal tropical garden city. The broad responses were:

- The built form, whether singularly or in aggregate, is shaped and orientated to maximum exposure to prevailing breezes and minimize exposure to sun.

- The planning of the buildings and their interiors permits through-ventilation and promotes air-flow.

- Vertical air-shafts are used to promote air-flow into the interior parts of the buildings. The transitional spaces for circulation and services, such as stair shafts, mechanical duct shafts, corridors and passageways are also used as wind conduits to bring ventilation into the inner parts of the buildings. This was the forerunner of the wing-wall idea introduced later in the MBf Tower and Menara UMNO.

Opposite

The site plan for the Spreeinsel
Competition.

Right

Conceptual urban form for the
Spreeinsel (Berlin) International
Urban Design Competition.

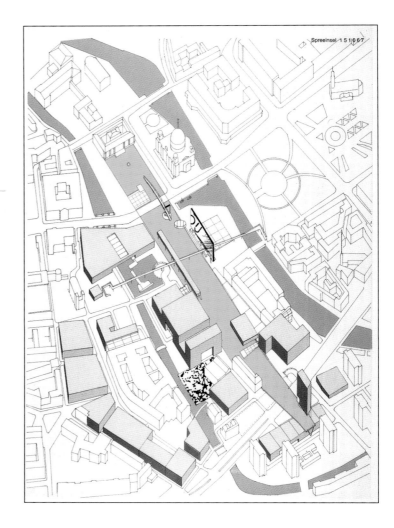

• The openings in the built form (e.g. windows, doors
and louvred walls and roofs) are orientated to facilitate
natural ventilation and cross-flow from the prevailing
winds. Accompanying this are higher floor heights to
facilitate wind-flow.

• Various devices are used as climatic modifiers
(e.g. overhangs, fins, louvres, and sun-shading devices)
to direct wind and to provide shade to the interior. This is
also to reduce insolation if the spaces are air-conditioned.
Other devices include shutters and blinds, walls (solar
walls and double walls), roofs (roof ponds and double
roofs) and thermal insulation.

• Landscaping and planting are used at different locations
and levels to reduce the ambient heat level.

• Transitional spaces are used to provide outdoor semi-
protected areas for climatic moderation (e.g. atria,
verandahs, corridors, plazas, terraces and balconies). There
are also open spaces in the upper parts of the buildings
such as roof-top gardens, sky-courts and sky-parks.

• Materials that do not absorb or store heat from the
sun are used.

• Roof ponds, water features and plantings are used
for the flat and near-flat surfaces of built forms for
evaporative cooling.

• Efforts are made to reduce air pollution and ambient heat.

• Building configurations are designed to reduce insolation
on the hot sides of the building.

• Neighbouring land forms, structures or vegetation are
used for the solar shading of buildings.

The ideas at this point in Yeang's development were all

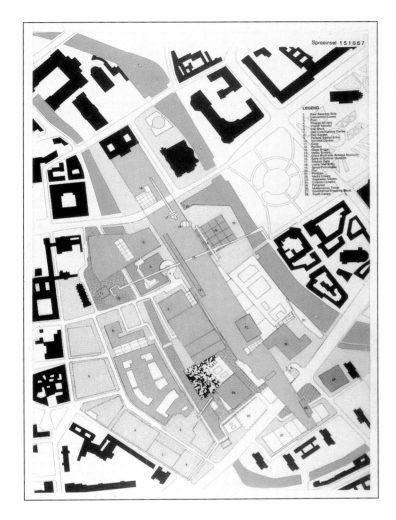

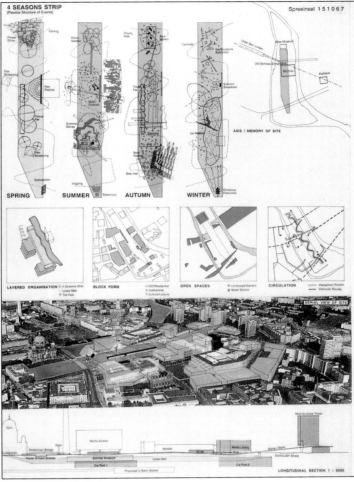

exploratory. It would be several years before he would get down to the specifics of how to achieve these general objectives.

URBAN DESIGN STUDIES
Spreeinsel (Berlin) International Urban
Design Competition (1993 – unplaced)

This urban design competition for a site in Berlin, prepared six years after the Bandar Sunway project, was conceptualized as a 'four-season strip'. In a location that has seasonal climatic variation, Yeang superimposed spring, summer, autumn and winter activities (programmes) upon the long rectangular site.

Thus in spring, there is a flower show, a film festival, a circus/fair, outdoor film screenings and a major convention; people bring out their bicycles after the winter. In summer, the activities of the 'strip' change to picnics, outdoor music concerts, summer games and outdoor speakers. In autumn there is the traditional German beer festival, dancing, a trade fair, flea markets and charity walks. In winter, there is ice-skating, Christmas festivities and sculpture exhibitions. There are all-year activities but essentially what Yeang did was to apply the principle of 'cultural activities related to climate' that is part of the culture in Southeast Asia. The four seasonal layers superimposed upon each other were then translated into conceptual built forms, parks and open spaces, pedestrian and vehicular circulation with associated below-ground parking, and an underground station. Connections were formed to the existing urban structure.

New Taichung Civic Centre (1995)

The New Taichung Civic Centre in Taiwan, carried out by Yeang in collaboration with Taiwan architect Ming Kuo Yu, was an entry for a 1995 UIA competition. There are four principles underlying the conceptual design. The first is the exploration of the seasonal and cultural activities that are generated within a public park located between a new city government building and a new city council building (in a similar manner to the Spreeinsel competition). A 'frame' connecting the two buildings supports interchangeable structures and components. The form and function of these structures change with the season and climate.

The second principle is to have continuous public landscape. The city government and the city council buildings are raised above the ground, allowing circulation beneath them. Continuous landscape is created from the southern to the northern extreme of the site. Security to the public building was the third consideration in the planning, and the fourth was the provision of circulation through naturally ventilated spaces.

The design sought to promote low-energy consumption, using daylight, sun, wind and diurnal temperature changes to the full. There is a high level of thermal insulation and maximum use of renewable and recyclable materials. The project aimed to collect and recycle rainwater and to recycle waste. All of these principles were part of an agenda for ecological sustainability, and the opportunity was taken to explore aspects of this agenda in urban design terms. The project contained a combined district

The New Taichung City Civic Center
Feng Shui Summary

Left

The city government building and the city council building are raised twelve metres above the ground, allowing landscaping to continue beneath them.

Opposite

A model of the New Taichung Civic Centre concept. A public park is located between the new city government building and the new city council building.

Top

A frame connects the two buildings and supports interchangeable structures and components.

Above

A *feng shui* summary of the New Taichung Civic Centre.

Right

A model of Yeang's entry for the
Marsham Street Urban Design
Competition in London.

cooling and electrical power system using agricultural fuels that
'have a reduced effect on the CO_2 emission into the atmosphere'.

The jury were appreciative of these strong theoretical
underpinnings and commented: 'The totality of the
government building and city council are strongly linked
together. The project is a powerful solution in its flexible use
of public space.' The design, driven by an ecological agenda,
was awarded third prize.

Marsham Street (London) Urban Design (1996)

Yeang's entry for a 1996 urban design competition for Marsham
Street in London was conceptualized as a 'three-dimensional
multi-layered matrix'. The nine-storey, mixed-use project
occupies a large rectangular site close to the Houses of
Parliament in the city's Westminster district. It incorporates
retail, commercial, office and residential spaces arranged
around a 1,800-square-metre central plaza.

In this project Yeang transferred the principles of vertical
urban design that he had developed in tropical Asia to the British
capital; and the bioclimatic responses for the winter, spring,
summer and autumn seasons that he had devised for the earlier
Spreeinsel Urban Design Competition entry effectively shape the
building and the central plaza, which has a fully retractable roof.
A 13,700-square-metre sky-court is introduced. The project is
remarkable for its careful analysis of climatic data and the

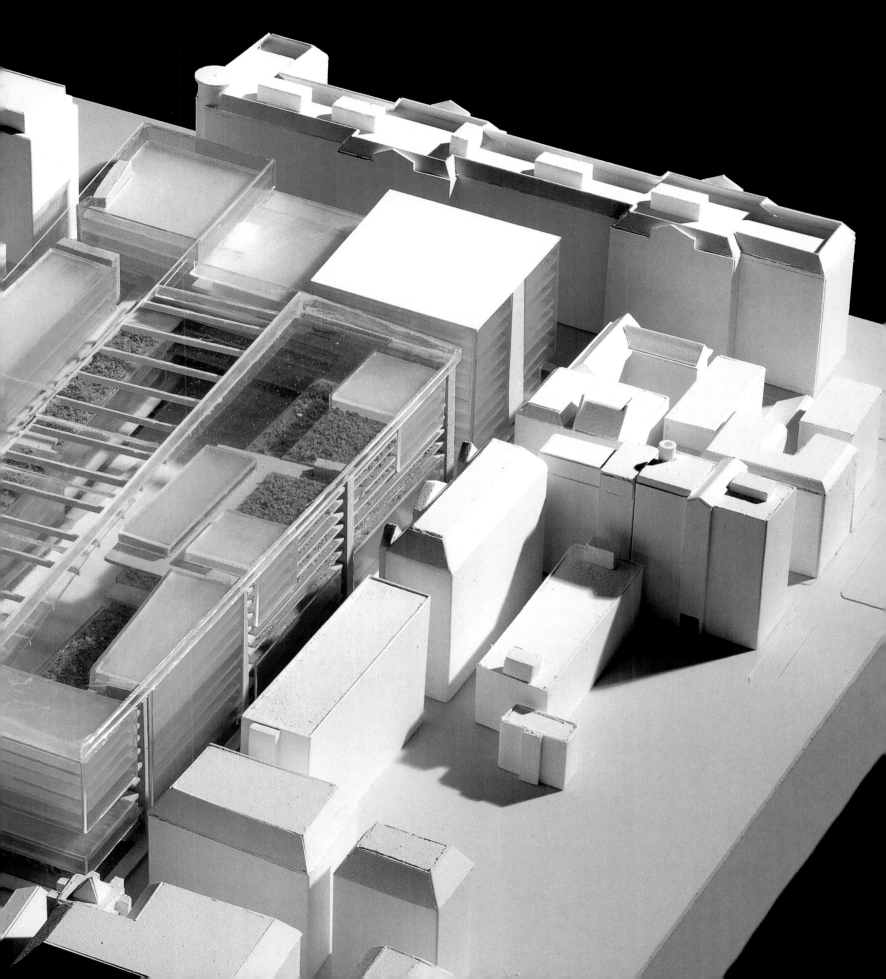

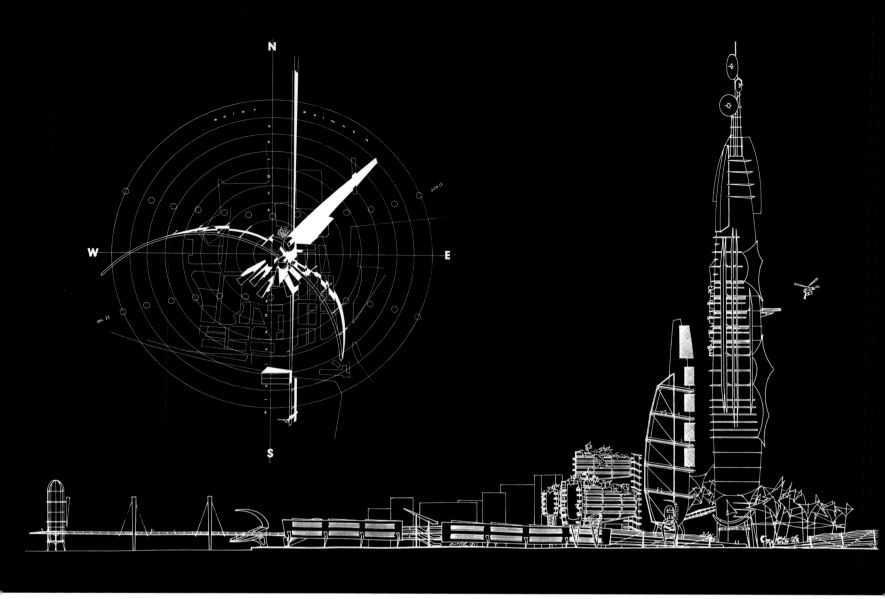

application of bioclimatic principles of design to an urban medium-rise building in the northern hemisphere. In the process, Yeang offers a unique insight into the possibilities for urban regeneration in London.

MASTERPLANNING

Johor Bahru 2005: The Bioclimatic City

Johor Bahru 2005 is a conceptual masterplan for Peninsular Malaysia's southernmost city, immediately north of the island of Singapore. The masterplan includes a sixty-storey tower with a plot ratio in excess of 1:10, but it is the conceptual ideas on the bioclimatic city that are particularly relevant.

'The bioclimatic city', writes Yeang, 'reacts like the human body, which adapts to its immediate environment. Just as the body maintains its stability by cooling via its extremities and by its homeostatic systems, so too can a city in the tropics employ cooling layers and use the principles of homeostasis to maintain levels of comfort.'

'The role of the architect and urban designer is to design structures and spaces to protect and enhance climatically the local urban environment. Additional layers are superimposed over the existing city. Some of the structures act as sun-shading devices over existing pedestrian routes. Urban spaces can be protected by canopy structures, creating shaded places for public gathering.'

Opposite and above

Johor Bahru 2005, conceptual drawings showing elevations and sun-path diagram.

Left

Johor Bahru 2005, conceptual sketch.

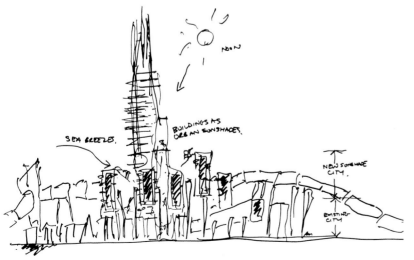

Vegetation on roofs and walls and in the various plazas provides recreation areas and assists in cooling the city's structures. Wind is channelled through pedestrian areas; evaporative cooling is introduced along the city streets; sea breezes off the Straits of Johor are harnessed; and the tower structure employs wing-walls to direct breezes and to create natural ventilation of the offices.

Lamankota Masterplan (1996)

The Lamankota masterplan was prepared for the Jalan Tun Razak-Cochrane/Jalan Perkasa area of metropolitan Kuala Lumpur. It is premised upon the Malaysian government's desire to have an integrated urban transport system. The masterplan provides a people-mover system with five stations that links with light rail transit (LRT) and personal rapid transit (PRT) systems at Star City and Maluri. A traffic-management concept gives priority to public transport and pedestrians.

The provision of an efficient public transit system is intended to reduce dependency on private motor cars and, consequently, the demand for fossil fuels. A commercial complex along the southern boundary of the site, bordering Jalan Tun Razak, is intended to form a noise-buffer between this heavily congested road and the residential areas. The programme details a wide range of industrial, commercial, residential, retail and institutional land uses.

The masterplan uses as its secondary organizing device the traditional Malaysian verandahs to encourage pedestrian movement with protection from the tropical climate. The continuous verandah forms a vital link between the residential, commercial and communal areas and is part of a network of pedestrian spaces. It is a theme that recurs in Yeang's work and relates to his 1985 competition entry for the Kuala Lumpur Golden Triangle and the subsequent publication of *The Tropical Verandah City*.[4]

The masterplan calls for extensive landscaping, and a design guide for buildings encourages developers and residents to landscape sky-courts, roof gardens and terraces. 'Sieve-mapping' of the existing site, using techniques appropriated

Opposite, top

The linear configuration of the Lamankota masterplan.

Opposite, bottom

The second organizing device of the Lamankota masterplan is its covered verandahway to encourage movement with protection from the tropical climate.

Above

A model of the Lamankota masterplan viewed from the west. The masterplan provides a people-mover system with five stations. This is intended to reduce reliance on private cars.

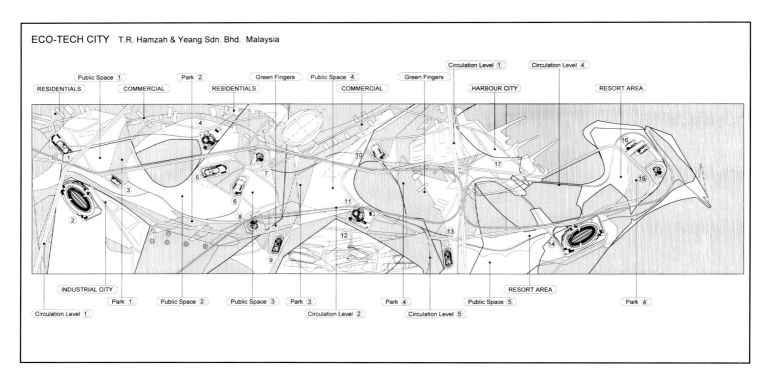

ECO-TECH CITY T.R. Hamzah & Yeang Sdn. Bhd. Malaysia

Public Space ① RESIDENTIALS COMMERCIAL Park ② RESIDENTIALS Green Fingers Public Space ④ COMMERCIAL Green Fingers Circulation Level ① HARBOUR CITY Circulation Level ④ RESORT AREA

INDUSTRIAL CITY Park ① Public Space ② Public Space ③ Park ③ Park ④ RESORT AREA Public Space ⑤ Park ④

Circulation Level ① Circulation Level ② Circulation Level ⑤

Above

The Eco-Tech City masterplan showing the circulation system.

Opposite

The huge model built for the Dortmund Exhibition of 1997 provides an image of a city of ecologically responsive high-rise towers.

from McHarg,[5] identified areas where existing vegetation will be conserved and protected by legislation. There is innovative use of indigenous trees and plants (e.g. *kayu manis*, *serai*, *buah pala* and *bunga melor*).

Eco-Tech City Masterplan (1997)

Eco-Tech City is a masterplan for a hypothetical site in Rostock, Germany. It was prepared for the Dortmund Exhibition of 1997. Yeang's bioclimatic towers are dispersed throughout the masterplan: there is a thirty-storey version and a forty-storey version of Menara TA1; three versions of Menara Mesiniaga (a twenty-storey version, a forty-storey version and a sixty-storey version); two versions of Central Plaza (twenty-seven and

fifty storeys); an eighty-storey signature tower modelled on the BATC project; two versions of the Shanghai Armoury Tower (thirty-six and fifty-five storeys); and three versions of the Gamuda HQ. The intention was to convey the urban form that could result from the use of high-rise towers in association with extensively landscaped parks. The towers in Eco-Tech City are connected by LRT systems and people-mover systems. This not only reduces the reliance on the motor car but also creates extensive parks and green spaces at ground level.

The huge model that was built for the exhibition gives a startling image of the form of a city driven by an ecological and high-technology agenda. It causes one to reflect on the reverse process that is shaping the skyline of many cities in Asia.

Multimedia Campus for Universiti Telekom Malaysia (1997)

The masterplan for the development of the multimedia campus of Universiti Telekom is located on a seventy-five-hectare site in Cyberjaya, an area of the Multimedia Super Corridor (MSC) that the Malaysian government intends to implement in the first two decades of the twenty-first century.

Above

The Eco-Tech City model viewed from the west.

Opposite

The Al-Hilali Office and Retail Complex in Kuwait City. The skin of the tower acts as an environmental filter.

The Universiti Telekom is seeking to become a state-of-the-art multimedia university promoting cooperation between researchers and leading players in the Malaysian IT industry. The basis for the masterplan is an IT-based educational strategy for the university, from which a design programme is formulated leading to urban design proposals and masterplan options.

Yeang had to adopt an abbreviated version of the McHarg model of landscape planning due to the local unavailability of land-use data to identify the salient features of the site's topography, geology, hydrology and microclimate. Following this, conclusions were drawn as to the land suitable for development. Yeang identified those areas that were suitable for intensive development, those suitable for moderate development, and those that should have limited development due to the vulnerability of the topography (e.g. severe slopes and dangers of erosion). Some areas were designated as being entirely unsuitable for development.

The analysis led to a masterplan with three options arising out of alternative programmes: Option One was a 'spine' development; Option Two favoured 'clusters' of development; while Option Three suggested a 'hub' form of development. All were related to the ecological analysis of the site and its context. This approach is now being used increasingly in Asia, but sadly it is still common to see huge tracts of undulating forested terrain

cleared and levelled to a series of 'platforms' with complete disregard for the damage to the environment. Siltation of rivers, erosion and slope slippage are some of the disastrous consequences that Yeang attempts to avoid.

Al-Hilali Office and Retail Complex (1997)

The Al-Hilali Office and Retail Complex in Kuwait City is a mixed-use programme containing retail facilities, a boutique hotel, a multi-purpose plaza, a club, a restaurant and a roof-top mini golf course. The project explores the notion of a 'flue-wall' with sun-shading on the west façade to act as a solar skin. The east façade of the tower has a double-layered 'flue-wall' as a ventilating space. Solar shading on the entire east façade gives protection

from the morning sun. The project is a demonstration of Yeang's principles of designing the bioclimatic skyscraper in a hot-dry location. It is driven by the same rationale of reconfiguring the tower to relate to the climate of the locality in which it is constructed.

Tianjin School of Civil Aviation Competition (1998)

The proposal for the School of Civil Aviation in Tianjin, China, was submitted in March 1998. The masterplan links the new accommodation to the existing campus to the north via a broad landscaped promenade. To the west of the promenade, in a security zone, is the school administration, a teaching complex, a library, a business centre, a computer centre, a science centre, an

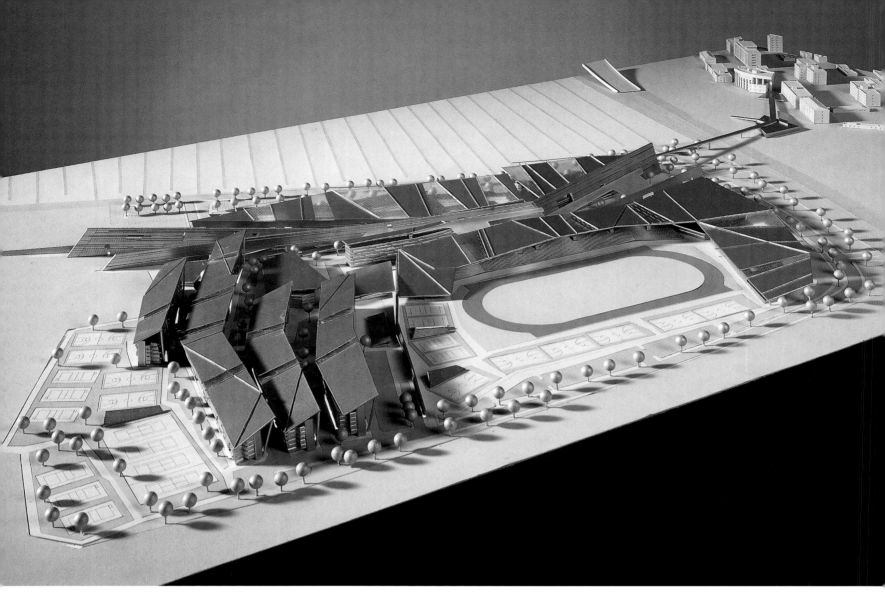

audio-visual centre, an international exchange centre and reserve land for a future research institute. To the east of the promenade is a sports hall, a swimming complex and a stadium with a variety of sports courts. On the southern end of the broad promenade is the staff and student accommodation, canteens and a bathhouse.

The plan is partly generated by security requirements that limit permeability between functional zones. The imagery of the conceptual plan is drawn from stealth aircraft at the 'cutting edge' of aeronautical design. Sharp angular forms and 'aerodynamic' planes strongly convey the building's purpose and functional complexity.

Business and Advanced Technology Centre Masterplan, Universiti Teknologi Malaysia (1998)

The masterplan is for a mixed development that includes an advanced management centre, a school for advanced education programmes, an integrated specific industry, research and development centre, a graduate centre, student residences, a convention and exposition centre, a management centre, an information and resource centre, a business hotel, retail shopping, offices, accommodation and service apartments. The development is scheduled to start in 2001 and will be gradually implemented over a period of ten to twelve years.

Eco-Cities

In the projects illustrated in this chapter, Yeang progressively extended the investigation of the 'green skyscraper' to the consideration of the implications of an ecological approach on urban planning. The development of low-energy, sustainable cities is highly relevant to the current interest in compact cities. Several studies have shown that the greater the intensity of urban population, and the more compact the urban form, the lower the energy consumption of a city. There is a proportional relationship in the reduction of energy consumption, notably in transportation fuel costs. Yeang cites this as one of the key justifications for the densification of development in the city and the *raison d'être* for the skyscraper. There are contradictory arguments that it is possible to build intensively for high-density residential development using medium-rise built forms with 'courtyard' layouts. But this, says Yeang, 'is true only up to a plot ratio of 1:4, beyond this the high-rise tower comes into its own'.

Arguments against compact cities tend to cite European and North American examples. The advocates of decentralization and dispersed models rarely confront the issue of the unparalleled growth in cities of Asia. The urban planning ideas illustrated in this chapter suggest new directions for Yeang to take in the next decade in order to develop ecologically sustainable, compact planning models as an alternative to those currently adopted in the rapidly growing cities in Asia and elsewhere in the tropical belt.

Opposite

The Tianjin School of Civil Aviation. The sharp angular and 'aerodynamic' forms suggest the design of state-of-the-art stealth aircraft and strongly convey the building's specialized purpose and functional complexity.

Above

A model of the BATC masterplan.

Right, below and opposite

The model of the six-hundred-metre Expo 2005 Nagoya Hyper-Tower. Yeang believes that towers should be imagined as 'cities in the sky'. Vertical transportation planning and a system of vertical parks, like those seen here, are integral parts of such a 'vertical city'. Significantly, Yeang's plan is in the form of a huge question mark: what form will the city take in the twenty-first century? (Ng)

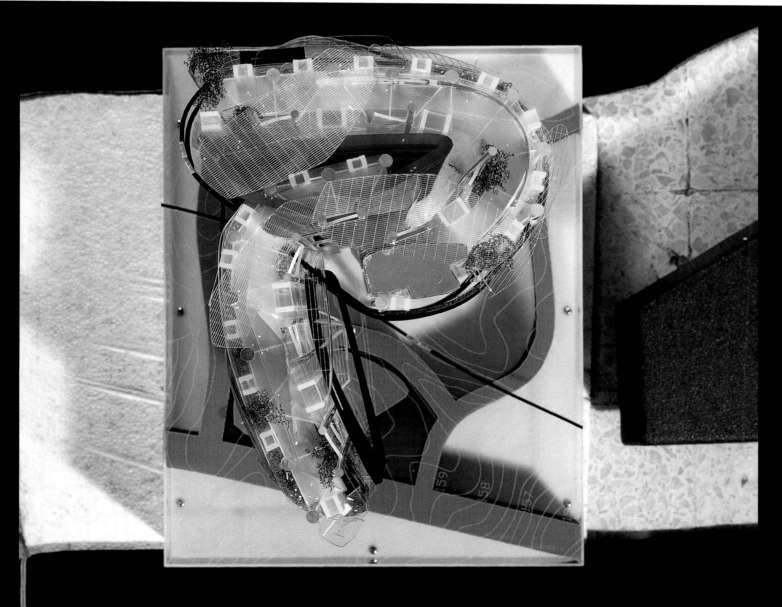

7 Thinking Vertically

THE FUTURE

In 1998, the work of T. R. Hamzah and Yeang was exhibited in Berlin; it has previously been on show in London, Tokyo and New York. And Yeang's designs have won several international architecture awards. Clearly, Yeang can no longer be defined as a Malaysian architect working in Southeast Asia. From the Kuala Lumpur office, he now operates an international practice in partnership with Tengku Robert Hamzah that has associated offices in Singapore, China and Australia. It is a transformation that no other Southeast Asian architect has managed to achieve. Yeang attributes his success to his having a focused ecological agenda independent of issues such as identity, tropicality and regionalism. Yeang would say that other Asian architects such as William Lim Siew Wai, Tay Kheng Soon and Jimmy Lim also have definable products, but none have sought to globalize their practice to the extent that he has.

His approach has not endeared him to some of his contemporaries, who dismissively put his success down to vigorous marketing of the practice. But it is more than that, for one can observe in the progressive refinement and continuous technical improvement of Yeang's skyscrapers the maturation of a set of ideas. By virtue of the generic validity of his work, he has progressed from a regionalist position to a global one. The international architectural community has embraced his ecological agenda because it offers solutions to many of the problems

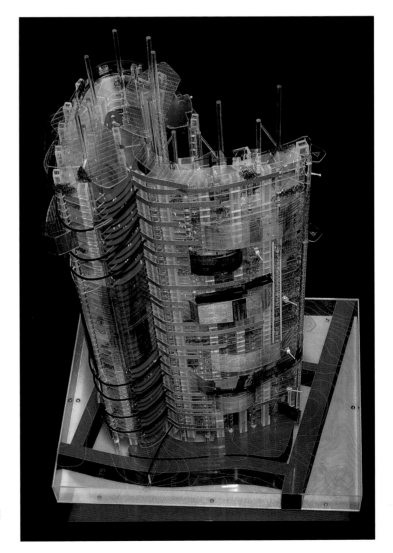

besetting humankind in the developed nations. At the 1998 Harvard Asia-Pacific Conference, Yeang chose 'environmental consciousness' as the theme of his presentation and reportedly it 'won over a predominantly Western middle-class audience'.[1]

Sixty per cent of the design staff of T. R. Hamzah and Yeang are non-Malaysians. Yeang explains this simply: 'I employ the very best young architects, whether they are from the UK, Europe, America, Australia or Asia; the 40 per cent of staff who are local "lads" know that they are among the best in the country, for their performance is measured against international standards. As a practice, we benefit from the "technology transfer" that comes about as a result of employing capable young designers from Europe and elsewhere, and they get the opportunity to optimize their talents here.'[2] Yeang maintains that architecture is analogous to manufacturing and one cannot be the 'best in the world' by simply relying on local resources.

THE 'GREEN SKYSCRAPER'

As Yeang has become increasingly focused upon the ecological sustainability of the high-rise building his terminology has undergone a further shift in emphasis. The term the 'green skyscraper' has superseded his earlier use of the less inclusive expression the 'bioclimatic skyscraper'. It marks more than just a change of nomenclature: it signifies a growing concern for ecologically sustainable design of large building types, and

bioclimatic design is seen as merely a subset of ecological design. In September 1998 Yeang completed the manuscript for a new technical book, *The Green Skyscraper: A Primer for Designing Ecologically Sustainable Large Buildings*.[3] It contains Yeang's current thinking and design agenda. The fundamental ideas have been introduced in previous publications by Yeang, but increasingly evident, as if sensing his and our own mortality, is an urgency in his language and the contention that without a concerted effort by humankind to incorporate ecological design 'our widespread activities as a species in the biosphere will in time overload the carrying capacity of the other species and the natural systems of the planet'.[4]

THE ECOLOGICAL APPROACH

The bioclimatic approach addresses the issues of conserving energy in an 'in-use' building and of reducing its waste products. 'In a more rigorous ecological approach,' says Yeang, 'the designer must also address the issue of the extent of delivered energy embodied in the materials and equipment used in the building.' The ecological approach adopted by Yeang considers the input of materials used in the operations of the building, as well as its outputs during the operational phase. 'The building's outputs must be non-polluting and be either recycled or reused or reintegrated into the biological cycle with little or no negative environmental impact.'[5]

Materials used in the building construction itself must also ideally be recycled or reused at the end of the useful life of the building. This affects the energy-embodiment values of the materials and the way in which they are fixed in the building. The level of embodied energy in a building is related significantly to its mass. The general indicator is that the lower the building's mass, the lower the total value of its overall embodied energy in its materials and equipment will be. A low-energy-embodied office tower should range from 8 to 13 gigajoules/m^2 of primary embodied energy.[6]

Often a value judgment needs to be made. Aluminium has a higher embodied energy than steel as a 'first cost'. However, at the end of its useful life in a building, it consumes considerably less energy in its recycling than steel. Reinforced concrete has almost the same amount of embodied energy as steel, but it is less recyclable at the end of its useful life. Steel can be virtually recycled into its original use, whereas concrete can be reused only in a downgraded form as rubble and cannot be recycled for structural uses.[7]

Life-Cycle Environmental Impacts

In the ecological design approach to the skyscraper advocated by Yeang, the impact of all the activities involved in the creation of a building from 'source to sink' are considered, in terms of their impact on the natural systems in the biosphere and of the related flow of energy and materials in the building's life-cycle. On recent projects Yeang assesses at the outset the extent of ecosystem analysis and mapping that is required, as demonstrated by the table below.

ECOSYSTEM HIERARCHY	SITE DATA REQUIREMENTS	DESIGN STRATEGY
Ecologically Mature	Complete Ecosystem Analysis and Mapping	• Preserve • Conserve • Develop only on no-impact areas
Ecologically Immature	Complete Ecosystem Analysis and Mapping	• Preserve • Conserve • Develop only on least-impact areas
Ecologically Simplified	Complete Ecosystem Analysis and Mapping	• Preserve • Conserve • Increase biodiversity • Develop on low-impact areas
Mixed Artificial	Partial Ecosystem Analysis and Mapping	• Increase biodiversity • Develop on low-impact areas
Monoculture	Partial Ecosystem Analysis and Mapping	• Increase biodiversity • Develop in areas of non-productive-potential-impact areas • Rehabilitate the ecosystem
Zeroculture	Mapping of remaining ecosystem components (e.g. hydrology, remaining trees, etc.)	• Increase biodiversity and organic mass • Rehabilitate the ecosystem

Ecosystem Hierarchy and Design Strategy. © 1998 Ken Yeang

Unless a skyscraper's design is fundamentally correct at the planning stage in all the bioclimatic and ecological aspects, no subsequent adjustments can make it function satisfactorily. The ecologically responsive skyscraper must be designed

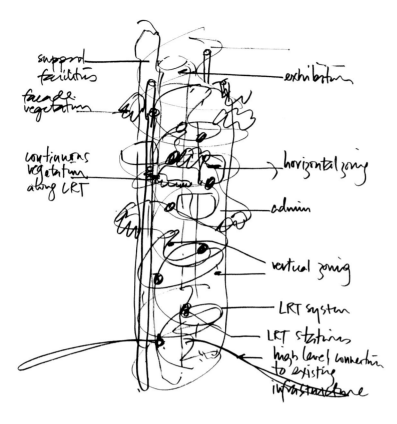

support facilities

facade vegetation

exhibition

continuous vegetation along LRT

horizontal zoning

admin

vertical zoning

LRT system

LRT stations

high level connection to existing infrastructure

from the outset rather than be a series of afterthoughts. While active energy-conserving devices can benefit energy performance, the skyscraper must be properly configured in a passive way. Any devices added on should contribute to its energy performance rather than being used to correct errors made earlier through poor design configuration and misuse of materials. These energy-efficient saving devices can contribute between eighteen and twenty per cent operational cost savings.[8]

'The full realization of the bioclimatic/ecological strategies', says Yeang, 'would be a skyscraper that is totally naturally ventilated and sun-lit. This is obviously dependent upon the users accepting a less consistent comfort level and accepting the inconvenience of having frequently to manipulate devices to respond to changing microclimate conditions, unless they are fully automated. Climate is not consistent, thus its realization hinges upon the level of comfort and convenience that is acceptable to the community and the acceptability of the ecological justifications.'[9]

The approach adopted by Yeang enhances users' well-being by enabling greater awareness of the external environment. Skyscraper occupants have the opportunity to experience the external environment and the seasonal changes throughout the working day. The green skyscraper that Yeang proposes encourages users to interact with the local external environment, instead of being encapsulated inside a hermetically sealed artificial environment.

Thinking Vertically

Yeang is intrigued by the notion of the skyscraper as a 'vertical city' embracing the concept of 'mapping the skyscraper'. 'Towers', says Yeang, 'should be imagined as "cities in the sky" with good pedestrian linkages, public realms, civic zones, vistas, and a sense of place extended upwards.' Some floors should have higher densities than others because of their use. 'You map a tall building the same way you do a city, with zones for parking, offices, and social spaces.'[10] The theoretical ideas in the 'green skyscraper' and the notion of the 'vertical city' were explored in two towers that Yeang designed in 1998.

Expo 2005 Nagoya Hyper-Tower (1998)

Expo 2005 in Nagoya, Japan, is to be a major event at the start of the next millennium. The exhibition's theme expresses the need to reconsider the natural world through the adoption of an

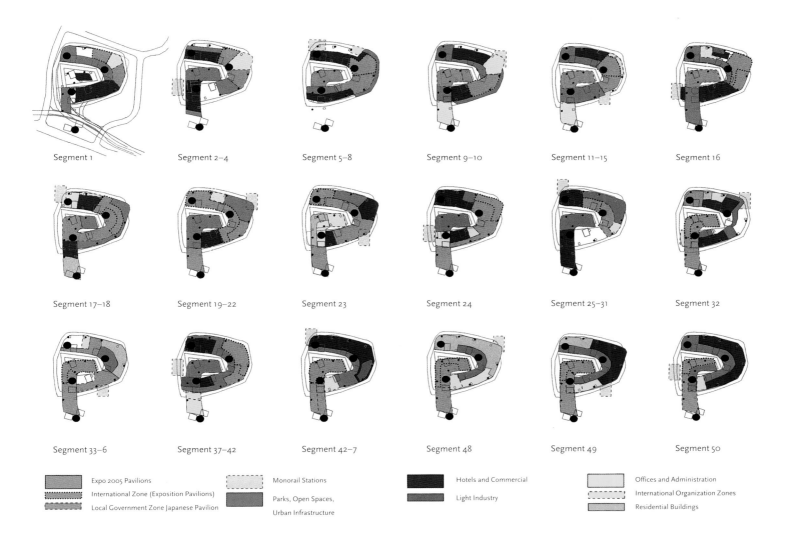

Segment 1   Segment 2–4   Segment 5–8   Segment 9–10   Segment 11–15   Segment 16

Segment 17–18   Segment 19–22   Segment 23   Segment 24   Segment 25–31   Segment 32

Segment 33–6   Segment 37–42   Segment 42–7   Segment 48   Segment 49   Segment 50

- Expo 2005 Pavilions
- International Zone (Exposition Pavilions)
- Local Government Zone Japanese Pavilion
- Monorail Stations
- Parks, Open Spaces, Urban Infrastructure
- Hotels and Commercial
- Light Industry
- Offices and Administration
- International Organization Zones
- Residential Buildings

innovative attitude to urban planning, infrastructure, building design and information, proposing new standards for quality of life in an ecologically friendly environment. The theme fits perfectly Yeang's current preoccupation with the ecologically sustainable large building set within an urban context.

Yeang addresses the issues of ecological sensitivity with a vertical masterplan. It is in the form of a prototype hyper-tower, six hundred metres in height. The fundamental premise of this proposal as a 'vertical masterplan' is that the hyper-tower would have a small footprint at the ground plane of just three hectares, but would have a gross floor area of 150 hectares – the equivalent of a city district measuring 1km × 1km at a gross plot ratio of 1:1.5.

Above

Expo 2005 Nagoya Hyper-Tower, a series of floor plans showing the function and zoning of the 'vertical city'.

Opposite

Expo 2005 Nagoya Hyper-Tower, generic design concepts.

The vertical masterplan would preserve much of the existing mature ecology of the locality. The building addresses the challenge to enter the twenty-first century with a respect for nature but also with a technological response, using clean and efficient energy technologies. This form of urban development creates an opportunity to integrate local resources, environmental demands and the specific needs of the international exhibition.

The generating principle of the Expo 2005 tower is vertical accessibility. The intersections of different transportation systems are intended to create activity nodes or behavioural settings, with green plazas and sky-courts animated by adjacent activities. The transportation planning in the hyper-tower includes an LRT system, a monorail circulating the outside of the tower (Yeang refers to it as a skin-crawler), high-speed inter-area lifts, district lifts and local lifts, travelators and gondolas.

The tower is integrated physically and systematically into the natural environment. Vegetation is an integral part of the external façade system giving shading and microclimate control. Tall trees are used to articulate double-volume spaces, and local plant species give a sense of place. The vertical park system is an exercise in planning equivalent to a substantial area of a city. The open spaces in the tower include promenades, thematic gardens, a 'ramp-park', observation gardens, sky-plazas, sky-courts, planted terraces, verandahs and roof gardens.

The rest of the programme is equally rich, including a transportation terminus, an information centre, auditoria, hotels, an amphitheatre, cultural institutions, a convention hall, LRT stations, a helipad, police stations, government buildings, an arts and crafts village, international exposition pavilions, administrative offices, commercial space and light industrial premises, in addition to residential accommodation.

The six-hundred-metre tower is divided into fifty segments, each twelve metres high. Within each segment, there is the possibility of constructing three- to four-storey-high buildings. The structure is envisaged as a megastructure with divisions of three blocks of fifteen segments and four megaplatforms supported by four technical floors. Constructional voids allow natural light to filter into the interior.

The Expo 2005 hyper-tower illustrates Yeang's intention of designing with nature. He pushes the boundaries for the advancement of the 'green skyscraper' beyond previous concepts. A vertical lifestyle is proposed, matching the dreams of his Archigram mentors at the AA in the 1960s.

Signature Tower,
Business and Advanced Technology Centre (1998)

Like the Expo 2005 tower, the sixty-five-storey BATC Tower is conceptually a high-rise park system with a hierarchy of landscaped 'places-in-the-sky'. These are distributed vertically throughout the tower and are related to a network of distribution and transportation systems. The open-space system includes a sky-plaza, sky-courts, a roof observation deck and terraces.

The tower is located within the second phase of a masterplan proposal for a nine-hectare campus for the Universiti Teknologi Malaysia that includes several high-rise towers. The signature tower incorporates a number of experimental features as a consequence of Yeang's ideas to develop a 'green skyscraper' that is a microcosm of the city. The masterplan for the mixed development, within which the BATC Tower is located, was illustrated in Chapter 6.

Behavioural Settings in High-Rise Buildings: A Theory of Vertical Urban Design

Simultaneous with the advancement of the ecological aspects of skyscraper design, greater attention now needs to be given to the internal spaces created. High-density living in compact urban environments will only be acceptable if privacy, security and lifestyle options are assured. In developing a new theory of vertical urban design, a methodology might be borrowed from Jon Lang (1994), Amos Rapoport (1977) and other researchers in the field of man-environment studies.[11] Empirical studies of the behavioural activities and their concurrent behavioural milieu would greatly assist our understanding of how public 'places-in-the-sky' can be created to sustain life in a hierarchy of situations.

Above

The BATC Signature Tower. (Ng)

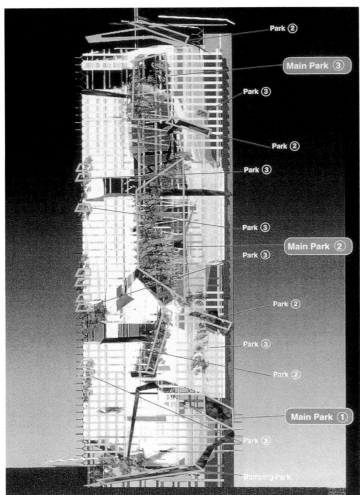

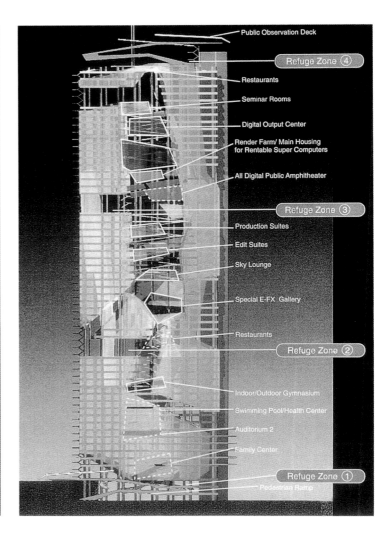

Above

The BATC Signature Tower, hierarchy of park systems. (Ng)

Above right

The BATC Signature Tower, vertical building programme. (Ng)

One might simultaneously investigate, in the manner of Gordon Cullen's *Townscape*,[12] elements of 'serial vision' incorporating compression, deflection, surprise, concealment, revelation, unfolding vistas, 'hereness' and 'thereness'. These are elements in the urban landscape that make 'horizontal' cities pedestrian-friendly, and at present they are relatively underdeveloped in Yeang's towers, which exhibit formal manipulation but in general fail to fulfill their promise in their internal environments.

The imageability of the vertical city might be considered using the terminology of Kevin Lynch.[13] This would include the location of 'nodes', the distinctive features of 'paths', the occurrence of 'landmarks' in the vertical morphology, the definition of 'districts-in-the-sky' and the articulation of 'edges'. This is not to suggest that 'places-in-the-sky' should resemble places at ground level: they would draw their distinctive character from the attributes of high-level habitation – the wind, breezes, expansive views, safety from street violence and vehicular pollution. It would be a celebration of 'high life'.

A methodology for vertical urban design must be derived that goes beyond the initial functional zoning of the Expo 2005 Nagoya Hyper-Tower or the BATC Signature Tower, otherwise, like the worst results of modernist planning, the spaces may be uninhabited. The development of vertical urbanism demands the creation of a richness in the public and private realms. It would respond to Mohsen Mostafavi's observations that, 'it is time to look more seriously at the quality of the internal spaces being produced'.[14] In this way, the behavioural activities of those who live and work in the towers would influence the form. It would make the process more holistic, adding to Yeang's ecological agenda.

Architecture for the Third Millennium

In June 1998, Asia Design Forum (ADF) No. 9 convened in Kuala Lumpur. The Forum took a different form from earlier meetings. On this occasion, Yeang invited leading architects and theorists to speak upon the theme of Asian architecture in the third millennium.

The views expressed were diverse but the identity issue, which dominated discourse in the 1980s, hardly surfaced. It was generally agreed that architecture in Asia would advance by acknowledging shared human values that are neither specifically Eastern nor Western. A number of the speakers addressed the theme of ecologically responsive architecture and the survival of the planet. Tao Ho from Hong Kong concluded that: 'Energy will be the shaping force of architecture in the twenty-first century'.[15]

The last decade of the twentieth century marks a symbolic transition in the pattern of human settlements. More than half of the estimated five billion people on the planet now live in cities. Vast numbers of people are clustered together in urban conglomerations.[16] They live in close proximity, preferring concentration rather than dispersal, attracted by the advantages of employment, services and goods. By the year 2025 it is estimated that the world's population will be 8.5 billion, and that seventy per cent will live in cities. Yeang's theoretical propositions and inventive solutions for the 'green skyscraper' typology set within an ecologically sustainable landscape offer a compelling vision of one form of urban habitation in the twenty-first century.

Chronology

1970

'Global Village', Shinkenchiku Residential Competition organized by Japan Architect magazine *(unplaced)*
The design proposal speculates on a housing form for the future. It consists of a megastructural A-frame surrounding a square courtyard as a repeatable planning module. Affixed to the sides of the A-frame is flexible, high-density housing. Under the A-frame is the commercial plaza. The central courtyard is landscaped, environmentally controlled, and covered by a tensile-skin structure. The influence of the Metabolists is evident in this student project.

1971

'Stylesville'
A design for a skyscraper in the form of an 'ice-cream sundae'. This is a conceptual design for a high-intensity city block. The city-block shapes parody consumer goods. The drawings were commissioned and reproduced in the form of a postcard published by *Architectural Design* magazine.

1972

Singapore Science Centre Competition, Jurong, Singapore, organized by the Singapore Institute of Architects *(unplaced)*
The building design is planned on a tartan grid with service towers located at the intersections of the grid. Shedlike enclosures are designed over the tartan grid for flexible-use exhibition spaces. Dish-shaped auditoria are placed above the sheds.

1976

Associated Battery Works, Petaling Jaya, Selangor
Interior renovation works for a battery factory.

Burmah Road Apartments, Burmah Road, Penang *(unbuilt)*
A seven-storey apartment development with commercial uses on the ground and first floors. The design explores the integration of planting with buildings by means of stepped planter-boxes that bring landscaping diagonally and continuously up the front of the building, across the roof and down the other façade. The ecological advantages of a continuous-planting concept is experimented with in this design.

Jalan Rahang Shophouse, Seremban *(unbuilt)*
A five-storey shophouse design with a mezzanine floor. The building is an early attempt to introduce planting into buildings. Planter-boxes of varying heights are located on all floors.

Tan Sri H. T. Ong House, Jalan Duta, Damansara, Kuala Lumpur
The built form is circular and tucked into the slope of a hillside.

Essene Administration Building, Gainesville, Florida, United States *(unbuilt)*
The circular built form is recessed partly into the ground. The building is four storeys high, encircling a central landscaped courtyard. Greenhouses are located at the entrance points along the north, south, east and west axes of the building. Movable curved solar-collectors are located along the outside walls. These cover part of the sides of the building and move to follow the sun's path.

Jalan Tunku Hassan Shophouse, Seremban *(unbuilt)*
A four-storey shophouse on a corner site. Planting is located in planter-boxes on the façade.

Ulysses House, Jalan Ampang Tengah, Ampang Hilir, Kuala Lumpur, for Mr and Mrs Leong Siew Wing
The house has a circular form around a central living space. Overlooking the living space is a gallery, above which is a stepped roof that brings light and

Taman Sri Ukay Housing and Shophouses.
T. R. Hamzah and Yeang's office is in the centre foreground.
Ken Yeang's residence, the Roof-Roof House, is at the extreme left.

ventilation into the inner spaces of the building. The internal spaces have a progression that extends from the main entrance to the living space, down to the terraces, and then to the poolside. Planning is based on two axes, one of which relates to the entrance from the south; the other relates to the pool and north-east view of the Ampang Hills.

Caunter Hall Apartments, Caunter Hall, Penang *(unbuilt)*

A five-storey apartment building in a low-income area. The design explores the use of a stepped section for the sun-shading of lower floors.

1977

Bishop Street/King Street Shophouse, Penang *(unbuilt)*

A five-storey shophouse on a narrow site.

Tenaga Suri Sports Complex, Taman Tun Dr Ismail, Damansara, Kuala Lumpur *(unbuilt)*

A small sports facility with a golf driving range.

Sunrise Shophouses, Jalan Ipoh, Kuala Lumpur

Two rows of five-storey shophouses located along a busy street. Verandahways are colonnaded and two storeys high. The upper floors are for residential use.

1978

Bricklin Road Apartments, Jalan Bricklin, Penang *(unbuilt)*

An apartment block with an octagonal plan facing a large free-form pool.

Taman Megah Shophouses, Taman Megah, Petaling Jaya

Three-storey shophouses in a dormitory suburb of Kuala Lumpur.

Jasin low-cost housing planning layout, Malacca *(unbuilt)*

A low-cost housing planning layout.

Taman Sri Ukay Housing, Apartments and Shophouses, Jalan Ulu Kelang, Ampang, Selangor

An upmarket housing development consisting of terraced houses, semi-detached houses, detached houses, apartments and shophouses. The design approach is to develop an abstraction of the vernacular Malay house. The stilts of the traditional houses are reinterpreted as sloping beams along the building façade. T. R. Hamzah and Yeang's office is located in the development.

Park Avenue Homes and Shophouses, Taman Seputeh, Kuala Lumpur

A housing development on an undulating site.

Institute of Public Administration Colleges,
Kluang, Kemaman, Sungei Patani
Three colleges built for the Institute for Public
Administration and financed by the World Bank.
The three colleges are of a prototype design and are
at different locations. Building configurations
are based on a courtyard layout with stepped-back
section and circular stairs at the corners of
the building. Building clusters are linked
by verandahways.

Playmore Apartments, Jalan Gurney,
Penang (unbuilt)
High-rise blocks with chevron-shaped floor plan
facing the sea. Single-loaded corridors give good
cross-ventilation to each unit. The units are double-
storey maisonettes.

1979

City Centre Urban Complex, Kuala Lumpur (unbuilt)
A mixed-use development consisting of a hotel,
shopping, apartments and offices. Vegetation is
brought down to the street level as a belt stretching
continuously from the top of the hill down to the
street pavement. The landscaped belt is used as a
buffer separating the hotel block from the stepped-
terraced shopping/commercial block. The stepped
terraces have planting up the building frontages.

Taman Arosa Housing and Shophouses,
Ulu Langat, Selangor
Mixed housing development. Internal courtyards
bring ventilation and light into the inner spaces of
the terraced houses.

Taman Kencana Housing and Shophouses,
Ulu Langat, Selangor
Mixed housing development that explores the use
of the roof of the two-storey link-houses as roof
gardens and terraces.

Taman Intan Shophouses, Klang, Selangor
Three-storey shophouses.

Ismail Sulaiman House, Section 17,
Petaling Jaya, Selangor
Detached house in Petaling Jaya. The house is on a
steep hillside. The design explores the interlocking
of two L-shaped building forms.

1980

ACW Ceramic Tile Factory, Klang, Selangor
A factory for the production of ceramic tiles, built on
a narrow rectangular site.

Tanming Housing, Petaling Jaya, Selangor
A terraced-housing project.

Wangsa Ukay Housing,
Jalan Ulu Kelang, Ampang, Selangor
A large housing development consisting of several
types of housing units. In the masterplan, the
terraced houses were planned with extra-wide
frontages. The subsequent designs give the
impression of semi-detached units with cross-
ventilating voids between each unit.

Wangsa Ukay Apartments,
Jalan Ulu Kelang, Ampang, Selangor
Three apartment blocks located on high
ground. Terraces are placed perpendicular to
the plan to bring cross-ventilation into the inner
areas of the apartments.

Wangsa Ukay Country Club,
Jalan Ulu Kelang, Ampang, Selangor
The design explores a number of filter-wall devices.
The cross-section combines a number of filtering
devices that include louvres, overlapping glass
panels, Z-shaped profiles, slats and canopies.

Wisma SMI, Lorong P. Ramlee, Kuala Lumpur
Yeang's first built skyscraper: a seventeen-storey
office tower located in Kuala Lumpur's Golden
Triangle area. Above the roof and mechanical
equipment is an experimental filterlike, Z-profiled
additional roof.

Westpoint Apartments/Leisure Holidays Apartments, Jalan Tanjung Bungah, Penang

The building is a twenty-storey apartment development facing the sea. Apartments are accessible by single-loaded corridors to give cross-ventilation to the units. Transitional spaces such as staircases have louvred ventilating walls. Ground-floor spaces are 'open to sky' and naturally ventilated.

Klang Industrial Lots, Klang, Selangor

Site-development plan for industrial shop units on the outskirts of Klang.

LYL Tower, Jalan Raja Chulan, Kuala Lumpur *(unbuilt)*

A multi-storey office building that explores the stepped-terraced façade.

TAF Housing, Petaling Jaya, Selangor

A terraced-housing development in Petaling Jaya. The design explores the idea of a cross-ventilating corridor that is placed perpendicular to each terraced house.

Sri Ferringhi Apartments, Tanjung Bungah Road, Penang *(unbuilt)*

The site planning explores the maintenance of the ecological continuity of landscaping from one side of the site to the other. The planning also demonstrates the possibilities of integrating planting with buildings at the horizontal low-rise

level. The planning segregates pedestrians from vehicular traffic. The overall configuration resembles the shape of a dragon, an auspicious image.

1981

Trellises Apartments, Taman Tun Dr Ismail, Damansara, Kuala Lumpur

The design has a set-back section facing a partly enclosed central court. The units have screens with movable louvres. This design was modified to allow for increased density while retaining the set-back section. To depart from the purist geometry of the modernist forms, less rigid geometry is used at the edges. Large tiled roofs at the entrances are combined with Z-shaped louvres to give through-ventilation to the atrium's community areas.

Warisan Tun Perak, Jalan Tun Perak, Kuala Lumpur

The design explores the extension of verandahways to the upper floors of the five-storey building, thereby increasing the transitional spaces at the face of the building. These ideas led to the development of the tropical verandah city and also provided the model for the landscaped terraces in the Menara Boustead.

Chan Leong Cheng Apartments, Klebang Besar, Malacca *(unbuilt)*

This is a seaside development in which the earlier concepts in the Sri Ferringhi apartments are used again. The building configuration combines low-rise units with a high-rise tower block.

Plaza Atrium

House, Jalan Ampang Hilir, Kuala Lumpur, for Mr and Mrs Quek Leng Chan

The major interior renovation of a private house. The renovation and extension consist of a number of design experiments in filter devices that provide the precedents for many later projects. The new entrance canopy explores the Z-profiled sections as a filtering device that permits ventilation but keeps out the rain. This provides the prototype for the Z-shaped profiled louvres used later in the roofs of Plaza Atrium. The poolside terrace overhangs have stepped slats placed at an angle. These devices provide the basic experimental prototypes used later for the inclined louvres at the top of the Plaza Atrium.

Plaza Atrium, Lorong P. Ramlee, Kuala Lumpur

A twenty-four-storey office-building complex located in Kuala Lumpur's Golden Triangle area. The building explores the idea of an atrium as the transitional space between the inside and outside of a building. The traditional shophouse verandahway is extended upwards to cover the entire face of the

Far left and left Menara Boustead

Bottom Menara Boustead,
sun-path diagram

building. Above the atrium space is a louvred
Z-shaped roof-form. The atrium of the building is
intended to act as a wind-shaft to cool the insides
of the building. (*See page 16 for further details.*)

Saratogoa Apartments, Johor *(unbuilt)*
Low- and medium-rise apartments. The building
configuration developed further the ideas in the
earlier Sri Ferringhi design. Planting is ecologically
linked through the periphery of the site and plants
are integrated with the buildings.

1982

Casuarina Hotel, Tanjung Bungah, Penang
Interior renovation works for the hotel.

Taman Tun Dr Ismail Local Masterplan
(revised design)
Masterplan preparation.

CWC Towers Development,
Jalan Ampang, Kuala Lumpur *(unbuilt)*
A mixed-use development on a prominent site in
Kuala Lumpur's Golden Triangle area. The design
for the tower blocks explores the idea of large
upper-floor terraces as sky-courts. These led to
the development of the high-level planting and
terraces used later in Menara Boustead.

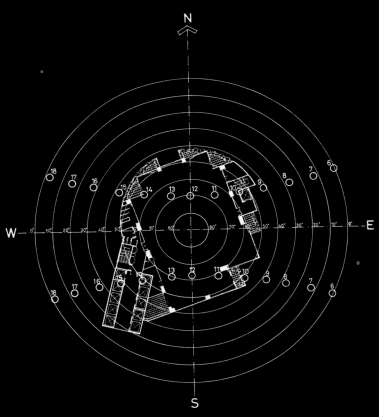

Datong Office, Johor Bahru *(unbuilt)*
Twin towers office development.

Bendahara Village, Kuantan, Pahang *(unbuilt)*
Masterplan for an urban village complex
development.

Menara Boustead, Jalan Raja Chulan, Kuala Lumpur
A thirty-two-storey office tower located in Kuala
Lumpur's Golden Triangle area. The tower explores
the idea of locating landscaped terraces on the
upper floors of an office building. The external wall
has a double skin and is clad with heat-sink
composite aluminium panels. The typical floor plan
develops the principles of a tropical high-rise
building type, e.g. provision of natural lighting and
ventilation to the lift- and stair-cores; service-cores
are located on the hotter sides of the building, being
the east and west sides; all window surfaces are
recessed unless facing exactly due north or south;
toilets are used as buffer zones, terraced balconies
are located at the corners with full-height glazing.
(*See page 30 for further details.*)

IBM Plaza, Taman Tun Dr Ismail,
Damansara, Kuala Lumpur
A twenty-four storey office tower linked to a two-
storey restaurant over a large plaza. The tower
incorporates the idea of escalating planter-boxes

IBM Plaza

IBM Plaza

along the façade of the building. The planters ascend
one face diagonally, traverse across the floor in the
mid-level and then ascend the other face to the
uppermost floor. The upper floors corbel outwards
to give an alternative form to the flat-surfaced
modernist tower slab. The design integrates
planting into the building as 'vertical landscaping'.
(*See page 24 for further details.*)

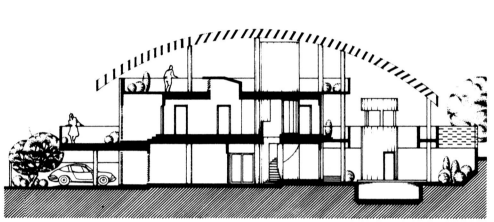

Roof-Roof House, section

ETM Apartments, Damansara,
Kuala Lumpur (unbuilt)
The design explores a curvilinear built form on the
edge of a sloping site.

Wisma Hong Leong Yamaha, Industrial Building and
Showroom, Jalan Semangat, Petaling Jaya, Selangor
A medium-rise warehouse-cum-showroom for
Yamaha motorcycles. The entrance canopy and
entrance lift lobbies use a Z-shaped profile, louvred
filter-roof form.

Taman Tun Dr Ismail Masterplan, Kuala Lumpur
The masterplan for the southern part of the Taman
Tun Dr Ismail (TTDI) site.

Singapore Island Country Club Competition
(unplaced)
A competition organized by the Singapore Institute
of Architects. The project provided the opportunity
to experiment with a number of roof forms:
Z-shaped louvred roof, egg-crate-grid roof pergola,
skylight roof form, glazed roofing and tiled roofing.
The ideas in this design led to the development of
the cross-sections of filter-wall devices in projects
that were concurrently under construction.

Sekemas Office Building (unbuilt)
An eighteen-storey office development. The design
explores the idea of a double-filter wall along the
façades and an atrium in the tenant's space.

MPD Housing, Pelentong, Johor
Low- and medium-cost terraced housing.

KEA Resort Masterplan,
Batu Ferringhi, Penang (unbuilt)
The masterplan for the development of a site in
Tanjung Bungah for a resort and country club.

Seapark Site Development Plan and Housing,
Petaling Jaya, Selangor
Mixed development.

Dason House, Jalan Beringin, Damansara,
Kuala Lumpur, for Mr and Mrs Tony Dason
A detached house located on a steep slope in an
upmarket residential area of Kuala Lumpur. The
design explores the fragmentation of the plan to
increase the external wall areas for cross-ventilation.

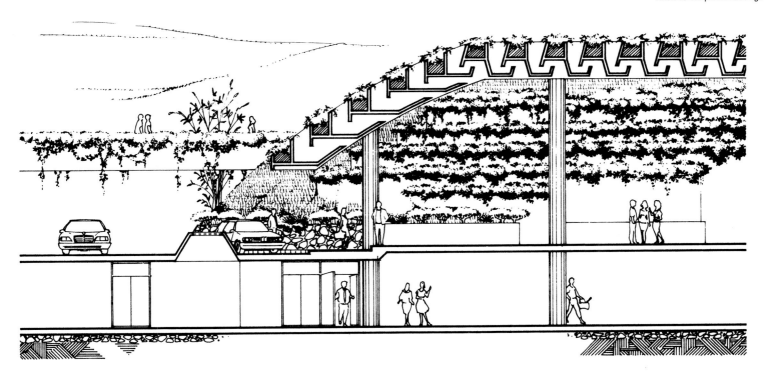

Wisma Kencana Tower, Kuala Lumpur (unbuilt)
The design is for a multi-storey office tower that
explores the ideas in Plaza Atrium. The atrium,
now located near the lift-cores, extends from
ground level to the louvred roof.

1984

Roof-Roof House, Taman Sri Ukay,
Jalan Ulu Klang, Ampang, Selangor
Yeang's attempt, in a house for his own use, to put
all his early ideas into practice and to test their
viability. (*See page 115 for further details.*)

KEA Resort Hotel Development,
Tanjung Bungah Road, Penang (unbuilt)
This project explores the use of verandahways
and the combination of the Z-profiled louvred
filter-roof form with tiled roofing in a composite
roof design.

MPD Housing Phase 2, Pelentong, Johor
An extension of the earlier scheme.

Kinta Apartments, Kuala Lumpur (unbuilt)
An apartment development that further extends the
ideas in the Saratogoa Apartments project.

ETM Apartments, Jalan Duta, Kuala Lumpur (unbuilt)
An apartment development that explores the idea of
the Z-profiled louvred roof form for an apartment
building and a set-back section.

1985

Lake Club Competition, Lake Gardens, Kuala
Lumpur, organized by the Malaysian Institute of
Architects (PAM) (unplaced)
Design for a competition organized by PAM. A
number of ideas are explored: the staircase as a wind
conduit, the waterfall atrium, the Z-shaped louvred

roof form combined with planter-box and continuous planting across the top of the building. The design brings together many of the concepts of early schemes. It is a benchmark for Yeang's development of ideas.

Kuala Lumpur Golden Triangle Urban Design Competition, Kuala Lumpur

Yeang's competition entry, which received an honorary mention, was for a 'linked city'. The concept used the verandah as a generic urban design device for linking buildings and for providing access between buildings. The ideas employed in this competition entry are published in Yeang's book, *The Tropical Verandah City*. (*See page 133 for further details.*)

Seapark Housing Phase 2, Petaling Jaya, Selangor

Further phases of the housing development on the SEA Housing site.

1986

SIAB Golf Hotel and Resort, River Donau, Hungary *(unbuilt)*

SIAB-ZAAL Building, Dubai, United Arab Emirates *(unbuilt)*

A small office tower with a central waterfall and atrium. The entire roof is covered by a louvred filter roof. The external wall is shielded by a lattice-louvred filter.

1987

Weld Atrium, Shopping Mall, Jalan Raja Chulan, Kuala Lumpur

Interior design for the public areas of a shopping mall in Kuala Lumpur's Golden Triangle area. The design explores the use of a louvred gypsum-plaster ceiling for the passageways and a louvred shading device for the atrium roof.

Northam City (Scheme 1), Northam Road, Penang *(unbuilt)*

The scheme explores the idea of a tower block with connecting sky-courts. The upper part of the tower is designed for a country club and is given a separate form. The entrance to the tower is a large public room that gives access to a court at the centre of the site. The apartments surround the central court and the passages are covered by a louvred roof.

Bandar Sunway Residential Competition *(unplaced)*

The design, in addition to fulfilling the competition's brief, explores ideas for a tropical garden city. (*See page 135 for further details.*)

1988

Wisma Sime Darby

Interior design for a penthouse and mezzanine floor for an advertising company. The design received an honorary mention in the Dupont Antron Interior Design Awards.

MacGin House, Kenny Hill, Kuala Lumpur

A detached house designed around a central motor-court. The roof form combines a slatted-louvre roof at an incline (similar to the profile on the uppermost roof of the IBM Plaza) with roofing tiles. The entrance porch has the Z-profiled roof form. Verandahways are used to link the north wing of the house with the south wing.

Raintree Club, Jalan Wickham, Kuala Lumpur

Interior renovation works for the coffee-house and games area of a country club.

Sunrise Apartments, Jalan Ipoh, Kuala Lumpur

Apartment development in Kuala Lumpur.

1989

Phase 6D, Taman Tun Dr Ismail, Kuala Lumpur *(unbuilt)*

Proposed masterplan and design for residential and shophouse development on existing temporary oxidation pond.

Joru Housing and Shophouses, Pelentong, Johor

A housing development for a rural site in Johor, consisting of double- and single-storey houses and industrial lots.

Office and Warehouse, Jalan 221, Petaling Jaya

Renovation works for three floors of an office block and adjoining warehouse.

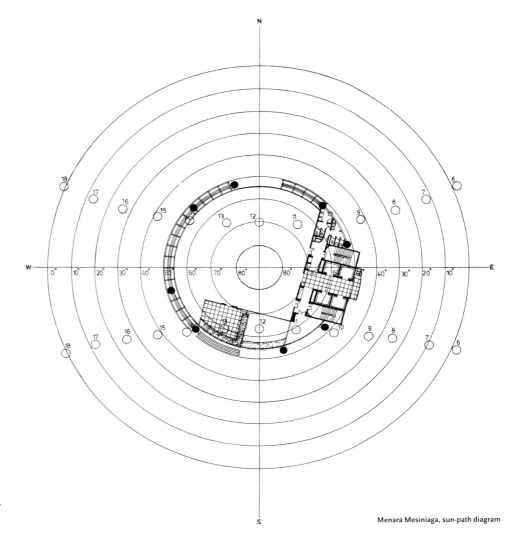

Menara Mesiniaga, sun-path diagram

Menara Mayban, Jalan Tun Perak, Kuala Lumpur
Interior design and space-planning for two floors in the Mayban Building.

Selangor Turf Club Grandstand and Racetrack, Sungei Besi, Selangor
A racetrack and grandstand on a green-field site south of Kuala Lumpur; Singapore Institute of Architects Design Awards 1995, Overseas Category: Honorary Mention. (*See page 122 for further details.*)

Terraces Apartments Phase 6E, Taman Tun Dr Ismail, Damansara, Kuala Lumpur
An apartment development consisting of a low-rise block with three tower blocks. It explores the use of set-back sections and the inverted court to bring sunlight and ventilation inside. The floor plans have cross-ventilation notches to ventilate the central-core areas.

Northam City, Penang (revised design) (unbuilt)
Revised design for the 1987 project. It explores means to bring ventilation and sunlight into the inner parts of the building.

1990

M. S. Tan House, Damansara, Kuala Lumpur
A detached house; Malaysian Institute of Architects Awards 1991, Single House Category.

Leisure Bay Condominium, Penang
A seventeen-storey condominium project.

Standard Chartered Bank, Penang
Additions and alterations to the Bank's Butterworth branch.

Standard Chartered Bank, Kuala Lumpur
Additions and alterations to the Bank's Jalan Ipoh branch.

Hannson Computers (M) Sdn Bhd, Taman Kencana, Ulu Langat, Selangor
Additions and alterations.

Selangor Turf Club, Sungei Besi, Kuala Lumpur
Relocation of stables and ancillary facilities.

1991

Walkway at Ampang Park, Kuala Lumpur (unbuilt)
New showroom and fitting-out of ground floor.

KL Plaza, Kuala Lumpur
Interior design of first storey of KL Plaza.

1992

Menara Mesiniaga, Subang Jaya, Selangor
Headquarters building of an IBM franchise located in Subang Jaya, near Kuala Lumpur. The fifteen-storey-high circular building has a tripartite

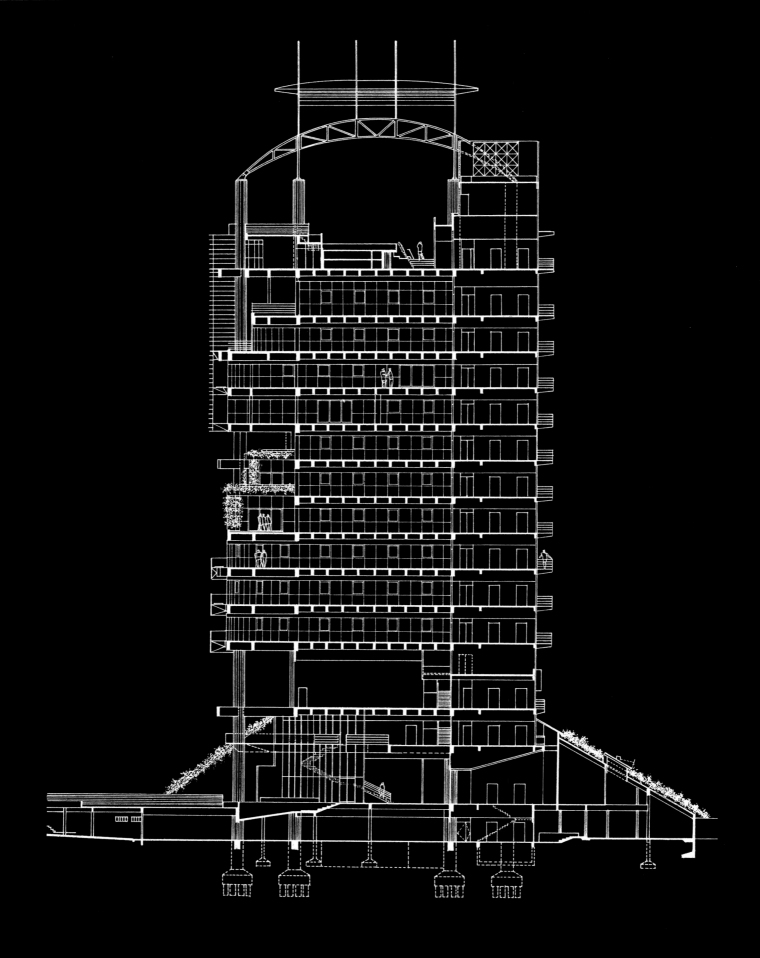

structure that consists of a sloping landscaped base, a spiralling body with landscaped sky-courts and external louvres that shade the offices, and an upper floor that houses recreational facilities, a swimming pool and a sun-roof; Aga Khan Award for Architecture 1996; and Royal Australian Institute of Architects International Award 1995. (*See page 41 for further details.*)

Euro Tower Competition, Glasgow, Scotland *(unplaced)*

A competition entry for a one-hundred-metre-high visitors tower. The structure is intended to create an urban icon to take a contemporary European city into the twenty-first century by building on its historic past. The public enclosure, relating to the environmental design considerations of the location, adapts to the bioclimatic variations of the inside/outside and day/night relationships, seasonal variations and solar orientation. These climate- and site-specific factors are addressed by the design of various kinetic solar-screening devices and heat-retention wraps.

Jalan Hang Lekiu, Kuala Lumpur

Office and retail development.

BP Malaysia, Jalan Damansara, Petaling Jaya, Selangor *(unbuilt)*

The head-office building for BP Malaysia. The design featured continuous vertical planting on the front face, stepping up the façade into a court on top of

Menara Mesiniaga
Opposite: Menara Mesiniaga, section on east–west axis

Menara Mesiniaga

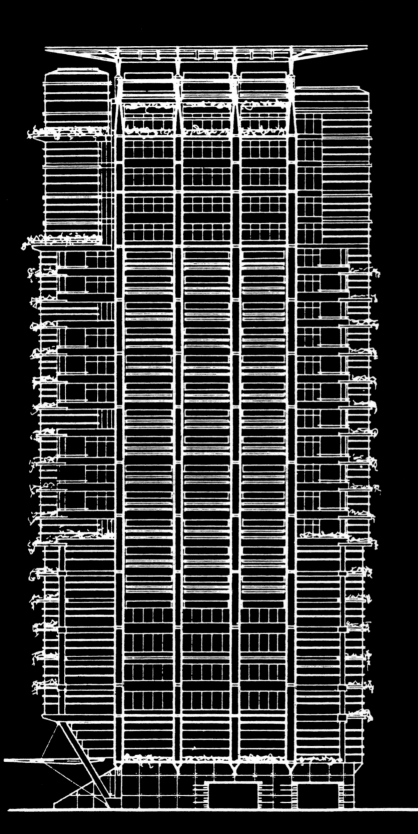

the car-park floors. The planting, besides contributing to the greening of the building, softens the impact of the car park facing the highway.

Taman Wangsa Puteri, Johor Bahru
Low-rise housing development.

Lido Cinema, Brickfields, Kuala Lumpur *(unbuilt)*
Renovation to existing cinema.

1993

**Autumnland Tower, Jalan Raja Chulan,
Kuala Lumpur** *(unbuilt)*
A twenty-four-storey tower in central Kuala Lumpur. The long sides of the building face east and west. To reduce the heat load on these façades a system of movable louvres and glass panels forms an environmentally active skin. The north and south faces have curtain-wall glazing. The lift lobbies are located on the hot east sides and are naturally ventilated, as are the stairways and toilets.

MBf Tower, Jalan Sultan Ahmad Shah, Penang
A thirty-one-storey building comprising a six-storey podium containing offices, retail spaces and a banking hall, above which are sixty-eight apartment units. (*See page 48 for further details.*)

**Taipan Crest, Taipan Triangle,
Subang Jaya, Selangor**
Three-storey shop and office project.

Spreeinsel International Urban Design Competition, Berlin, Germany (unplaced)
(*See page 137 for further details.*)

Super Sandwiches (M) Sdn Bhd, Wisma Kewangan, Jalan Raja Chulan, Kuala Lumpur
A renovation project.

Bandar Pelabuhan Kelang, Jalan Kem, Klang
An industrial development in the Klang Valley.

1994

*Menara Lam Son Square,
Ho Chi Minh City, Vietnam* (unbuilt)
The twenty-six-storey Menara Lam Son Square is circular in plan. The sun-path and the wind-rose determine the configuration of the floor-plates. The east side of the tower has a variety of sun-shading devices, while the west side has deeply cut-out sky-terraces. The terraces have clear glazing and sliding glazed doors, which give the option of natural ventilation in the event of the shutdown of mechanical and electrical services. (*See page 73 for further details.*)

*Cardiff Bay Opera House Competition,
Cardiff, Wales, United Kingdom* (unplaced)

China Tower No. 1, Haikou, Hainan, China (unbuilt)
The thirty-five-storey hotel tower's design is part of a continuing investigation of the use of wind as an ambient bioclimatic component. It explores the use of the predominant north-easterly and south-easterly winds. In the middle of the tower (oval in plan) is an atrium punctuated on both sides by cut-out sky-courts with sun scoops reflecting daylight inside. The tower's aerodynamic shape is orientated so that the tip of the oval faces towards the prevailing wind, which is then ducted through ceiling plenums to ventilate the inner parts of the building. The wind is controlled by adjustable louvres that are externally sensor-controlled and monitored. A wind-powered generator is situated at the top of the building; the electricity produced is stored in batteries and provides water heating and lighting.

China Tower No. 2, Haikou, Hainan, China (unbuilt)
Two thirty-six-storey upmarket apartment towers facing the sea. Most floors have four apartment

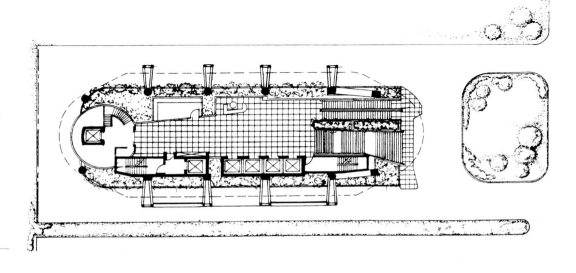

Autumnland Tower, ground-floor plan
Opposite Autumnland Tower, elevation

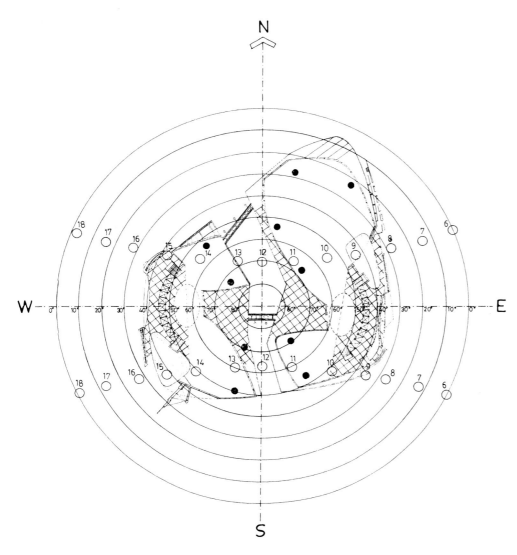

Tokyo-Nara Tower, typical floor plan related to the sun's path

units; others have three with the remaining space used as sky-courts and communal spaces-in-the-sky. All the apartments have external walls on three sides and large balconies, with movable typhoon shutters facing the sea. Lift lobbies and staircases are naturally ventilated and the top floor houses penthouse swimming pools, a sun-deck and wind-powered generators.

China Tower No. 3, Haikou, Hainan, China

This thirty-six-storey office tower has an elliptical floor-plate orientated to receive wind, which is then channelled into the building for ventilation. A number of wind-collection devices are proposed. One system is used to ventilate naturally the public lift lobbies, stairs and toilets. Another is adopted for the usable office areas. The external wall design is solar responsive, using the principle of decreasing density of sun-shading. The north- and south-facing facets of the wall are unshaded. At the top of the building is a revolving restaurant. This is combined with a large wind scoop.

Menara Seacorp, Penang

A seventeen-storey corporate headquarters for a financial institution. The design features a semi-enclosed public verandahway at ground level, solar shading, sky-courts and terraces and naturally ventilated and lit lift lobbies, staircases and toilets.

MSG Pavilion, Kuala Lumpur

Interior structure.

Johor Bahru 2005 Tower, Johor Bahru
Johor Bahru 2005 is a conceptual masterplan for Peninsular Malaysia's southernmost city, which lies immediately north of the island of Singapore. The plan includes a sixty-storey tower with a plot ratio in excess of 1:10. (*See page 142 for further details.*)

SJCC Masterplan, Subang Jaya, Selangor
An eighteen-storey tower.

Penggiran Towers,
Taman Tun Dr Ismail, Kuala Lumpur (*unbuilt*)
A twenty-eight-storey tower.

Menara PanGlobal, Johor Bahru (*unbuilt*)
A sixteen-storey tower.

Malaysian Credit Finance, Wisma Kewangan,
Jalan Raja Chulan, Kuala Lumpur
Interior design of the eleventh floor and ground floor.

Bonia Headquarters, Jalan Midah,
Taman Midah
Warehouse and office.

Ngee Ann City, Orchard Road, Singapore (*unbuilt*)
Interior design.

KTM Seremban
A masterplan for a new urban centre.

Bukit Tunku House
Renovation to an existing house.

1995

The New Taichung Civic Centre,
Taiwan, UIA Competition
The New Taichung Civic Centre in Taiwan, carried out in collaboration with Taiwan architect Ming Kuo Yu, was an entry for a 1995 UIA competition. (*See page 138 for further details.*)

Tokyo-Nara Tower,
urban site between Tokyo and Nara, Japan
This eighty-storey tower was a conceptual project prepared for the 1995 World Architecture Exposition in Japan. (*See page 81 for further details.*)

Puncak Sri Hartamas F6, Kuala Lumpur
Three twenty-five-storey towers and two twenty-two-storey towers.

Conoco Office, Wisma Goldhill,
Jalan Raja Chulan, Kuala Lumpur
Interior design of Conoco offices.

Hitechniaga HQ, Bandar Hartamas,
Kuala Lumpur
The nineteen-storey Hitechniaga HQ tower is to be the corporate headquarters of Hitechniaga, a Malaysian company dealing in data communication. (*See page 75 for further details.*)

The AIA Building, Washington, United States,
Integrated Photovoltaic Competition (*unplaced*)

Jaya Jusco Shopping Complex,
Taman Tun Dr Ismail, Kuala Lumpur (*unbuilt*)
Renovation to an existing commercial development.

Commerce Square, Petaling Jaya Selatan
Office and retail development with tower.

Komplek Kewangan, Kuala Lumpur
Interior design to part of floors 17, 18 and 19.

State Cinema, Petaling Jaya (*unbuilt*)
Commercial development.

1996

Marsham Street Competition, London,
United Kingdom (*unplaced*)
Yeang's entry for a 1996 Urban Design Competition for Marsham Street, London. (*See page 140 for further details.*)

Casa-Del-Sol, Bukit Antarabangsa, Kuala Lumpur
An eleven-storey residential tower situated at Bukit Antarabangsa, on the outskirts of Kuala Lumpur. (*See page 63 for further details.*)

Lamankota Masterplan, Kuala Lumpur
A masterplan prepared for the Jalan Tun Razak-Cochrane/Jalan Perkasa area of

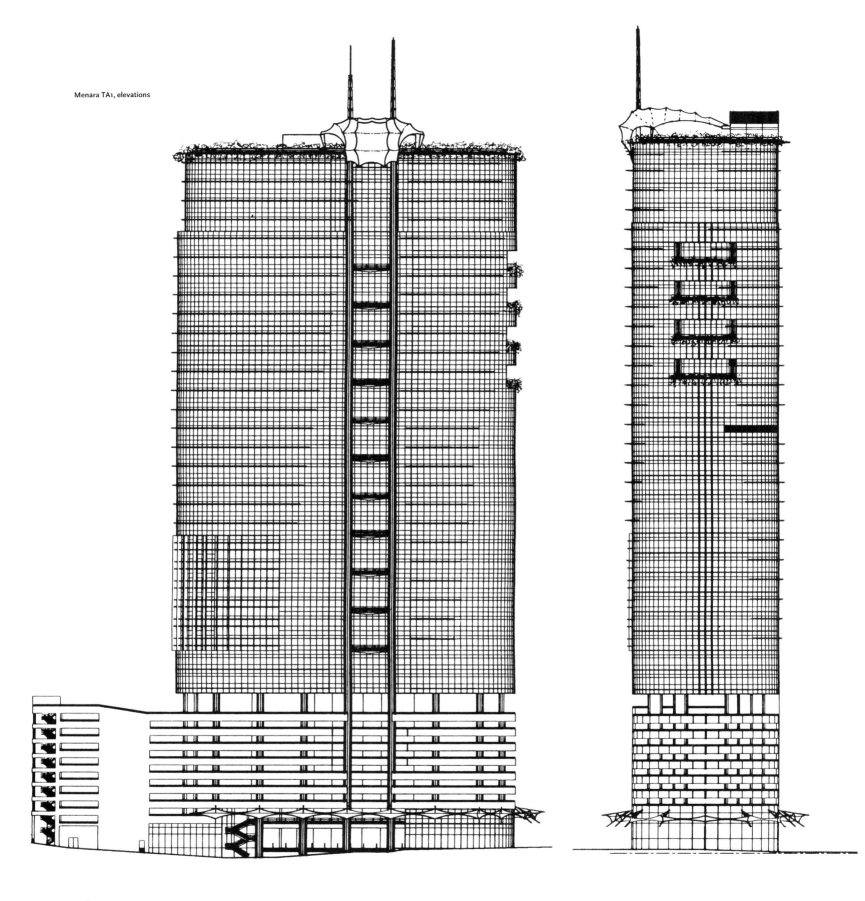

Menara TA1, elevations

metropolitan Kuala Lumpur. (*See page 144 for further details.*)

Central Plaza, Jalan Sultan Ismail, Kuala Lumpur
A twenty-nine-storey tower located on a long narrow site in Kuala Lumpur; Malaysian Institute of Architects Design Award 1996. (*See page 57 for further details.*)

Menara TA1, Kuala Lumpur
A thirty-seven-storey skyscraper occupying a narrow rectangular site in Kuala Lumpur. (*See page 61 for further details.*)

Samling Institute of Technology and Research, Miri, Sarawak (*unbuilt*)

Wirrina Cove Hotel, Adelaide, Australia
Condominium and hotel upgrading.

Eco-Media City for FACB Berhad (*unbuilt*)
A masterplan for a forty-one-acre site.

Hipa Masterplan, Laos
Conceptual masterplan for a mixed-use development.

Banker's Club Penthouse, Kuala Lumpur (*unbuilt*)
Renovation.

Menara Boustead
Renovation to floors 7, 14, 21, 26 and 27.

Bukit Unggul (*unbuilt*)
Mixed development of a 170-acre site.

Kang Keng Airport, Sihanoukville, Cambodia (*unbuilt*)
Roof design.

Bukit Ceylon, Kuala Lumpur (*unbuilt*)
Proposed development.

1997

SD Headquarters and Condominium Competition, Bukit Kiara, Kuala Lumpur (*unplaced*)
The roof of this building is designed to act as a giant trellis to filter the sun. The intention is to create indoor/outdoor spaces within which people are able to interact. A promenade connects the two condominium parcels and passes through the office complex. The separation between the condominium and offices is achieved by changes in the landscape. The use of a trellis will reduce the amount of solar gain the building will receive, thus resulting in a low-energy structure.

Megan Corporate Park, Desa Petaling, Kuala Lumpur
All blocks have a north–south orientation. This

A variety of sun-shading devices are employed on the west façade of Menara TA1. (Ng)

minimizes the solar heat gain to the long façades of its rectangular configuration. The sky-lit, oval-shaped internal atrium space extends all the way up to the roof. This provides natural lighting and ventilation to the interior corridor spaces, as well as providing an internal focus to the office spaces upon entry to the building. The detached canopy over the atrium allows hot air to escape, thus enabling natural ventilation to cool the upper floor lobbies. All lift lobbies and staircases have natural cross-ventilation and have natural lighting. The two rows of buildings are tiered to follow the natural topography of the site, thus minimizing its impact on the environment.

Bar Council, Jalan Loke Yew, Kuala Lumpur
Lecture hall and library interior design.

Bar Council, Jalan Tun Perak, Kuala Lumpur
Office renovation.

Eco-Tech City, Rostock, Germany
A masterplan for a hypothetical site in Rostock in Germany, prepared for the Dortmund Exhibition of 1997. (*See page 146 for further details.*)

The eighteen-storey Menara MISC HQ tower rises alongside a
four-storey common facilities wing. Aluminium louvred sun-shading
is wrapped around the elliptically shaped tower. (Ng)

Menara MISC Headquarters, Shah Alam, Selangor
An eighteen-storey elliptical-shaped tower for the
Malaysia International Shipping Corporation Berhad
(MISC) located in Shah Alam town centre. (*See page
91 for further details.*)

Shanghai Armoury Tower, Pudong, Shanghai, China
A thirty-six-storey tower located in the Pudong
district of Shanghai, built for the Northern Pudong
Open Economy. (*See page 92 for further details.*)

Maybank Tower Competition, Singapore (*unplaced*)
Competition for the redevelopment of the existing
Maybank site in Singapore, a fifty-four-storey tower.

TA2 Service Apartments, Kuala Lumpur (*unbuilt*)
A forty-six-storey tower. (*See page 110 for further
details.*)

**San Francisco Community Centre Design
Competition, San Francisco, United States** (*unplaced*)

Kota Kemuning Business Park, Selangor
Masterplan of a twelve-acre site.

**Bukit Gedung Division 2 Army Camp,
Penang** (*unbuilt*)

Multimedia Campus, Universiti Telekom Malaysia, Cyberjaya, MSC
A masterplan for Universiti Telekom, located on a seventy-five-hectare site in Cyberjaya within Malaysia's proposed Multimedia Super Corridor (MSC). (*See page 146 for further details.*)

Imperial Sheraton Hotel, Jalan Sultan Ismail, Kuala Lumpur
A thirty-three-storey tower.

Jalan Ulu Kelang
Housing development.

Bukit Unggul and Country Resort Sdn Bhd
Golf driving range canopy.

Wirrina Cove, Adelaide, Australia
Proposed development of service apartments.

Standard Chartered Bank, Jalan Ampang, Kuala Lumpur (*unbuilt*)
Interior design and renovation of the Jalan Ampang branch.

Standard Chartered Bank, Petaling Jaya, Selangor (*unbuilt*)
Interior design and renovation of the Petaling Jaya branch.

Menara Choy Fook On Tower, Kuala Lumpur (*unbuilt*)
Addition and alteration.

Kuala Lumpur International Airport, Sepang
Proposed fitting-out of five food and beverage outlets at Kuala Lumpur International Airport.

Al-Hilali Office and Retail Complex, Kuwait City
(*See page 149 for further details.*)

FACB HQ, Bukit Unggul, Selangor
A twenty-nine-storey hemispherical tower with a central atrium. (*See page 107 for further details.*)

Taman Tun Dr Ismail-6D (TTDI-6D)
A residential development in Kuala Lumpur consisting of 320 units of apartments in two twenty-eight-storey towers. (*See page 111 for further details.*)

1998

Guthrie Pavilion, Shah Alam, Selangor
A three-storey office and golf clubhouse designed for Guthrie Property Development Holding. (*See page 126 for further details.*)

Business and Advanced Technology Centre Masterplan, UTM, Semarak
A masterplan for a nine-hectare campus for the Universiti Teknologi Malaysia. (*See page 150 for further details.*)

Signature Tower, Business and Advanced Technology Centre, UTM, Semarak
A signature office tower located within the second phase of the masterplan proposal for the nine-hectare campus for the Universiti Teknologi Malaysia. (*See page 158 for further details.*)

Gamuda Headquarters, Kota Kemuning Business Park, Shah Alam, Selangor
A ten-storey office building with an elliptical atrium created by the tower's two curved wings. (*See page 103 for further details.*)

Menara UMNO, Jalan MacAlister, Penang
A twenty-one-storey tower built on the island of Penang as the headquarters of Malaysia's ruling party; Singapore Institute of Architects Awards 1998: Honorable Mention; and Royal Australian Institute of Architects International Award 1998. (*See page 83 for further details.*)

Hotel Imperial, Jalan Sultan Ismail, Kuala Lumpur
Renovation of level 12 of the existing hotel.

Tianjin Civil Aviation School Competition, Pin Hai Airport, Tianjin, China
A proposal for the School of Civil Aviation in Tianjin linking new accommodation to the existing campus via a broad landscaped promenade. (*See page 149 for further details.*)

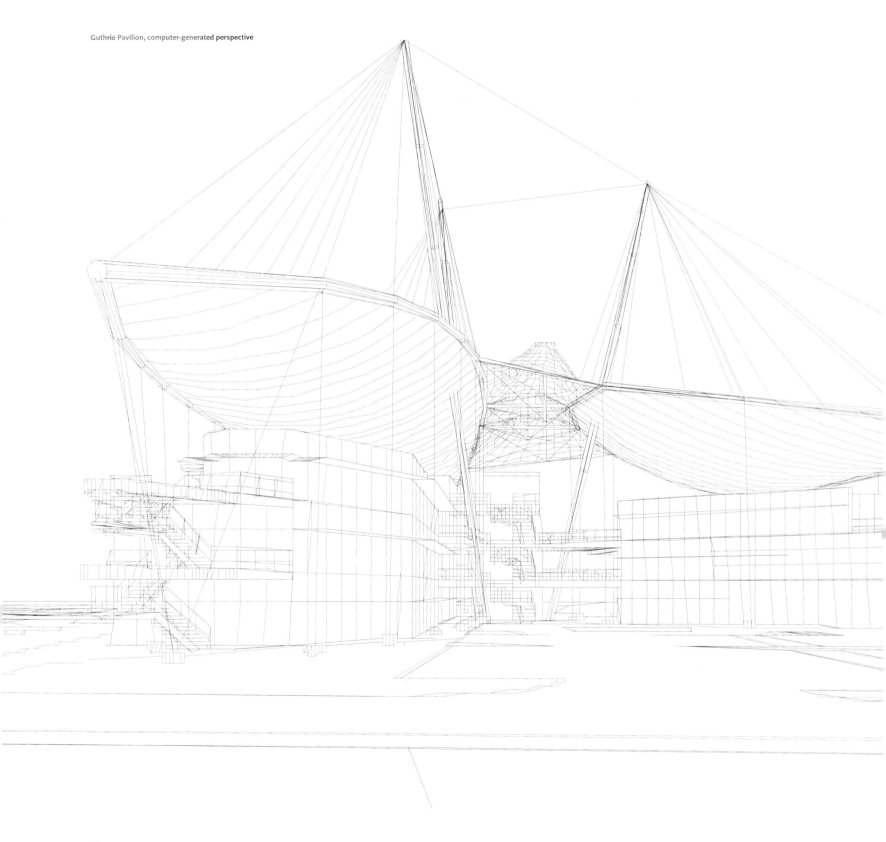

Guthrie Pavilion, computer-generated perspective

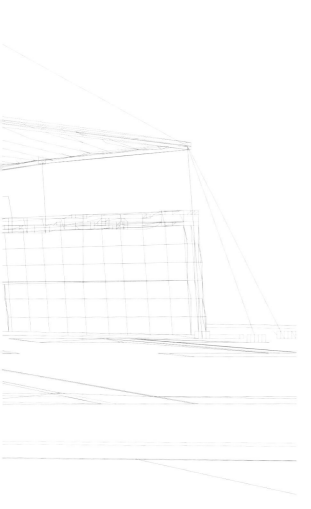

Permasteelisa Technological Campus, San Vendemiano, Italy

A three-storey experimental building with a façade integrating bioclimatic features. (*See page 124 for further details.*)

Ladang Puchong Town Centre

A conceptual urban design project for Ladang Puchong town centre.

Selangor Turf Club, Sungei Besi, Kuala Lumpur

Interior design and renovation within Selangor Turf Club.

Metrolux Sdn Bhd

A terraced-housing project.

Sri Hartamas, Kuala Lumpur

Shops and offices.

Hartamas F6 Towers, Kuala Lumpur

This project is a further exploration of the 'residential-units-in-sky' ideas. Five residential towers are connected by a sky-bridge to the recreational level (the clubhouse and pool) on the second storey and to the car-parking blocks. Each storey of the residential towers has four apartment units that are arranged around a central service-core containing elevators, access stairs and fire-escape stairs. Each apartment unit is detached in a similar manner to those in the MBf Tower in Penang. This maximizes the external wall surface, allows air to penetrate between the units and permits better cross-ventilation. Each unit has a generous balcony accessed from the living space.

Expo 2005 Nagoya Hyper-Tower

A six-hundred-metre-high megastructure, including a transportation terminus, an information centre, auditoria, hotels, an amphitheatre, cultural institutions, a convention hall, LRT stations, a helipad, police stations, government buildings, an arts and crafts village, international exposition pavilions, administrative offices, commercial space and light industrial premises, in addition to residential accommodation. (*See page 156 for further details.*)

Project Data and Collaborators

PLAZA ATRIUM (1981–4)

Principal Dr Ken Yeang

Project Architect Yeoh Soon Teck

Design Architect Mak Meng Fook

Project Team Rahim Din, David Fu

Project Manager Timuran

Civil Engineer Reka Perunding Sdn Bhd

Structural Engineer Reka Perunding Sdn Bhd

M. and E. Engineer Jurutera Perunding LC Sdn Bhd

Quantity Surveyor Baharuddin Ali and Low Sdn

Client Ban Seng Development Sdn Bhd

No. of Storeys 24

Gross Floor Area 10,700m²

Site Area 2,023m² (0.20ha)

Plot Ratio 1:5.07

Completion Date 1984

ROOF-ROOF HOUSE (1984)

Principal Dr Ken Yeang

Project Architect Rahim Din

Design Architect Rahim Din

Project Team Mak Meng Fook, David Fu,
Rahimah Lasim, Kon Liam

Project Manager T. R. Hamzah and Yeang Sdn Bhd

Civil Engineer Reka Perunding Sdn Bhd

Structural Engineer Reka Perunding Sdn Bhd

M. and E. Engineer Jurutera Perunding LC Sdn Bhd

Quantity Surveyor Baharuddin Ali and Low Sdn

Client Ken Yeang

No. of Storeys 2

Gross Floor Area 350m²

Site Area 604m²

Completion Date 1984

**KUALA LUMPUR GOLDEN TRIANGLE
URBAN DESIGN COMPETITION (1985)**

Principal Dr Ken Yeang

Project Architect Anthony Too

Design Architect Vincent Lee

MENARA BOUSTEAD (1986)

Principal Dr Ken Yeang

Project Architect Yeoh Soon Teck

Design Architect Chee Soo Teng

Project Team Mak Meng Fook, Mun Khai Yip,
Joe Khoo

Civil Engineer Khanafiah YL Sdn Bhd

Structural Engineer Khanafiah YL Sdn Bhd

M. and E. Engineer Khanafiah YL Sdn Bhd

Quantity Surveyor Baharuddin Ali and Low Sdn

Landscape Architect Lip Leow and Associates

Client Boustead Holdings Bhd

No. of Storeys 32

Gross Floor Area 45,470m²

Plot Ratio 1:6.97

Completion Date 1987

IBM PLAZA (1985)

Principal Dr Ken Yeang

Project Architect Chee Soo Teng

Design Architect Woon Chung Nam

Project Team Mak Meng Fook, David Fu

Project Manager TTDI Development Sdn Bhd

Civil Engineer Wan Mohamed and Khoo Sdn Bhd

Structural Engineer Wan Mohamed and
Khoo Sdn Bhd

M. and E. Engineer JuaraConsult Sdn Bhd

Quantity Surveyor Juru Ukur Bahan Malaysia

Landscape Architect T. R. Hamzah and
Yeang Sdn Bhd

Client TTDI Development Sdn Bhd

No. of Storeys 24

Gross Floor Area 41,868.45m²

Plot Ratio 1:4.106

Completion Date 1987

MENARA MESINIAGA (1992)

Principal Dr Ken Yeang

Project Architect Too Ka Hoe

Design Architect Seow Ji Nee

Project Team Don Allan Ismail, Sacha Noordin,
Lyn Yap, Yusof Zainal Abidin, Philip Tan Hui Lee,
Ooi Poh Lye, Rahimah Lasim, Tomas Quijano,
Mohamad Pital Maarof

Project Manager Client in-house

Civil Engineer Reka Perunding Sdn Bhd

Structural Engineer Reka Perunding Sdn Bhd

M. and E. Engineer Norman Disney and
Yong Sdn Bhd

Quantity Surveyor Baharuddin Ali and Low Sdn

Interior Design T. R. Hamzah and Yeang Sdn Bhd

Landscape Architect Lap Consultancy
General Contractors Siah Brothers Sdn Bhd
Steelwork Sediabena Sdn Bhd
Client Mesiniaga Sdn Bhd
No. of Storeys 15
Gross Floor Area 12,345.69m²
Site Area 6,503m² (0.65ha)
Plot Ratio 1:1.6
Start Date June 1989
Completion Date August 1992

SELANGOR TURF CLUB (1992)

Principal Dr Ken Yeang
Project Architects Ahmad Kamil Mustapha,
  Chong Voon Wee, Lim Peik Boon, Charles Peh
Design Architect Ng Kim Teh
Project Team Mah Lek
Project Manager WTW Consultants Sdn Bhd
Civil Engineer Engineering and Environmental
  Consultants Sdn Bhd
Structural Engineer Tahir Wong Sdn Bhd
M. and E. Engineer E. R. Nair Associates/Norman
  Disney and Yong Sdn Bhd
Landscape Consultant Malik Lip and Associates
Client Selangor Turf Club
No. of Storeys 4
Gross Floor Area 30,266.94m²
Site Area 103.6ha
Completion Date 1992

MBF TOWER (1993)

Principal Dr Ken Yeang
Project Architects Yap Lip Pien, Laurent Lim
Design Architects Haslina Ali, Normala Ariffin,
  Don Allan Ismail
Project Team Haslinda Hashim, Rahimah Lasim,
  Ooi Poh Lye, Sneha Mathews, Shamsul Baharin
Project Manager MBf Property Services Sdn Bhd
Civil Engineer Reka Perunding Sdn Bhd
Structural Engineer Reka Perunding Sdn Bhd
M. and E. Engineer Jurutera Perunding LC Sdn Bhd
Quantity Surveyor Baharuddin Ali and Low Sdn
Landscape Architect Malik Lip and Associates
Client MBf Holdings Bhd
No. of Storeys 31
Gross Floor Area 17,531.18m²
Site Area 7,482.39m² (0.74ha)
Plot Ratio 1:2.34
Start Date 1990
Completion Date 1993

SPREEINSEL (BERLIN) URBAN DESIGN COMPETITION (1993)

Principal Dr Ken Yeang
Project Architect Ng En Long
Design Architects Ang Chee Cheong,
  Ibrahim (Lawrence) Liau
Project Team Derick Ng, Ng Wai Tuck
Completion Date 1993

MENARA LAM SON SQUARE (1994)

Principal Dr Ken Yeang
Quantity Surveyor Juru Ukur Bahan Malaysia
No. of Storeys 26
Gross Floor Area 19,684m²

NEW TAICHUNG CITY CIVIC CENTRE (1995)

Principals Dr Ken Yeang, Ming Kuo Yu
Project Architect Eddie Chan Kin Leong
Design Architect Houston Morris
Project Team Ming Kuo Yu, Roshan Gurung,
  Rajiv Ratnarajah, Alvise Simondetti,
  Tim Mellor, Adlin Shauki bin Aksan, Andrew Piles,
  Tan Wah Aik, Margaret Ng, Loh Mun Chee,
  Yap Yow Kong, Yvonne Ho Wooi Lee
Civil Engineer Battle McCarthy Consulting Engineers
Structural Engineer Battle McCarthy
  Consulting Engineers
M. and E. Engineer Battle McCarthy
  Consulting Engineers
Gross Floor Areas
  City Government Building: 140,120m²
  City Council Building: 63,343m²
Site Areas
  City Government Site: 50,986m²
  City Council Site: 14,985m²

HITECHNIAGA HQ TOWER (1995)

Principal Dr Ken Yeang

Project Architect Don Allan Ismail

Design Architects Sacha Noordin, Guy Westbrook,
Margaret Ng, Tomas Quijano

Owner Hitechniaga Sdn Bhd

No. of Storeys 19

Gross Floor Area 6,724.94m²

Site Area 1,308.032m²

Plot Ratio 1:5.14

MARSHAM STREET
URBAN DESIGN COMPETITION (1996)

Principal Dr Ken Yeang

No. of Storeys 10

Gross Floor Area 86,000m²

Site Area 20,000m²

Plot Ratio 1:4.6

LAMANKOTA MASTERPLAN (1996)

Principal Dr Ken Yeang

Project Architect Eddie Chan Kin Leong

Design Architects Yvonne Ho Wooi Lee,
Aidan Hoggard, Chew Tick Wah,
Stephanie Lee, Leow Aik Boon

Project Manager Umi-Ross Project Management

Planner and Landscape Consultant T. R. Hamzah
and Yeang Sdn Bhd

Traffic and Transport Consultant Jurutera Perunding
Zaaba Sdn Bhd

Civil Engineer Perunding Teras Sdn Bhd

Structural Engineer Perunding Teras Sdn Bhd

Quantity Surveyor MTM Bersekutu

Property Consultant and Valuer Jurunilai Iktisas
Henry Butcher Sdn Bhd

Financial Consultant KAF Discount Bhd

No. of Storeys Varies from 5 to 15

Gross Floor Areas
Residential: 1,075,782m² (8,500 units)

Other Facilities
Commercial: 1,099,007m²
Community Facilities: 6.88ha
Education: 4.05ha
Landscaping: 6.88ha
Infrastructure: 10.52ha

Site Area 70.39ha

Plot Ratio 1:6.8

Completion Date 1996

CENTRAL PLAZA (1996)

Principal Dr Ken Yeang

Project Architects Lim Piek Boon, Yew Ai Choo

Design Architects Rachel Atthis, Heng Jee Seng

Project Team Ooi Poh Lye, Margaret Ng,
Loh Mun Chee, Yap Yow Kong, Russell Harnett,
Hannah Cherry, Paul Brady

Project Manager Client in-house

Civil Engineer Reka Perunding Sdn Bhd

Structural Engineer Reka Perunding Sdn Bhd

M. and E. Engineer Jurutera Perunding LC Sdn Bhd

Quantity Surveyor Baharuddin Ali and Low Sdn

Client Malview Sdn Bhd

No. of Storeys 29

Gross Floor Area 57,863m²

Site Area 2,982.5m²

Plot Ratio 1:7.5

Start Date June 1992

Completion Date June 1996

MENARA TA1 (1996)

Principal Dr Ken Yeang

Project Architects Seow Ji Nee,
Chong Voon Wee, Ahmad Kamil

Design Architects Normala Ariffin,
Ken Wong, Paul Mathews

Project Team David Fu, Ooi Poh Lye,
Margaret Fu, Loh Mun Chee

Project Manager MBf Property Services Sdn Bhd

Civil Engineer Reka Perunding Sdn Bhd

Structural Engineer Reka Perunding Sdn Bhd

M. and E. Engineer Jurutera Perunding LC Sdn Bhd

Quantity Surveyor Baharuddin Ali and Low Sdn

Landscape Architect Malik Lip and Associates

Main Contractor Sri Hartamas Builders Sdn Bhd

JV Partner Mul-T-Plex Engineering (M) Sdn Bhd

Client ERF Properties Sdn Bhd

No. of Storeys 37

Gross Floor Area 43,888m²

Site Area 4,868.5m² (0.47ha)

Plot Ratio 1:10.6

Start Date July 1992

Completion Date June 1996

CASA-DEL-SOL APARTMENTS (1996)

Principal Dr Ken Yeang

Project Architect Andy Chong Soon Onn

Design Architect Mohamad Pital Maarof

Project Team Ooi Poh Lye

Project Manager MBf Property Services Sdn Bhd

Civil Engineer H. P. Lee & Rakan-Rakan

Structural Engineer H. P. Lee & Rakan-Rakan

M. and E. Engineer Suffian Lee Perunding

Quantity Surveyor Kumpulan KuantiKonsult

Landscape Architect Malik Lip and Associates

Client Metrolux Sdn Bhd

No. of Storeys 11

Gross Floor Area 26,903.84m²

Site Area 1.83ha

Plot Ratio Total: 160 units apartment

Completion Date 1996

FACB HQ (1997)

Principal Dr Ken Yeang

Project Architect Seow Ji Nee

Design Architects Grace Tan, Joakim Lyth

Civil Engineer H. S. Liao Sdn Bhd

Structural Engineer H. S. Liao Sdn Bhd

M. and E. Engineer Ranhill Bersekutu Sdn Bhd

Quantity Surveyor Jurus Kos

No. of Storeys 27

Gross Floor Area 33,929m²

Site Area 8,528m²

Plot Ratio 1:4.0

TAMAN TUN DR ISMAIL-6D (1997)

Principal Dr Ken Yeang

Client TTDI Development Sdn Bhd

No. of Storeys 28 (× 2)

Gross Floor Area 66,640m²

SHANGHAI ARMOURY TOWER (1997)

Principal Dr Ken Yeang

Project Architect Eddie Chan Kin Leong

Design Architects Ahmad Ridzwa Ahmad Fathan, Norindar International

Project Team Roshan Gurung, Yvonne Ho Wooi Lee, Margaret Ng, Loh Mun Chee

Civil Engineer Battle McCarthy Consulting Engineers

Structural Engineer Battle McCarthy Consulting Engineers

M. and E. Engineer Battle McCarthy Consulting Engineers

Client Northern Pudong Open Economy Company

No. of Storeys 36

Gross Floor Area 46,750m²

Site Area 9,100m²

Plot Ratio 1:5.13

**MULTIMEDIA CAMPUS
FOR UNIVERSITI TELEKOM MALAYSIA (1997)**

Principal Dr Ken Yeang

Project Architect Azri Yahya

Design Architects Chuck Yeoh, Sam Jacoby

ECO-TECH CITY MASTERPLAN (1997)

Principal Dr Ken Yeang

TA2 (1997)

Principal Dr Ken Yeang

Project Architect Eddie Chan Kin Leong

Design Architects Ahmad Ridzwa Ahmad Fathan, Tim Wort, Alun White

Civil Engineer Ranhill Bersekutu Sdn Bhd

Structural Engineer Ranhill Bersekutu Sdn Bhd

M. and E. Engineer C. Y. Tau Perunding

Quantity Surveyor Juru Ukur Bahan Malaysia

Landscape Architect Jurukur Perunding Services Sdn Bhd

No. of Storeys 46

Gross Floor Area 39,346.029m²

Site Area 6,058m² (0.61ha)

Start Date October 1997

Completion Date 2000

MENARA MISC HQ (1997)

Principal Dr Ken Yeang

Project Architect Lim Piek Boon

Design Architects Joshua Levine, Carlo Matta, Alberto Bonnour, Alex Wright, James Lai, Turlough Clancy, Sacha Ramlan Noordin

Civil Engineer Tahir Wong Sdn Bhd

Structural Engineer Tahir Wong Sdn Bhd

M. and E. Engineer Norman Disney and Yong Sdn Bhd

Quantity Surveyor Juru Ukur Bahan Malaysia
Client Malaysia International Shipping Corp Bhd
No. of Storeys Office 18, Common facilities wing 4
Gross Floor Area 38,248.97m²
Site Area 9,797m²
Plot Ratio 1:4.16

AL-HILALI OFFICE AND RETAIL COMPLEX (1997)
Principal Dr Ken Yeang
Project Architect Seow Ji Nee
Design Architects Ahmad Ridzwa Ahmad Fathan,
    Tim Wort, Alun White, Zainal
Civil Engineer Buro Happold
Structural Engineer Buro Happold
M. and E. Engineer Buro Happold
Quantity Surveyor Juru Ukur Bahan Malaysia
No. of Storeys 20
Gross Floor Area 19,085m²
Plot Ratio 1:3

SD HQ AND CONDOMINIUM
COMPETITION (1997)
Principal Dr Ken Yeang
Project Architect Ahmad Ridzwa Ahmad Fathan
Design Architects Ahmad Ridzwa Ahmad Fathan,
    Tim Wort, Alun White, Vivian Chang
No. of Storeys 2 to 6
Gross Floor Area
    Offices: 81,194.6m²
    Condominium: 49,546.44m²

Start Date 1997
Completion Date 2001

GUTHRIE PAVILION (1998)
Principal Dr Ken Yeang
Project Architect Seow Ji Nee
Design Architects Ian Morris, Mike Jamieson
Project Team Ahmad Ridzwa Ahmad Fathan,
    Anton Pertschy, Richard Coutts,
    Loh Mun Chee, Warren Williams,
    Margaret Ng, Yap Yow Kong
Project Manager Client in-house
Civil Engineer Tahir Wong Sdn Bhd
Structural Engineer Tahir Wong Sdn Bhd
M. and E. Engineer PCR Sdn Bhd
Quantity Surveyor Azhar Rouse and Hisham Sdn
Landscape Consultants
    Guthrie Landscaping Sdn Bhd
Main Contractor Syarikat Abdul
    Rahman-Sediabena Sdn Bhd JV
Roof Specialists Sediabena Sdn Bhd-Flontex JV and
    Engineers IPL Ingenierplanung Leichtbau Gmbf
Client Guthrie Property Development
    Holdings Sdn Bhd
No. of Storeys 3
Gross Floor Area 5,666m²
Site Area 26,694m² (2.69ha),
    351,719.95m² including golf course (35.17ha)
Plot Ratio 1:0.212
Start Date July 1995
Completion Date 1998

HARTAMAS TOWN CENTRE (1998)
Principal Dr Ken Yeang
Project Architect Jay Low
Design Architects Mariani Abdullah, Philip Tan
Project Team Ho Eng Ling, Sow Sun Fong,
    Paul Brady, Simon Doody, Derick Ng
Project Manager MBf Property Services Sdn Bhd
Civil Engineer H. S. Liao Sdn Bhd
Structural Engineer H. S. Liao Sdn Bhd

MENARA UMNO (1998)
Principal Dr Ken Yeang
Project Architect Shamsul Baharin
Design Architects Ang Chee Cheong, Tim Mellor
    Warren Williams, Anthony Ogden
Project Team Ooi Poh Lye, Margaret Ng,
    Yap Yow Kong, Haslinda Hashim, Azizan,
    Mah Lek, Loh Mun Chee, Deborah Rogger,
    Tomas Quijano, Jason Ng, Richard Coutts
Project Manager Client in-house
Civil Engineer Tahir Wong Sdn Bhd
Structural Engineer Tahir Wong Sdn Bhd
M. and E. Engineer Ranhill Bersekutu Sdn Bhd
Quantity Surveyor Juru Ukur Bahan Malaysia
Main Contractor JDC (M) Corporation Sdn Bhd
Natural Ventilation Consultant Professor Phil Jones,
    Welsh School of Architecture, University of Wales,
    Cardiff (UK)
Wind Consultant Professor Richard Ainsley,
    Anarhralun Institute of Tropical Architecture,
    Queensland (Australia)

Landowner Majlis Agama Islam Negara P. Pinang
Owner South East Asia Development
   Corporation Bhd
No. of Storeys 21
Gross Floor Area 13,776.884m²
Site Area 1,920m²
Plot Ratio 1:5.5
Start Date 1995
Completion Date March 1998

HARTAMAS F6 TOWERS (1998)
Principal Dr Ken Yeang
Project Architect Andy Chong Soon Onn
Design Architect Jane Fare
Project Manager MBf Property Services Sdn Bhd
Civil Engineer Jurutera Perunding Tegap Sdn Bhd
Structural Engineer Jurutera Perunding
   Tegap Sdn Bhd
M. and E. Engineer EAB Consultant Sdn Bhd
Quantity Surveyor KBC Quantity Surveyors Sdn Bhd
Landscape Architect G. L. Ong Consultant
No. of Storeys 25 (×3) and 22 (×2)
Gross Floor Area 59,650m²
Site Area 2.54ha

GAMUDA HEADQUARTERS (1998)
Principal Dr Ken Yeang
Project Architect Eddie Chan Kin Leong
Design Architects Anne Save Beavereail,
   Tim Mellor

Civil Engineer Ranhill Bersekutu Sdn Bhd
Structural Engineer Ranhill Bersekutu Sdn Bhd
M. and E. Engineer Ranhill Bersekutu Sdn Bhd
Quantity Surveyor Juru Ukur Bahan Malaysia
Landscape Architect Sabit-ACLA Sdn Bhd
Client Gamuda Bhd
No. of Storeys 10
Gross Floor Area 31,800m²
Site Area 12,104.4m²

EXPO 2005 NAGOYA HYPER-TOWER (1998)
Principal Dr Ken Yeang
Project Architect Ahmad Ridzwa Ahmad Fathan
Design Architect Laura Tze Ling

**BUSINESS AND ADVANCED TECHNOLOGY
CENTRE (BATC) (1998)**
Principal Dr Ken Yeang
Project Architect Tim Mellor
Design Architects Ahmad Ridzwa Ahmad Fathan,
   Chuck Yeoh, Sam Jacoby, Ravin Ponniah,
   James Douglas Gerwin, Zainal Mohammed,
   Vivian Chang
Civil Engineer Battle McCarthy
   Consulting Engineers
Structural Engineer Battle McCarthy
   Consulting Engineers
M. and E. Engineer Battle McCarthy
   Consulting Engineers
Quantity Surveyor Juru Ukur Bahan Malaysia

No. of Storeys 60 (signature office tower) and 30
   (office towers × 5)
Gross Floor Area 707,898m²
Site Area 167,220m²

TIANJIN SCHOOL OF CIVIL AVIATION (1998)
Principal Dr Ken Yeang
Project Architect Yvonne Ho
Design Architects Yvonne Ho,
   Ahmad Ridzwa Ahmad Fathan
Civil Engineer Battle McCarthy
   Consulting Engineers
Structural Engineer Battle McCarthy
   Consulting Engineers
M. and E. Engineer Battle McCarthy
   Consulting Engineers
No. of Storeys 6
Gross Floor Area 191,921m²
Site Area 330,000m²

**PERMASTEELISA
TECHNOLOGICAL CAMPUS (1998)**
Principal Dr Ken Yeang
Project Architect Seow Ji Nee
Design Architects Sacha Ramlan Noordin

T. R. Hamzah and Yeang Staff 1975–1998

Adlin Shauki bin Aksan
Adrian Hazizi Hashim
Ahmad Kamil Mustapha
Ahmad Mirza Hamzah
Ahmad Nazri Jaafar
Aidan Hoggard
Aileen Sew
Alberto Bonnour
Alex Wright
Alvise Simondetti
Amy Goh
Andrew Piles
Ang Chee Cheong
Ania Stolinska
Anthony Ogden
Anthony Too
Anton Pertschy
Asmadi bin Jusoh
Azahari Muhammad Vedo
Azhar Hj Sidek
Azizan bin Murad
Azmin Abdullah
Brian Rogers
Carlo Matta
Chan Ah Choon
Chan Soo Seng
Chan Tai Ngok
Chan Yue yee
Chang Sin Seng
Charles Peh
Charles Poh

Chee Soo Teng
Chew Loo See
Chew Tick Wah
Chong Kim Yong
Chong Soon Onn
Chong Tiam Fook
Chong Tiew Lee
Chong Voon Wee
Chow Kin Hoong
Chow Kok Cheong
Christina Mary
Christina Wong
Chua Caik Leng
Chuck Yeoh
Dang Wei Dong
David Fu
Deborah Rogger
Derick Ng See Leng
Desmond Ng
Don Allan Ismail
Eddie Chan Kin Leong
Edward Jackson
Ellir W. Sheryn
Emmy Lim Ying-Li
Erica Gilbert
Ernest Teh
Fadzillah Mohd Fadzil
Fong Lee Tian
Foo Chong Yee
Foo Yoke Ling
Frederieke van Ellen

Fu Kam Sang
Gillian Chew
Gillian Wan
Goh Bee Lian
Goh Tai Foong
Goon Li Chin
Guy Westbrook
Hannah Cherry
Haslina Ali
Haslina Yaakob
Haslinda Hashim
Heng Jee Seng
Ho Eng Ling
Houston Morris
Ian Morris
Idrani E. Vanniasingham
Idris Clywd
Irene Ching Sow Lin
Isa bin Abdullah
Ismail Awab
James Allan Finnie
James Chin Wei Mean
James Chua
James Douglas Gerwin
James Lai
James Ng
James Phillips
Janet Yue Yoon Wa
Jay Low
Jeanie Lim
Jeffri Merican

Joe Khoo
Joshua Levine
Kamariah
Kassim bin Ramli
Kayate bte Sukadis
Ken Wong
Khoo Cheng Khean
Kiang I. Peng
Kon Liam
L. Selvasubramaniam
Lai Chee Keong
Lai Chooi Ming
Lam Chow Yuen
Lau Sing Foo
Laurence Liauw
Laurent Lim
Lee K. Y.
Len Beng Hooi
Leow Ai Boon
Leow Shian Kee
Liew Kiang Meng
Lim Kim Huat
Lim Oh Seng
Lim Pay Chye
Lim Piek Boon
Linda Gan
Loh Mun Chee
Loo Chiew Koy
Lucille Lim
Lyn Yap
Mah Lek

Mak Fook Chin
Mak Meng Fook
Mak Wei Mun
Margaret Fu
Margaret Ng
Mariani Abdullah
Mark Gurney
Mary Lim
Mary Lui
Masjuita
Megat Rozlan Abd Rahman
Megat Sharizal
Michael Simmons
Mike Jamieson
Mimi Alhabshi
Mohamad Pital Maarof
Mohd Fizal
Mohd Sabri
Mohd Zolsamsuri Hassan
Mun Khai Yip
Nadarajan a/l Nadesan
Ng Boon Teck
Ng En Long
Ng Kim The
Ng Van Yain
Ng Wai Tuck
Ng Yu Thian
Ngooi Voon Fong
Noor Aliyah Md Ali
Nor Zaini Musti
Noraini bte Ahmad

Norasman Mohd Hashim
Nordin
Normala Hj Ariffin
Normala Ismail
Norziana Yusoff
Oh Siew Choo
Ong Boon Hing
Ooi Poh Lye
Pan Chee Seng
Patricia Tan Kim Tho
Paul Brady
Paul Mathews
Peter Ho
Philip Tan
Philip Tan Hui Lee
Poon Chee Pak
Puvan Selvanathan
Quaik Lian See
Rachel Atthis
Rahim Din
Rahimah Mohd Lasim
Raja Hidzir bin Raja Khalid
Rajiv Ratnarajah
Rashidah Omar
Ravin Ponniah
Razidah bte Mohd Sharif

Richard Coutts
Ahmad Ridzwa Ahmad Fathan
Rohailan Mohammad
Rohani Sulaiman
Roshan Gurung
Roslan Mohamed Amin
Ruby Loo
Rukiyah Samsuddin
Russell Harnett
Sacha Ramlan Noordin
Sam Jacoby
Sarangapany a/l Muniandy
See Tho Loong Yow
Seow Ji Nee
Shahrina Intan
Shahrom bin Omar
Shamsul Bahair
Shamsul Baharin
Shanmuganathan a/l Perumal
Shanmungam
Sharifah Alhabshi
Simon Doody
Sneha Anne Mathews
Soh Soon Chong
Song Guofu
Sow Sun Fong

Srazali Aripin
Stephanie Lee
Suhaimi
Suriati Hassan
Suriyanti bt Mohd Tahir
Tai Fong Teng
Tam Chooi Leng
Tan Bee Woan
Tan Beng Kay
Tan Hai Choo
Tan Kim Tho
Tan Kooi Yan
Tan Shn Hee
Tan Wah Aik
Tay Lee Lee
Tham Pak Chee
Tham Seow Swee
Theresa Fu
Thomas Chin Weng Yin
Tim Mellor
Tomas Quijano
Tommy Phuah
Too Kah Hoe
Travis Cooke
Turlough Clancy
Vincent Le Feuvre

Vincent Lim
Voon Quek Wah
Voon Sin Fatt
Warren Williams
William Jude
Wong Choon Heng
Wong Suit Wah
Wong Tung Ken
Woo Yiw Po
Woon Choon Neng
Woon Chung Nam
Woon Yoke Wei
Yap Lip Pien
Yap Siat Lin
Yap Yow Kong
Yeap Lean ee
Yeaw Kiew
Yeoh Gim Seong
Yeoh Soon Teck
Yeong Kwong Meng
Yew Ai Choo
Yip Phaik Yoon
Yong Siew Fong
Yusmanisa Yusoff
Yusof Zainal Abidin
Yvonne Ho Wooi Lee

Zainal Mohammed
Zakiah bt Hj Abdullah
Zurinah bt Hussein

Drawings
Adrian Hazizi Hashim
Alex Cheong
Derick Ng See Leng
Emmy Lim Ying-Li
Mariani Abdullah
Noraini bte Ahmad
Peter Ho
Raymond Soh
Srazali Aripin
Yeoh Gim Seong

Models
J. M. Kiang
　(J. M. Kiang Modeller)
Lim Swee Eng (Technibuilt)
Mohd Nor Abdullah
　(Excell Matrix)

Teaching and Advisory Positions, Exhibitions and Awards

Teaching Positions, External Examinerships, Professorships and Advisory Positions

Professor (Graham Willis Chair), University of Sheffield (1994–8).

Adjunct Professor, Royal Melbourne Institute of Technology (1993–8).

External Examiner, Universiti Sains Malaysia, Penang (1988 and 1989).

External Examiner, University of Moratuwa, Sri Lanka (1986 and 1987).

Occasional Teacher, Universiti Teknologi Malaysia and Institut Teknologi Mara, Malaysia.

Lectured at various schools of architecture in Asia, Europe and the United States.

Editorial Advisory Board, Building Research and Information (E. & F. N. Spon, United Kingdom).

Editorial Advisory Board, Singapore Institute of Architects Journal (1997).

Editorial Advisory Board, Hong Kong Institute of Architects Journal (1997).

Exhibitions

1985 'Houses – 7 KL Architects', Tokyo Ginza Pocket Park Gallery, Tokyo.

1990 'Tropical Skyscrapers', Tokyo Designers Space, Tokyo, 9–20 January.

1992 'Contemporary Architects Exhibition', Nara Town Hall, Triennale Nara, Japan.

1994 'Bioclimatic Skyscrapers', Aedes Galerie und Architekturforum, Berlin, 11 February–11 March.

1995 'Bioclimatic Skyscrapers', The Building Centre, London, February.

1997 'The Skyscraper Bioclimatically Considered', The Architectural League of New York, The Urban Center, New York, 9 January.

1998 'Expo 2005 Tower', AA School, London, May.

1998 'Energetics', T. R. Hamzah and Yeang Sdn Bhd and Yeo Lee Inc, Aedes East Architekturforum und Galerien, Berlin, 22 May–19 June.

1998 'Energetics', T. R. Hamzah and Yeang Sdn Bhd and Yeo Lee Inc, NAI, Rotterdam, September.

Awards

1984 Penang Swimming Club Masterplan and Extension Design Competition: First Prize.

1985 Dewan Bandaraya, Kuala Lumpur: Urban Design Citation.

1987 Commonwealth Association of Architects, London: Commendation (for *The Tropical Verandah City*).

1988 Antron Design Award, United States: Honorable Mention.

1989 Malaysian Institute of Architects (PAM) Award for Excellence in Design and Building (for IBM Plaza).

1989 PAM Award for Excellence in Design and Building (for the Weld interior).

1989 Antron Design Award, United States: Honorable Mention.

1991 PAM Award for Single Residential Buildings (for the M. S. Tan House).

1992 The Norway Award for outstanding contribution to quality in the field of architecture.

1992 PAM Award for Commercial Buildings.

1993 PAM Award for Excellence in Design for Commercial Buildings (for Menara Mesiniaga).

1993 PAM Award for Conservation: Honorary Mention (for Standard Chartered Bank, Penang).

1993 International Award for Innovative Technology in Architecture (IATA), Quaternario, Italy: Top Twenty Finalist.

1993 Second Malaysian Institute of Interior Designers (MSG/MSID) Commercial Interior and Display Design Award (for the Seacorp light fittings).

1995 International Association for Sports and Leisure Facilities Award, Germany (for Selangor Turf Club).

1995 Singapore Institute of Architects (SIA) Design Award (Overseas Category): Honorary Mention, Singapore (for Selangor Turf Club).

1995 Kenneth F. Brown Asia Pacific Culture and Architecture Design Award, Hawaii: Merit Award (for Roof-Roof House).

1995 Royal Australian Institute of Architects (RAIA) International Architecture Award (for Menara Mesiniaga).

1996 Aga Khan Award for Architecture, Geneva (for Menara Mesiniaga).

1997 PAM Award for the Best Commercial Building (for Central Plaza).

1998 SIA Design Award (Overseas Category): Honorary Mention (for Menara UMNO).

1998 RAIA International Award (for Menara UMNO).

1998 Far Eastern Economic Review, Asian Innovation Awards: Bronze Award.

Bibliography

Publications by Ken Yeang

1972

'Bases for Ecosystem Design', *Architectural Design*,
July, Architectural Press, London.

1974

'Bionics: The Use of Biological Analogies in Design',
Architectural Association Quarterly (*AAQ*), No. 4,
London.
'The Energetics of the Built Environment', *Architectural
Design*, July, Architectural Press, London.

1976

'The Architect as Stylist', *The Economic Bulletin*,
November/December, Academic Publishers,
Malaysia, pp. 8–9.

1977

'Architecture in Malaysia: In Praise of Innovation',
The Economic Bulletin, January, Academic
Publishers, Malaysia, pp. 24–5.

1979

'The Identity Crisis', *Architecture Malaysia*, 4:79,
Malaysian Institute of Architects Journal,
Kuala Lumpur.

1981

'Notes on Regional Influences Affecting Design',
in proceedings of the seminar 'Kearah Identiti
Kebangsaan Dalam Senibina', Kuala Lumpur,
20–3 January 1981, Ministry of Youth and
Culture, Malaysia.

1982

'A Theoretical Framework for the Incorporation of
Ecological Considerations in the Design and
Planning of the Built Environment', doctoral thesis,
University of Cambridge (published as *Designing
with Nature*, McGraw-Hill, New York, 1995).

1984

'Architecture in Malaysia: In Praise of Innovation', in
R. Poon (ed), *ARCASIA FORUM 1: Innovation in
Architecture*, Architect in Asia Publication,
Hong Kong, pp. 11–14.
'Notes for a critical vernacular in contemporary
Malaysian architecture', *UIA International
Architect*, 6/1984, London, pp. 16–17.

1985

'Project Management in Relation to Design and Cost
Control', *The Surveyor*, The Professional Journal
of the Institution of Surveyors Malaysia, Vol. 20,
No. 3, Malaysia, pp. 54–63.

1986

'Landuse, Climate and Architectural Form', in
M. B. Sevcenko (ed), *Design For High-Intensity
Development*, proceedings of the International
Conference On Urban Design, Aga Khan Program
for Islamic Architecture, United States, pp. 75–80.
Contemporary Asian Architecture: A Selective Review,
editor, Commonwealth Association of
Architecture Publication, Malaysia.
The Tropical Verandah City, Longman, Malaysia.

1987

*The Tropical Verandah City: Some Urban Design
Ideas for Kuala Lumpur*, (second edition), Asia
Publications, Kuala Lumpur.
*Tropical Urban Regionalism: Building in a South-East
Asian City*, a MIMAR book, Concept Media Pte
Ltd, Singapore.
'A Review of Malaysian Architecture', in *Post
Merdeka Architecture*, catalogue of exhibition
organized by the Malaysian Institute of
Architects, Kuala Lumpur.

1988

'On Dilettantes and Exclusivists', *South East Asia
Building*, February, Singapore, pp. 92–4.
'There are Interior Designers and there are *Interior
Designers*', *South East Asia Building*, March,
Singapore, pp. 92–4.

'Foreign Affairs', *South East Asia Building*, Singapore, April, pp. 65–71.

'Asian Architecture: A Battleground for the Cultural Imperative', *South East Asia Building*, June, Singapore, pp. 74–6.

'Thinking About Architecture', *South East Asia Building*, August/September, Singapore, pp. 44–6.

'What they didn't teach you in architectural school', *South East Asia Building*, November, Singapore, pp. 79–82.

ARCASIA, The Architecture & Design Magazine, No. 1, August, editor, Arcasia Publication, Malaysia.

'A Review of Malaysian Architecture', in *Post-Merdeka Architecture Malaysia 1957–1987*, Malaysian Institute of Architects Publication, pp. 13–25.

1989

'Urban Design Ideas for the Tropical City', in proceedings of the seminar 'Perancangan: Satu Mekanisme Pengurusan Perubahan Persekitaran', 14–15 January, Fakulti Alam Bina, Universiti Teknologi Malaysia, Malaysia.

'Towards a Comprehensive Architectural Education Policy', in proceedings of 'Seminar on Architectural Education', January, Universiti Sains Malaysia, Penang.

1990

'The Idea of the Intelligent Building', in *'Development of Intelligent Buildings in the Tropics' Conference Papers*, The Total Building Conference, 12–13 July, Singapore, pp. 72–82.

1991

'High-Rise Design for Hot-Humid Places', *Building Research and Information*, Vol. 19, No. 5, September/October, London, pp. 274–81.

'Tropical Skyscrapers', in proceedings of 'Asia '91 Construction: New Frontiers', CEMS, Singapore, pp. Arch-13–Arch-25.

'Review of B. Botond, *The New Japanese Architecture*, Rizzoli, 1990', *Mimar*, No. 41, Concept Media Ltd, London, pp. 79–81.

1992

'The Tropical Skyscraper', in P. G. Raman, *Criticism and Growth of Architectural Ideas*, Asia Design Forum, Singapore.

'Designing the Tropical Skyscrapers', *Mimar*, No. 42, Concept Media Ltd, London, pp. 40–5.

'The Tropical Skyscraper', *Journal of the Indian Institute of Architects*, Vol. 57, Issue 7, December, pp. 32–7.

The Architecture of Malaysia, Pepin Press, Holland.

Louisiana Heights, workshop at Louisiana State University, Malaysia.

'The Malaysian Skyscraper Reconsidered', *Solidarity 131–132*, July–December, Solidarity House, Philippines, pp. 16–31.

1993

'Forward', in Lillian Too, *Feng Shui*, Konsep Books, Kuala Lumpur, pp. 13–15.

'Designing the Asian Skyscraper', in *2020 Magazine*, Malaysia, July/August, pp. 34–42.

1994

'Asia by Design', *Space*, September, South Korea, pp. 99–105.

1995

'Above the Gucci Syndrome', *The Edge*, 7 August, Kuala Lumpur, pp. 18.

'Leadership in the Pacific Rim must be seized', *Building Property Review*, September/October, Kuala Lumpur, pp. 94–7.

'The Bioclimatic Skyscraper', in proceedings of the symposium 'Architektur-Energie-Komfort', 22 November, Haus der Wirtzchaft, Stuttgart.

'The Bioclimatic Skyscraper', in proceedings of the 'Symposium in Glashaus, Kulturzentrum Herten', 27–8 October, Germany, pp. 40–9.

'Look East, Go West', *Building Property Review*, November/December, Kuala Lumpur, pp. 86–8.

'On Sustainable Design', in *JIA Sustainable Design*

Guide, Japan Institute of Architects, Tokyo, Japan, pp. 13–15.

Section 3.1 in M. M. Ali, and P. J. Armstrong (eds), *Architecture of Tall Buildings*, McGraw-Hill, New York, pp. 143–53, 306–7, 518–19.

Designing with Nature, McGraw-Hill, New York.

1996

'The Big Picture', *Building Property Review*, January/February, Kuala Lumpur, pp. 97–8.

'Mystical Insurance: Review of Evelyn Lip, *Feng Shui Environments of Power: A Study of Chinese Architecture*, Academy Editions', in *World Architecture*, No. 43, February, pp. 123.

'Competing in the Asian Century', *Building Property Review*, March/April, Kuala Lumpur, pp. 78–80.

'Design Innovations: Explorers or Pirates', *Building Property Review*, May/June, Kuala Lumpur, pp. 62–4.

'Malaysian Designers boleh!', *The Edge*, 3 June, Kuala Lumpur.

'AICR, The Dreaded Architectural Identity Chain Reaction', *Building Property Review*, July/August, Kuala Lumpur, pp. 95–7.

'The Bioclimatic Skyscraper', *Journal of Architecture and Building Service: Architectural Institute of Japan*, No. 12, Vol. 111, No. 1398, Tokyo, pp. 34–7.

'Incidents at the Supermarket', *Building Property Review*, November/December, Kuala Lumpur, pp. 84–6.

'Habe Ich etwas nicht verstanden?', *Stat Bauwelt*, No. 48, December, Germany, pp. 2744.

1997

'The Asian Architect', *Shinkenchiku*, 1997, No. 72/1, Tokyo, pp. 90–3.

'To Be or Not To Be an Architect', *Building Property Review*, January/February, Kuala Lumpur, pp. 72–4.

'To Whom Does Modern Technology Belong?', *Building Property Review*, March/April, Kuala Lumpur, pp. 42–4.

'Against Parochialism', *Building Property Review*, May/June, Kuala Lumpur, pp. 46–8.

'The Fickle Finger of Fame', *Building Property Review*, July/August, Kuala Lumpur, pp. 50–2.

'Designing the Green Skyscraper', *Architecture Malaysia*, September/October, Kuala Lumpur, pp. 68–78.

'On Asian Cities', *Building Property Review*, September/October, Kuala Lumpur, pp. 42–6.

'Designing the Green Skyscraper', in H. R. Viswanath, J. J. A. Tolloczko and J. N. Clarke, *Multi-Purpose High-Rise Towers and Tall Buildings*, proceedings of the Third International Conference 'Conquest of Vertical Space in the 21st Century', organized by The Concrete Society, London, 7–10 October, E. & F. N. Spon, London, pp. 13–27.

'Designing the Green Skyscraper', in proceedings of the 'International Symposium Commemorating 50th Anniversary of the Architectural Institute of Pusan', Kyongnam, South Korea, pp. 63–77.

'Supertower North East', *Materia + Factura = Construction*, Newcastle School of Architecture, University of Newcastle, United Kingdom, pp. 47–50.

The Skyscraper Bioclimatically Considered: A Design Primer, Architectural Design, Academy Editions, London.

'Technology for Housing: Past and Future Trends', in *Housing The Nation: A Definitive Study*, Cagamas Berhad, Kuala Lumpur, pp. 499–512.

'Tropical Urban Regionalism' and 'Bioclimatic Skyscrapers', in C. Jencks and K. Kopf (eds), *Theories and Manifestoes of Contemporary Architecture*, Architectural Design, Academy Editions, London, pp. 146–8, 164–6.

'Three Strategies for the Greening of Hong Kong', in H. Hanru and H. U. Obrist (eds), *SECESSION: Musée d'Art Contemporain de Bordeaux*, Verlag Gerd Hatje, Germany, Section 78.

1998

'The Architect and His Business', *The Edge*, 23 February, Kuala Lumpur, p. 18.

'The Malaysia City of the Future: Some Physical Planning and Urban Design Ideas', *Architecture Malaysia*, March/April, Malaysia Institute of Architects Journal, Kuala Lumpur, pp. 70–5.

'On Rapid-Prototyping and Product Development', unpublished essay, May.

'Singapore's Architects and Architecture in the World's Market Place', in P. Bay (ed), *Contemporary Singapore Architecture*, Page 1 Publishing Pte Ltd, Singapore, pp. 269–77.

1999

The Green Skyscraper: A Primer for Designing Ecologically Sustainable Large Buildings, Prestel, Munich and New York.

Publications with References to and Projects by T. R. Hamzah and Yeang

1982

Necdet Teymur, 'Environmental Discourse', London, pp. 143, 208.

1983

D. Teh (ed) et al, 'MA Interviews: Interview of Ken Yeang', *Architecture Malaysia*, 3:83, Malaysian Institute of Architects Journal, Kuala Lumpur, pp. 36–43.

1984

K. Y. Lee, 'The Roof-Roof House', *Architecture Malaysia*, 2:84, Malaysian Institute of Architects Journal, Kuala Lumpur, pp. 2–26.

Haig Beck (ed), 'Hamzah & Yeang Architects, Roof-Roof House, Kuala Lumpur', *UIA International Architect*, Issue 6/1984, pp. 16–17.

1985

D. Teh et al, 'Ken Yeang', in *Houses – 7 KL Architects*, exhibition catalogue, Tokyo Ginza Pocket Park Gallery, 21 February–19 March, Tokyo, pp. 46–53.

Interview, *Nikkei Architecture*, Issue 4-8, pp. 146–7.

'Plaza Atrium', *Interior Digest*, Vol. 2, No. 1, MPH Magazines Sdn Bhd, Malaysia, pp. 3-6.

Annie Ooi, 'The Roof-Roof House', in Fong Peto (ed), *Her World Annual '85*, Berita Publishing, Kuala Lumpur, pp. 64–9.

1986

Tomoyoshi Kato, 'Regionality of Contemporary Architecture: Malaysia', *A&U*, 86:03, Japan, pp. 5–9.

Angie Ng, 'A House in the Valley', in *Her World's Homescene*, Berita Publishing, Kuala Lumpur, pp. 33–5.

Sheila Cheong (ed), 'The Roof-Roof House', *Design & Decor Annual '86*, Metropolitan Publishing Sdn Bhd, Malaysia, pp. 73–7.

'The Tropical Verandah City', *Ginza Pocket Park News*, No. 11, Summer, pp. 7–8.

Norfan Yusoff et al, *Tall Buildings of the World*, Council of Tall Buildings and Urban Habitat, Lehigh University, Bethlehem, Pennsylvania, p. 93 (Menara Boustead).

1987

Robert Powell, 'Book Review: *Tropical Urban Regionalism*', in *SIAJ*, September/October, Singapore Institute of Architects, Singapore, p. 51.

Udo Kultermann, 'Architecture in South-East Asia 4: Malaysia', in *Mimar*, No. 26, December, Concept Media Pte Ltd, Singapore, pp. 69–71.

1988

Editorial, 'An Unsentimental Artist', *Asiaweek*, 15 July 1988, Asiaweek Ltd, Hong Kong, p. 55.

H. B. Tan, 'Designer Profile: Ken Yeang', *Interiors Quarterly*, September–November, pp. 40–3.

John Arbouw (ed), 'IBM Malaysia: Emergent Regionalist Architecture', *South East Asia Building*, August/September, pp. 17–25.

1989

Mabel Yeung, 'Architecture: Kenneth Yeang', *AD International*, ADI Publications Ltd, Hong Kong, pp. 54–61.

Diana Shooman, 'Cool Oasis in the Tropics', *Beautiful Home*, No. 5, October–November, 1989, pp. 60–3.

'IBM Plaza', *AT Architecture Magazine*, November, Japan, p. 79.

Dennis Sharp, 'Tropical Heights', *RIBAJ*, August.

Dennis Sharp, 'Transformation of the Traditional', *Building Design*, 3 November, pp. 22–7.

Jack King (ed), 'Tropical Heights', *Wolfson College Cambridge*, No. 16, pp. 28–37.

Robert Powell, *Ken Yeang: Rethinking the Environmental Filter*, Landmark Books Pte Ltd, Singapore.

Kurokawa, Kisho, 'The Conversion of the Modernist Paradigm and the Architecture of Ken Yeang', in Robert Powell, *Ken Yeang: Rethinking the Environmental Filter*, Landmark Books Pte Ltd, Singapore, pp. 7–8.

1990

'Eaves, Overhangs and Other Protection from Sun and Rain', *Design and Decor Annual*, August (Roof-Roof House).

Omar Zakiah, 'Modern Inclinations', *Malaysian Tatler*, February, pp. 124–6 (Dason House).

'Tropical Skyscrapers Exhibition', *AT Architecture Magazine*, February, Japan, pp. 8–9.

P. G. Raman, 'Tropical Heights at Tokyo Designer's Space', *A & U*, 90:04, No. 235, April, Japan, pp. 6–7.

'World Pulse', *Axis (Quarterly Trends in Design)*, Spring, Japan, p. 35.

P. G. Raman, 'Ken Yeang's garden cities in the sky', *Blueprint*, April, No. 66, London, p. 12.

Neal Morris, Paradigms Lost in the Tropics', *AJ*, 25 April, London, p. 14.

Hugh Aldersey-Williams, 'Design in a different climate', *Interior Design*, April, pp. 66–8.

Binu Thomas, 'Hairy Buildings and Sky Gardens', *Asiaweek*, 11 May, p. 49.

Ken Lou, 'Asian Visions', *The Straits Times*, 16 May, Singapore, pp. 1–3.

A. Krafft (ed), 'T. R. Hamzah & Yeang, Roof-Roof House, Ampang Selangor, T. R. Hamzah & Yeang, Plaza Atrium, Kuala Lumpur', *Contemporary Architecture*, Vol. 12, 1990/1991, Presses Polytechniques at Universitaires Romandes, E. & F. N. Spon, London, pp. 62–5, 158–61.

C. S. Lim (ed), 'Private Investigations', *Architecture Malaysia*, November/December, 11/12:90, Malaysian Institute of Architects Journal, Kuala Lumpur, pp. 52–7.

P. G. Raman, 'The web of tradition: Ken Yeang's buildings in Malaysia', in Giancarlo de Carlo (ed), *Spazio Società*, No. 51, Milan, pp. 96–105.

Colin Amery, 'Lesson to be learnt from a tropical climate', *Financial Times*, 14 June, London, p. 13.

1991

C. S. Lim (ed), 'MacGin House', 'Roof-Roof House', 'Metrolux Double-Storey Linkhouse', *Architecture Malaysia*, November/December, 11/12:91, Malaysian Institute of Architects Journal, Kuala Lumpur, pp. 27–9, 39, 61.

S. Nair, 'Cool Comfort', *Malaysian Tatler*, March, pp. 68–70 (Roof-Roof House).

S. Nair, 'Formal Living', *Malaysian Tatler*, May, pp. 72–4 (MacGin House).

Norulhoda Salleh, 'Generating efficiency in fantasy', *New Straits Times*, April 23, p. 25.

Brenda Polan, 'The Green House Effect', *Joyce*, No. 13, Spring, pp. 233–6.

Jacquelin Ho, 'Yeang and Exuberant', *Malaysian Business*, 16–30 September, pp. 62–3.

1992

'Contemporary Architect Exhibition', catalogue, Triennale Nara.

P. Selvanathan, 'Tropical Aspirations', *Malaysian Tatler*, February, pp. 54–5.

L. T. Ngiom (ed), 'Mesiniaga Building', *Architecture Malaysia*, May/June, 5/6:92, Malaysian Institute of Architects Journal, Kuala Lumpur, pp. 11–13.

P. Selvanathan, 'A World of Concrete Intelligence', *Visage*, June, Accent Publishing Sdn Bhd, Kuala Lumpur, pp. 56–8.

Kaneki Tile, 'IBM Plaza, Malaysia', *Kaneki Tile Catalogue*, Kaneki Tile, Japan, p. 74.

'Kenneth Yeang', *AT Architecture Magazine*, August, Japan, pp. 8–15.

Jessica Loon, 'The Trophy Building: Menara Mesiniaga at Subang Jaya, Selangor', *What's New in Building*, Vol. 11, No. 11, November, Toucan Publishing Pte Ltd, Singapore, pp. 22–4.

Tej Fernandez (ed), 'Menara Mesiniaga', *Building*

Journal, June/July, Global Motive Sdn Bhd, Kuala Lumpur, pp. 34–40.

Eddy Koh (ed), 'Architecture: Sowing on Concrete', *IQ, Interiors Quarterly*, September/November, Shusse Publishing, Singapore, pp. 48–52.

Yuki Fuchigami, 'Ken Yeang: Architect on the Scene', *Kenchiku Bunka*, Japan, pp. 13–15.

Malaysian Institute of Architects, 'T. R. Hamzah & Yeang Sdn Bhd', *Towards Johor Bahru 2005 Urban Design Competition*, p. 20.

'Menara Mesiniaga: Laminated Glass', *MSG (Malaysian Sheet Glass Berhad) Product Catalogue*, p. 18

Steven Groak, *The Idea of Building*, E. & F. N. Spon, London, p. 39.

1993

Alison Nadel, 'KL Skyline', *Wings of Gold* (MAS inflight magazine), February, Kuala Lumpur, pp. 16–17.

Tej Fernandez, 'T. R. Hamzah & Yeang: Designers of High Rises', *Building Journal,* January/February, Global Motive Sdn Bhd, Malaysia, pp. 69–71.

L. T. Ngiom (ed), 'Selangor Turf Club, Sungei Besi', *Architecture Malaysia*, Vol. 5, No. 2, March/April, Malaysian Institute of Architects Journal, Kuala Lumpur, pp. 20–5.

Ivor Richards, 'Tropic Tower', *Architectural Review*, February, pp. 26–30.

Jacquelin Loon (ed), 'Warisan Tun Perak: From Traditional to Contemporary', *What's New in*

Building, Vol. 12, No. 2, February, pp. 34–6.

Graham Vickers, 'Far East Wizard', *World Architecture*, No. 22, March, pp. 72–7.

C. Pearson, 'Tropical Modern', in *Architectural Record*, McGraw-Hill, New York, pp. 27–31.

Philip Arcidi, 'Menara Mesiniaga Tower', *Progressive Architecture*, March, p. 109.

Udo Kultermann, *Architecture in the 20th Century*, Van Nostrand Reinhold, New York, p. 240.

Roef Hopman, 'Cool Comfort in a Tropical Skyscraper', in *Commercial Design Trends*, Vol. 1, Singapore, pp. 52–5.

K. Akihiro (ed), 'Bio-Climatic High-Rise Design as Orientation for 21st Century: Ken Yeang', *ECIFFO*, Vol. 21, Summer, pp. 4–7.

'Nara, and Triennale, Nara, 1992', *The Japan Architect*, special issue.

Jacquelin Loon (ed), 'Standard Chartered Bank Building, Penang', *What's New in Building*, Vol. 12, No. 4, April, pp. 28–30.

Jacquelin Loon (ed), 'New Turf for Punters: Selangor Turf Club' in *What's New in Building*, Vol.12, No. 8, August, pp. 48–9.

M. Tan (ed), 'Central Plaza', *Building Review Journal*, Vol. 8, No. 6, p. 74.

J. Sanders, 'Book of Note: *The Architecture of Malaysia* by Ken Yeang', in *Progressive Architecture*, August, p. 90.

'T. R. Hamzah & Yeang Sdn Bhd, Selangor: Menara Mesiniaga', *Quaternario Award*, IATA 93, Electa, Milan, pp. 70–3.

Robert Powell, *The Asian House*, Select Books Pte

Ltd, Singapore, and Thames and Hudson, London, pp. 162–5 (Roof-Roof House).

1994

D. Devoss, 'High-Rise Revolution', *Asia Inc*, January, pp. 38–45.

T. Ikeda et al, 'Bioclimatic Skyscrapers: Recent Works of T. R. Hamzah & Yeang Sdn Bhd', *SD (Space Design)*, No. 94:03, March, pp. 5–44.

M. Pawley, G. Battle and C. McCarthy, 'Profile: Ken Yeang', *World Architecture*, No. 28, March, London, pp. 24–47.

A. Balfour and I. Richards, *Bioclimatic Skyscrapers: Ken Yeang*, Artemis, London.

Fay Sweet, 'Climate Shaping in the Cities', *New Scientist*, October.

Susan Berfield, 'Skyscrapers for the Tropics: Jumping Out of the Glass Box', *The Asian Wall Street Journal*, p. 9.

Hugh Pearman, 'Rising in the East', *The Sunday Times*, 13 March, the 'Culture' supplement, pp. 12–13.

'The Great Leap Skyward', *Architectural Record*, March, p. 32.

Chris Abel, 'Cool High-Rise', *Architectural Review*, March, pp. 26–31.

Bryan Lawson, 'Ken Yeang', in *Design in Mind*, Butterworth Architecture, Oxford, pp. 119–30.

KIRA (Korean Institute of Architects), *Contemporary Architecture in Asia,* KIRA Publication, South Korea.

David Calhoun (ed), *Encyclopaedia Britannica 1995 Yearbook of Science and the Future*, Encyclopaedia Britannica Inc, Chicago, p. 290 (Menara Mesiniaga).

Klaus Daniels, *The Technology of Ecological Building*, Birkhauser Verlag, Berlin, Germany, pp. 28–33, 284–5 (Tokyo-Nara Tower).

J. Glancey, 'Booming Far East reaches for the sky', *The Independent on Sunday*, 10 July, p. 13.

Charles de Ledesma, Mark Lewis and Pauline Savage, *The Rough Guide: Malaysia, Singapore and Brunei*, Penguin, United Kingdom, p. 87.

Jessica Loon, 'MBf Tower', *What's New in Building*, Vol. 13, No. 3, March, Singapore, pp. 27–8.

M. Fuchigami, 'Kenneth Yeang (Malaysia)', in *Cross-Currents: Fifty-One World Architects*, Japan, pp. 218–21.

1995

Martin Pawley (ed), 'Yeang probes photovoltaic glazing', *World Architecture*, No. 38, London.

Maggie Toy, 'T. R. Hamzah & Yeang' and 'Reaching for the Skies', *Architectural Design*, Profile No. 116, Academy Group, pp. 66–77 (Menara Mesiniaga, MBf Tower, China Tower).

Cynthia Davidson (ed), *Architecture Beyond Architecture*, Architectural Design, Academy Editions, London, pp. 94–101.

Movin' 143, Osaka, pp. 8–9.

Adele Weder, 'The Greening of the Skyscraper', *INSITE*, January, Ontario, Canada, pp. 45–7.

Dwight Holling, 'Sustainable Skyscrapers', *Tomorrow*, No. 4, Vol. 5, October–December.

Dieter Schempp, 'Menara Mesiniaga', in *Glasforum 3.95*, Germany, pp. 5–10.

Klaus Daniels, 'Klima and Gebaincoform' in *Technologie des Okologischen Bauens*, Germany, pp.18-33.

Peter Davey (ed), 'Menara Mesiniaga; Aga Khan Award for Architecture', *Architectural Review*, November, p. 70.

Zaini Zainuddin, 'Pakar Binaan Bio-iklim', *Anjung Seri*, May, Kuala Lumpur, pp. 78–83.

Tang, Eugene, 'Above the Gucci Syndrome', *The Edge*, 7 August, Kuala Lumpur, p. 18.

Mathew Demetros, 'Yin and Yeang', in *AJ*, 13 July, London, pp. 18–19.

Clifford Pearson (ed), *Architectural Record*, Pacific Rim, p. 25.

Sheryll Stothard, 'Who died ... and made you the designer', *Men's Review*, January, Kuala Lumpur, pp. 33–7.

H. Kuzon and J. Search, 'Architects of Change', *Wired*, July/August, London, p. 111.

Charles Jencks, *The Architecture of the Jumping Universe*, Architectural Design, Academy Editions, London, p. 95.

C. Mierop, *Skyscrapers: Higher And Higher*, Institut Français d' Architecture, Norman Editions, Paris, France, pp. 156–9 (Tokyo-Nara Tower).

'The New Taichung Civic Center International Competition Entries', Leader of the Garden AD, Taiwan, pp. 56–62 (Third Prize Entries).

T. Bhaskaran (ed), 'The 1995 Aga Khan Award for Architecture', *South East Asia Building*, Singapore, p. 12.

Hasan-Uddin Khan, *Contemporary Asian Architecture*, Taschen, Kolu, Germany, pp. 106–11.

Miyake Richi (ed), *581 Architects In The World*, Toto Shuppan, Tokyo, Japan, p. 488.

Rendow Yee, *Architectural Design Drawing*, Demand Printing Solutions, San Francisco, p. 286.

1996

D. K. Dietsch, 'Muslim Architecture Honoured by Aga Khan', *Architecture*, January, United States, p. 32.

Nicola Turner (ed), 'Aga Khan Award for Architecture', *World Architecture*, No. 42, January, London, p. 66.

Pietro Chianchiano (ed), 'L'ippodromo di Selangor in Malaysia', *TSPORT*, No. 186, January–February, Milan, Italy, pp. 40–5.

Seth Mydans, 'Malaysia Looks Down on World From 1,483 feet', *New York Times*, 5 February, New York, p. 11.

D. Danner (ed), 'AIT-Symposium Intelligent Building Design', *AIT* (*Architektur, Innenarchitektur, Technischer Ausban*), March, Leinfelden-Echterdingen, pp. 6–7.

Mary Blume, 'In Asia Skyscrapers Reach for Records', *International Herald Tribune*, 30–1 March (Tokyo-Nara Tower).

Lin Jing, 'Ken Yeang and his Bioclimatic

Skyscrapers', *World Architecture*, No. 45, April, London, pp. 23–31.

Nicola Turner (ed), 'Business Parks', *World Architecture*, No. 46, May, London, p. 117 (Kota Kamuning Business Park).

Andrew Auker, 'Review of *Designing with Nature: The Ecological Basis for Architectural Design*', *Architectural Record*, May.

Jo Newson, 'Awarding Alternatives', *World Architecture*, No. 47, June, London, p. 43 (Menara Mesiniaga).

Friedrich Dasler, 'Vielfalt', *AIT (Architektur, Innenarchitektur, Technischer Ausban)*, July, Leinfelden-Echterdingen, pp. 31–2.

Rowan Moore, 'Towering Ambitions', *The Daily Telegraph*, 16 July, p. 17 (Tokyo-Nara Tower).

Clifford Pearson (ed), 'Pacific Rim', *Architectural Record*, July, p. PR15 (Central Plaza).

Sea-Young Chang (ed), 'Architect of Malaysia: Ken Yeang', *Space*, Vol. 323, 1994:09, Space Group of Korea, pp. 98–101.

Nicola Turner (ed), 'Centre of it All', *World Architecture*, No. 51, November, London, pp. 42–7 (Central Plaza).

C. Casati (ed), 'Ken Yeang: New Basis', *L'Arca*, November, Milan, Italy, pp. 14–23.

C. Brensing, 'Bioclimatische Hochhauser', *DB (Deutsche Bauzeitung)*, November, Stuttgart, p. 18.

Rowan Moore (ed), 'Letter from Bali', *Blueprint*, November, London, p. 14.

Davina Jackson, 'International Award: Menara Mesiniaga, Malaysia', *Architecture Australia*, November/December, Melbourne, Australia, pp. 52–3.

J. Lee, 'Menara Budaya has the highest rooftop canopy in the world', *Building Review Journal*, November, Kuala Lumpur, pp. 39–45.

P. C. Lim, 'Menara TA One', *Architecture Malaysia*, November/December, Malaysian Institute of Architects Journal, Kuala Lumpur, pp. 22–8.

Ignasi de Sola-Morales and X. Costa, *Present and Futures: Architecture in Cities,* 'XIX Congress of the International Union of Architects UIA Barcelona 1996', catalogue, Cornite d'Organitzacio' del Congress UIA Barcelona 96, Collegi d'Arquitectes de Catalunya, Centre de Cultura Contemporanie de Barcelona and ACTAR, pp. 248–51 (Menara Mesiniaga, Hitechniaga HQ Tower).

T. S. Phillips et al, *Advanced Technology Facilities Design: 1996 Review*, The American Institute of Architects, Washington, pp. 2–5.

Leon van Schaik, 'Ushida Findlay: an essay', in E. Ushida and R. Findlay, *Parallel Landscapes*, Gallery MA, Book 02, Tokyo, p. 75.

Leon van Schaik, 'Asia Design Forum 6', *Transition*, 52/53, RMIT, Melbourne, Australia, pp. 106–11.

Dan Cruickshank (ed), *Sir Bannister Fletcher's 'A History of Architecture'*, Architectural Press, Butterworth-Heinemann, Oxford, pp. 1601–2.

Y. Kaneko (ed), *ROOTS*, Delphi Inc, Tokyo, Japan, pp. 012–013.

M. Watanabe, S. Muramatsu and T. Furuichi, 'Innovative Architecture in Asia', Architectural Institute of Japan, Tokyo, pp. 5–16.

1997

Z. Othman, 'Rangka 'K' Terbalik', *Anjung Seri*, January, Kuala Lumpur, pp. 105–7 (Central Plaza).

P. C. Lim, (ed), 'Casa-Del-Sol Tower', *Architecture Malaysia*, January/February, Malaysian Institute of Architects Journal, Kuala Lumpur, pp. 34–7.

Roef Hopman, 'Cool Building Suit the Tropics', *Design Trends*, Vol. 13, No. 1, Singapore, pp. 68–73.

Nicola Turner (ed), 'Servicing the Green Skyscrapers', *World Architecture*, No. 53, February, London, United Kingdom, pp. 108–9.

Makoto S. Watanabe, 'A High-Rise Building and a Boy who cares for an Elephant', *SD (Space Design)*, No. 38a, February, p. 100.

Budi, Tulus, Setyo, Moersid, A, 'Arsitektur Bioclimatik Ken Yeang', *Matra*, Majalah Tred Pria, February, Jakarta, Indonesia, pp. 120–3.

L. H. Chio, 'One Singular Pursuit', *ID*, Vol. 15, No. 2, Singapore, p. 71.

Jayne Merkel, 'The Skyscraper Bioclimatically Considered', *Oculus*, AIA New York Chapter, Vol. 59, No. 7, March, New York, pp. 13–14.

Penny Lewis, 'Carry on Stormin', Norman', in *LM*, No. 98, March, London.

V. Yoges, 'A Malaysian Architectural Breakthrough', *Malaysia Design*, First Quarter, Malaysia Design Council, Kuala Lumpur, pp. 41–5.

P. C. Lim (ed), 'Megan Corporate Park', *Architecture Malaysia*, March/April, Malaysian Institute of Architects Journal, Kuala Lumpur, pp. 14–19.

Angeline Ch'ng (ed), 'Ken Yeang, A World-Class Player', *Città Bella*, May, Kuala Lumpur, Malaysia, pp. 48–9.

A. G. Ahmad, 'The Chronological Biography of Arthur Charles Alfred Norman', *Journal of the Malaysia Branch of the Royal Asiatic Society*, Vol. 70, Part I, No. 272, June, Kuala Lumpur, p. 21.

June Cummings (ed), 'ESD in Cyberspace', *Building Innovation and Construction Technology*, No. 16, June/July, CSIRO Australia, p. 14.

Ji-Seong Jeong (ed), 'Ken Yeang & T. R. Hamzah: The Skyscraper Bioclimatically Considered', *Contemporary Architecture (CA)*, July, CA Press Co, Seoul, South Korea, pp. 10–17.

Yong-Soo Cho, 'Bioclimatic Architectural Design by Ken Yeang', *Ideal Architecture*, 97:12, Pusan, South Korea, pp. 146–75.

Rob Mead, 'The Mile High Club', *Tomorrow's Technology Today (T3)*, No. 9, July, Bath, United Kingdom, p. 37.

Louise Kennedy, 'ESD Guru builds green future', *The Australian Financial Review*, 14 August, Property Section, p. 48.

Leo Gullbring, 'Skyscraper', *Goteborgs-Bosten*, 25 August, Sweden, p. 41.

Marcos de Sousa, 'Arquitectura Bioclimatica', *Architectura & Urbanismo*, No. 12, August/September, No. 73, PINI, São Paulo, Brazil, p. 38.

P. Kasi et al (eds), 'Central Plaza', *Architecture Asia*, September/October, Arcasia, Kuala Lumpur, pp. 30–6.

A. Koch (ed), 'Solar-Streiter', *AT Special Intelligente Architektur*, Leinfelden-Echterdingen, Germany, p. 48–52.

P. Morgan, 'Seeking Middle Ground: Green Buildings and People-Friendly Streets', *Asiaweek*, 5 December, Hong Kong, p. 55.

Francis Duffy, *The New Office*, Conran Octopus Ltd, London, pp. 70–1 (Menara Mesiniaga).

W. S. Wong (ed), *Monument for 1997*, Hong Kong Institute of Architects, Hong Kong, p. 7.

C. Davidson and I. Serageldin (eds), *Arsitektur Di-Luar Jangkanan Arsitektur*, Jakarta, Indonesia, pp. 76–81.

Rendow Yee, 'Diagramming the Design Press', in *Architectural Drawing*, John Wiley & Sons Inc, New York, United States, pp. 458–61.

Chris Abel, *Architecture and Identity: Towards a Global Eco-Culture*, Architectural Press, Butterworth-Heinemann, Oxford, pp. 190–3.

Francisco Asensio Cerver, *The Architecture of Skyscrapers*, Arco, for Hearst Books International, New York, pp. 36–55 (Menara Budaya, Central Plaza).

D. Mackenzie, *Green Design: Design For The Environment*, Laurence King Publishing (Calmann & King Ltd), London, pp. 60–3 (Menara Mesiniaga).

Max Fordham, 'Thinking Big' in *Architectural Review*, August 1997, London, pp. 87–8 (Review of *The Skyscraper Bioclimatically Considered: A Design Primer*).

Ivor Richards, 'Singapore Super Tower: Bioclimatic High-Rise on the Singapore Skyline', *Journal of Southeast Asian Architecture*, 1:47-61, pp. 47, 57.

Mark Pimlott, 'New Urbanisms', *AA News*, Autumn, Architectural Association, London, p. 15.

James Steele, *Architecture Today*, Phaidon Press, London, pp. 296–8, 383.

M. Toy, *Architectural Design Profile No. 125: The Architecture of Ecology*, Academy Group, London, pp. 70–5.

C. Jencks and K. Kropf, *Theories and Manifestoes of Contemporary Architecture*, Academy Editions, London, pp. 146–8, 184–6.

1998

C. Fukagawa (ed), 'Creator's Work: Ken Yeang', *Axis*, Vol. 71, 1 and 2, January and February, p. 80.

Jon Ignatowicz, 'The Guthrie Pavilion', *Singapore Architect*, No. 197/98, January–March, Singapore.

Leon van Schaik, 'Big Chill', *RIBA International*, May, London, pp. 6-11.

Melissa Drier, 'Yeohlee Hits the Road', *WWD*, 10 June.

Weijen Wang, 'Writing Between the Generic: Neo-orientalization and Deorientalization Reflected at the Harvard Asia-Pacific Design Conference', *Dialogue*, June, Taipei, Taiwan, p. 102.

A. Koor, 'Naturally Cool', *Hinge*, Vol. 44, June, Hong Kong, pp. 50–1.

Hugh Pearman, *Contemporary World Architecture*, Phaidon Press, London, pp. 18, 202, 210, 278–9, 413, 484–6.

V. M. Schobeth, 'Lahjahre bei ... Ken Yeang, *AIT (Architektur, Innenarchitektur and Technischer Ausban)*, Leinfelden-Echterdingen, pp. 34–5.

Harriet Grind, 'Golf Umbrella', *Architectural Review*, London, pp. 56–9 (Guthrie Pavilion).

Jonathan Hill, 'Child's Play', in Sarah Dyson (ed), *AA News*, London, p. 2.

T. Davis, 'Ken Yeang's Green Skyscrapers', *Canadian Consulting Engineer*, June–July, Vol. 39, No. 3, pp. 60–1.

Fujiki Laboratory (Tokyo Metropolitan University), 'The fusion of high technology and regional culture', *Detail*, No. 137, July, Japan, p. 110 (Menara Mesiniaga).

Peter Wisloki, 'Fairway to Heaven', *Building Design*, 10 July, London, pp. 20–2. (Guthrie Pavilion).

'T. R. Hamzah & Yeang: The Greening of Hong Kong', in Hou Hanru and Hans Obrist (eds), *Cities on the Move*, Hatje, Vienna.

Russel Fergusan (ed), *At the End of the Century (One Hundred Years of Architecture)*, Museum of Contemporary Art, Los Angeles, Harry N. Abrams Inc, New York, p. 72.

Jeremy Melvin, 'My Greatest Design ...', *HighLife*, BA inflight magazine, August, p. 25 (Menara UMNO).

Gene King, 'T. R. Hamzah & Yeang Sdn Bhd', *Dialogue*, August, Taipei, Taiwan, pp. 51–81.

Gene King, 'Menara UMNO', *Dialogue*, September, Taipei, Taiwan, pp. 58–89.

K. Chandran (ed), 'Towering Beyond the Millennium', *The Peak*, Vol. 9, No. 3, Singapore, pp. 60–1.

Jonathan Hill 'Ke Da Ke Xiao/Mei Da Mei Xiao', in Mary Wall (ed), *AA Files 36*, London, p. 67 (Nagoya 2005 Tower).

Tzi Ling Li, 'Inside the Bioclimatic Skyscraper: A Critical Analysis', Master of Architecture thesis, unpublished, National University of Singapore.

Andrew Harrison et al (eds), *Intelligent Buildings in South-East Asia*, E. & F. N. Spon, London, p. 172 (Menara Mesiniaga).

Dietmar Steiner (ed), *Domus*, No. 808, October, Milan, pp. 22–5 (Menara UMNO).

Robert Harley, 'Building the Green Factor', *The Australian Financial Review Magazine*, October, p. 38 (Menara UMNO).

John Branton, 'Highly Fashionable', *Going Places*, Malaysian Airlines inflight magazine, October, p. 31.

Graham Humphries, 'Bring on the Millennium', *The Australian Magazine*, 3–4 October, p. 48 (Menara UMNO).

Murray Hiebert, 'Feel the Heat', *Far Eastern Economic Review*, 8 October, pp. 74–5 (Menara Mesiniaga).

M. Griffiths, 'Hypertower Proposed for Expo 2005 in Japan', *Engineering World*, Vol. 8, No. 5, October/November, Melbourne, pp. 42–3 (Expo 2005 Nagoya Hyper-Tower).

Murray Hiebert, 'Catch Some Breezes', *Far Eastern Economic Review*, 22 October, p. 50.

Peter Ward, 'Cutting Edge in Stark Relief', *The Australian*, 13 November, p. 40 (Menara Mesiniaga).

Kumpulan Guthrie Berhad, 'Annual Report 1997–1998', front cover (Guthrie Pavilion).

Hidenori, 'The Asian Way', *Trendy*, November, Japan, p. 254 (Menara Mesiniaga).

Paola Ramirez, 'Al rescate del diseno ecologico', *La Nacion*, 3 November, Costa Rica, p. 6 (Menara UMNO).

F. D. Sedlacek (ed), *Award-Winning Architecture: International Yearbook 1998/99*, Prestel, Germany, p. 97 (Central Plaza).

Voon Fee Chan (ed), *The Encyclopedia of Malaysia (Volume 5: Architecture)*, Archipelago Press, Singapore, pp. 115, 125.

Clifford Pearson, 'A Lofty Idea for Expo Facilities: The World's Tallest Tower', *Architectural Record*, New York, p. 48 (Expo 2005 Nagoya Hyper-Tower).

Clifford Pearson, 'Guthrie Pavilion', *Architectural Record*, New York, pp. 80–5.

Lee Chor Wah (ed), 'Guthrie Pavilion', *Architecture Asia*, Kuala Lumpur, pp. 44–7.

Richard Lorch (ed), 'Guthrie Pavilion', *Building Research & Information*, Vol. 26, No. 6, November/December, E. & F. N. Spon, London.

Robert Powell, 'Vertical Aspirations: Menara UMNO', *Singapore Architect*, No. 200/98, December, Singapore, pp. 66–71.

Acknowledgments

A decade ago, in 1989, I wrote the first monograph of Ken Yeang and his practice T. R. Hamzah and Yeang, *Ken Yeang: Rethinking the Environmental Filter*.[1] The book was an important benchmark in the development of Yeang's ideas and it was my first engagement with architectural discourse in Southeast Asia. We both grew as a result of the collaboration and I have followed his subsequent development closely.

A number of individuals have given me insights into the significance of Yeang's recent work including William Lim Siew Wai, Professor Leon van Schaik (Dean of the Faculty of the Constructed Environment at the Royal Melbourne Institute of Technology, Australia); Associate Professor Lam Khee Poh (Dean of the Faculty of Architecture, Building and Real Estate at the National University of Singapore), Dr Charles Jencks, Professor Peter Tregenza (School of Architecture, University of Sheffield), Christopher McCarthy of Battle McCarthy Consulting Engineers, Dr P. G. Raman (School of Architecture, Edinburgh University), and Professor Phil Jones (Centre for Research in the Built Environment, University of Wales, Cardiff). My long-time assistant Lynda Lim gave invaluable help with numerous drafts of the book produced in a relatively short time. She indexed and cross-referenced all the photographs and drawings.

The book would not have been possible without the enthusiastic cooperation of Ken Yeang's partner Tengku Robert Hamzah and Lucy Chew, Yeang's secretary, who gave me access to the office library and archives, located illustrations and organized access to buildings.

I am indebted to Jamie Camplin of Thames and Hudson and commissioning editor Professor James Steele from the University of Southern California for the opportunity to write this entirely new monograph of Yeang's work.

ROBERT POWELL
Singapore, November 1998

Notes

Introduction

1. This chapter is based on interviews carried out with Yeang in 1989. I have subsequently updated the information in this new publication on the basis of other published sources, discussions and correspondence with Yeang over the last decade. I am also appreciative of the comments of James Steele on the opening paragraphs.
2. Alan Balfour, 'Architecture for a New Nation', in *Bioclimatic Skyscrapers: Ken Yeang*, Artemis, London, 1994, pp. 7–8.
3. Yeang's analytical axonometric drawings of Le Corbusier's houses at Poissy and Pessac appear in Charles Jencks's *Le Corbusier and the Tragic View of Architecture*, Penguin, London, 1973, pp. 88–9.
4. Leon van Schaik in correspondence with the author, 25 September 1998.
5. Ken Yeang, 'Bionics: The Use of Biological Analogies in Design', in *Architectural Association Quarterly (AAQ)*, No. 4, London, 1974.
6. Alan Balfour, 1994, p. 8.
7. Ken Yeang in correspondence with the author, 30 July 1998.
8. Robert Powell, *The Urban Asian House*, Select Books, Singapore, and Thames and Hudson, London, 1998, p. 19.
9. Yeang uses this phrase in *The Architecture of Malaysia*, Pepin Press, Amsterdam and Kuala Lumpur, 1992, p. 261.
10. Ken Yeang, *Tropical Urban Regionalism: Building in a South-East Asian City*, a MIMAR book, Concept Media Pte Ltd, Singapore, 1987.

Chapter 1

1. Yeang writes on the search for Malaysian architectural identity in *The Architecture of Malaysia*, Pepin Press, Amsterdam and Kuala Lumpur, 1992, p. 273.
2. This chapter is based on interviews with Ken Yeang in 1989. It has been updated with reference to later publications by Yeang in which the 'Primary-Level Design Experiments' are retrospectively referred to as the 'Series 1' towers.
3. Ken Yeang, 'Notes on Regional Influences Affecting Design', in proceedings of the seminar 'Kearah Identiti Kebangsaan Dalam Senibina', Ministry of Youth and Culture, Kuala Lumpur, 20–3 January 1981.
4. Paul Ricoeur, on 'Universal Civilisation and National Cultures', in *History and Truth*, Evanston, 1965, pp. 271–84.
5. A. Tzonis and L. Lefaivre, 'The Grid and the Pathway', in *Architecture in Greece*, No. 5, 1981.
6. Kenneth Frampton, 'Towards a Critical Regionalism', in H. Foster (ed), *The Anti-Aesthetic*, Bay Press, Port Townsend, 1983.
7. I am indebted to James Steele for his comments, in correspondence with the author, 8 November 1998.
8. Subsequently, I edited *Architecture and Identity*, the proceedings of an AKAA seminar held in Kuala Lumpur in 1983, jointly sponsored by the Malaysian Institute of Architects. The proceedings were published by Concept Media, Singapore.
9. Robert Powell (ed), *Architecture and Identity*, AKAA and Concept Media Pte Ltd, Singapore, 1983.
10. Eric Lye in Robert Powell (ed), 1983.
11. Robert Powell (ed), 1983.
12. Robert Powell, *Line Edge and Shade: The Search for an Architectural Design Language for Tropical Asia*, a monograph of the work of Tay Kheng Soon and Akitek Tenggara II, Page One Publishing, Singapore, 1997.
13. Charles Correa commenting on Ken Yeang's paper entitled 'Land Use, Climate and Architectural Form' at the 1985 seminar 'Design for High-Intensity Development', hosted by the Malaysian Institute of Architects and the Aga Khan Program for Islamic Architecture at Harvard University and Massachusetts Institute of Technology; proceedings published in 1986, p. 79.
14. Robert Powell, *Ken Yeang: Rethinking the Environmental Filter*, Landmark Books, Singapore, 1989.
15. Ken Yeang, 1987.
16. Ibid.
17. This idea is articulated with greater precision in Robert Powell, 1989.
18. Ken Yeang, 'The Architect and His Business', *The Edge*, Kuala Lumpur, 23 February 1998, p. 18.

Chapter 2

1. Robert Powell, 1989.
2. In 'Singapore Super Tower: Bioclimatic High Rise on the Singapore Skyline', *Journal of Southeast Asian Architecture* 1997, 1:47–61, Professor Ivor Richards records a workshop conducted by Yeang at the University of Newcastle-upon-Tyne, United Kingdom, in 1996.
3. In correspondence with the author, 30 July 1998, Yeang argues that his, '*modus operandi* has changed much since 1989 (i.e. from simply talking about a bioclimatic concept and interpreting it generally, to a more professional and precise level of working with a more quantitative approach using collaborators from all over the world'. In this quantitative approach, architecture becomes now 'an art that is engineered' rather than an 'art that has engineering'.
4. Asia Design Forum was founded by Ken Yeang in 1990. The coordinator of the first two meetings was Dr P. G. Raman. Dr Raman now teaches in the School of Architecture at Edinburgh University, United Kingdom.
5. P. G. Raman (ed), *Criticism and the Growth of Architectural Ideas*, Singapore, 1992.
6. Ibid.
7. In the *Singapore Architect*, No. 196/97, Singapore, 1997, pp. 84–6, Associate Professor Lam Khee Poh, Dean of the Faculty of Architecture, Building and Real Estate at the National University of Singapore, points out the need to initiate R. & D. endeavours to study the actual performance of completed buildings and to compare this with the behaviour envisaged at the design stage. Professor Tunney Lee also made this point in discussion with the author, 11 November 1998.

8. In correspondence with the author, 30 July 1998.

9. Ibid.

10. Cynthia Davidson (ed), *Architecture Beyond Architecture*, AKAA and Academy Editions, London, 1995.

11. Charles Jencks in correspondence with the author, May 1998.

12. Ibid.

13. Peter Eisenmann, in Cynthia Davidson (ed), 1995.

14. Alan Balfour, 1994.

15. Ibid.

16. Ken Yeang in *World Architecture*, London, February 1997.

17. Ivor Richards, 'The Tropical High-Rise Tower', in *Bioclimatic Skyscrapers: Ken Yeang*, 1994, p. 11.

Chapter 3

1. W. White, *Third World Planning Review*, 16 (2), 1994.

2. Ken Yeang, 'Designing the Green Skyscraper', *Malaysia Architect*, Kuala Lumpur, September/October 1997.

3. Ibid.

4. William Lim Siew Wai and Tan Hock Beng, *Contemporary Vernacular*, Select Books, Singapore, 1997.

5. Ken Yeang, 1994.

6. Alan Balfour, 1994.

7. Ibid.

8. Ivor Richards, 1994.

9. Klaus Daniel, *The Technology of Ecological Building*, Birkhauser Verlag, Berlin, 1994. Menara Mesiniaga is included, and there is also a section contributed by Yeang on 'Climate and Built Form: A Global Perspective'.

10. Ken Yeang, 1997.

11. Ibid.

12. Ken Yeang, *Designing with Nature: The Ecological Basis for Architectural Design*, McGraw-Hill, New York, 1995. The book is based upon Yeang's doctoral thesis at Cambridge entitled 'A Theoretical Framework for the Incorporation of Ecological Considerations in the Design and Planning of the Built Environment'.

13. Ken Yeang in correspondence with the author, 30 July 1998.

14. Ibid.

15. Ken Yeang, 1995.

16. Ken Yeang, 'Designing the Green Skyscraper', *Malaysia Architect*, Kuala Lumpur, September/October 1997, pp. 80–2.

17. Leon van Schaik in correspondence with the author, 23 September 1998.

18. William Lim Siew Wai in conversation with the author, 21 August 1998.

19. Alan Balfour, 1994.

20. Simulation of the wind performance was carried out by Professor Phil Jones of the University of Wales, Cardiff, United Kingdom.

21. Leon van Schaik, 'Big Chill', *RIBA International*, London, March 1998, pp. 6–11.

22. Asia Design Forum No. 6, Hokkaido, Japan, 1995.

23. Leon van Schaik in *Transitions 52/53*, RMIT, Melbourne, 1996.

24. Asia Design Forum No. 7, Bali, Indonesia, 1997.

25. Ken Yeang, 'Notes on Practice and Architecture', unpublished internal memorandum, 1998.

26. Ken Yeang, 'Malaysian designers boleh!', *The Edge*, Kuala Lumpur, 3 June 1998.

Chapter 4

1. Ken Yeang, 'On Rapid-Prototyping and Product Development', unpublished essay, June 1998.

2. Ken Yeang, *The Skyscraper Bioclimatically Considered: A Design Primer*, Academy Editions, London, 1997.

3. Lam Khee Poh, 'Review of *The Skyscraper Bioclimatically Considered: A Design Primer*', *Singapore Architect*, 196/97, Singapore, 1997, pp. 84–6.

4. Yeang's response to Lam Khee Poh's review, *Singapore Architect*, 197/97, Singapore, 1997, pp. 18–19.

5. Christopher McCarthy of Battle McCarthy Consulting Engineers, United Kingdom, in correspondence with the author, 14 September 1998.

6. Leon van Schaik in correspondence with the author, 15 September 1998.

7. Ken Yeang in correspondence with the author, 21 January 1998.

Chapter 5

1. Haig Beck, 'Hamzah and Yeang Architects, Roof-Roof House, Kuala Lumpur', *UIA International Architecture*, 6/1984, pp. 16–17.

2. Lee Kwong Yan, writing on the Roof-Roof House in *UIA International Architect*, 6/1984.

3. A. H. Rosenfield et al, 'Painting the Town White and Green', *Technology Review*, February–March 1997, pp. 52–4.

4. Ibid.

5. M. Hough, *Cities and Natural Processes*, Routledge, London, 1995.

6. D. M. Kurn, S. E. Bretz, B. Huang and H. Akbari, *The Potential for Reducing Urban Air Temperature Through Vegetative Cooling*, Lawrence Berkeley Laboratory Report No. LBL-35320 1994, Berkeley, California, 1994.

7. B. C. Wolverton, A. Johnson and K. Bounds, *Interior Landscape Plants for Indoor Air Pollution Abatement*, Final Report, September 1989, National Aeronautical and Space Administration, John Stennis Space Center, MS 39529.6000, 1989, p. 22.

8. Ken Yeang, 'Designing the Green Skyscraper', *Architecture Malaysia*, Kuala Lumpur, September/October 1997, pp. 75–6.

9. Ibid.

10. Jon Ignatowicz, 'Guthrie Pavilion', *Singapore Architect*, 197/98, Singapore, 1997, pp. 90–5.

Chapter 6

1. Ken Yeang, *The Tropical Verandah City*, Longman, Kuala Lumpur, 1986.

2. Julian Beinhart in *Design for High-Intensity Development*, Malaysian Institute of Architects and the Aga Khan Program for Islamic Architecture at Harvard University and Massachusetts Institute of Technology, 1986, p. 89.

3. Kevin Lynch, *Image of the City*, MIT Press, Cambridge, Massachusetts, 1960.

4. Ken Yeang, 1986.

5. Ian L. HcHarg, *Design with Nature*, Doubleday/Natural History Press, New York, 1969, is a widely influential publication on designing with respect to the natural environment and ecology.

Chapter 7

1. A review of the 1998 Harvard Asia-Pacific Conference appeared in *Dialogue*, Taiwan, June 1998.

2. Ken Yeang in conversation with the author, October 1998.

3. Ken Yeang, *The Green Skyscraper: A Primer for Designing Ecologically Sustainable Large Buildings*, Prestel, Munich and New York, 1999.

4. Ibid.

5. R. Aynsley, 'Natural Ventilation in Passive Design', in *RAIA Environment Design Guide*, May 1996, p. 1.

6. Ken Yeang, 'Designing the Green Skyscraper', *Architecture Malaysia*, Kuala Lumpur, September/October 1997, p. 77.

7. N. P. Howard, 'Embodied Energy in Different Buildings' (Table), Building Research Establishment, United Kingdom, 1996.

8. Ken Yeang, 'Designing the Green Skyscraper', *Architecture Malaysia*, Kuala Lumpur, September/October 1997, p. 77.

9. Ibid., p. 73

10. Jayne Merkel, 'Review of Ken Yeang's lecture "The Skyscraper Bioclimatically Considered" at AIA, New York Chapter, 1997'. The lecture was accompanied by an exhibition of the work of T. R. Hamzah and Yeang at the Architecture League, New York City.

11. Jon Lang, *Urban Design: The American Experience*, Van Nostrand Reinhold, New York, 1994, and Amos Rapoport, *Human Aspects of Urban Form*, Pergamon Press, Oxford, 1977.

12. Gordon Cullen, *Townscape*, Architectural Press, London, 1971.

13. Kevin Lynch, 1960.

14. Asian Design Forum No. 7, Bali, Indonesia, 1997, p. 27.

15. Tao Ho speaking at Asia Design Forum No. 9, Kuala Lumpur, Malaysia, 13–14 June 1998.

16. David Clark, 'Global Patterns and Perspectives', in *Urban World – Global City*, Routledge, London, 1996.

Acknowledgments

1. In 1985, the Malaysian Institute of Architects (PAM) jointly hosted, with the Aga Khan Program for Islamic Studies at Harvard University and Massachusetts Institute of Technology (MIT), a seminar entitled 'Design for High-Intensive Development'. A reception was held in Yeang's residence – the Roof-Roof House – during which I was introduced to Yeang. Four years later, I wrote the monograph *Ken Yeang: Rethinking the Environmental Filter*.

Index